Testing
IN
LANGUAGE
PROGRAMS

JAMES DEAN BROWN

Prentice Hall Regents
Upper Saddle River, New Jersey 07458

Library of Congress Cataloging-in-Publication Data

Brown, James Dean.
    Testing in language programs / James Dean Brown.
       p. cm.
    Includes bibliographical references (p.   ) and index.
    ISBN 0-13-124157-5
    1. Language arts—Ability testing. 2. Examination—Design and
construction. 3. Examinations—Validity. I. Title.
    LB1576.B856   1996
    372.6'044—dc20

Director of Production: Aliza Greenblatt
Editorial Production/Design Manager: Dominick Mosco
Interior Design and Electronic Production: Noël Vreeland Carter

Art Director: Merle Krumper
Cover Design: Jerry Votta
Manufacturing Manager: Ray Keating

 © 1996 by PRENTICE HALL REGENTS
Prentice-Hall, Inc.
A Simon & Schuster Company
Upper Saddle River, New Jersey 07458

Printed in the United States of America
10 9 8 7 6 5 4

ISBN 0-13-124157-5

Prentice-Hall International (UK) Limited, *London*
Prentice-Hall of Australia Pty. Limited, *Sydney*
Prentice-Hall of Canada Inc. *Toronto*
Prentice-Hall Hispanoamericana, S.A., *Mexico*
Prentice-Hall of India Private Limited, *New Delhi*
Prentice-Hall of Japan, Inc. *Tokyo*
Simon & Schuster Asia Pte. Ltd., *Singapore*
Editora Prentice-Hall do Brasil, Ltda., *Rio de Janeiro*

CONTENTS

PREFACE

Testing in Language Programs has its roots in a class that I teach quite regularly—a course in Language Testing that I have taught many dozens of times. While many books exist on language testing, none seemed to offer the types of information that I wanted to present in my class. I felt that some books were too technical and complex to be thoroughly covered in one semester, while others were too practical—offering many ideas for different types of language test questions, but very little on test construction, analysis, and improvement. *Testing in Language Programs* is designed to cover the middle ground. It provides a balance between the practical and technical aspects of language testing that is neither too complex nor too simplistic.

This book provides information about language testing that would not only be immediately useful for making *program-level decisions* (for example, admissions, proficiency, and placement decisions) but also information about testing for *classroom-level decisions* (that is, assessing what the students have learned through diagnostic or achievement testing). These two categories of decisions and the types of tests that are typically used to make them are quite different.

The category of tests most useful for program-level decisions consists of tests specifically designed to compare the performances of students to each other. These are called *norm*-referenced tests because interpretation of the scores from this category of tests is linked closely to the notion of the normal curve (also known as the *bell curve*). Such tests are most commonly used to spread students out along a continuum of scores based on some general knowledge or skill area so that the students can be placed, or grouped, into ability levels. The administrator's goal in using this type of test is usually to group students of similar ability in order to make the teacher's job easier. In other situations, the administrator may be interested in making comparisons between the average proficiency levels of students in different levels, between different language institutions or among students across the nation. Norm-referenced tests are also appropriate for these kinds of language proficiency testing. Notice that the purpose of the tests in the norm-referenced family is to make comparisons in performance either between students within an institution (for placement purposes) or between students across courses or institutions (for proficiency assessment purposes). In short, sound norm-referenced tests can help administrators (and to some degree teachers) to do their jobs better.

In contrast, the *criterion*-referenced family of tests is most useful to teachers in the classroom (though administrators should be interested in these tests as well). Criterion-referenced tests are specifically designed to assess how much of the material or set of skills taught in a course is being learned by the students. With criterion-referenced tests, the purpose is not to compare the performances of students to each other but, rather, to look at the performance of each individual student vis-à-vis the material or curriculum at hand. They are called *criterion*-referenced tests because interpretation of the scores from this category of tests is intimately linked to assessing well-defined criteria for what is being taught. Such tests are often used to diagnose the strengths and weaknesses of students with regard to the goals and objectives of a course or program. At other times, criterion-referenced tests may be used to assess achievement, in the sense of "how much each student has learned." Such information may be useful for grading student performance in the course, or for deciding whether to promote them to the next level of study, as well as for improving the materials, presentation, and sequencing of teaching points. In short, sound criterion-referenced tests can help the teacher to do a better job.

My primary motivation in writing this book was to provide practical and useful testing tools that will help language program administrators and teachers to do their respective jobs better. The distinction between the norm-referenced and criterion-referenced categories of tests will help administrators and teachers to focus on the respective types of tests most appropriate for the kinds of decisions that they make in their work. Hence, the topic of each chapter will be approached from both norm-referenced and criterion-referenced perspectives. After all, the decisions made by administrators and teachers all affect students' lives, sometimes in dramatic ways, involving a great deal of time and money, and at other times in more subtle ways, including psychological and attitudinal factors.

I assume that teachers, though most interested in classroom tests, will also take an interest in program-level decisions. Similarly, I assume that administrators, though primarily interested in program-level decisions, will also take an interest in classroom-level tests. Each group is inevitably involved in the other's decision making—perhaps in the form of teachers proctoring and scoring the placement test, or perhaps in the form of an administrator evaluating the effectiveness of teachers' classroom tests. The types of decisions discussed in this book may interact in innumerable ways, and I think that any cooperation between administrators and teachers in making decisions can be very healthy for the curriculum in general and test development in particular.

Regardless of whether the reader is a teacher or an administrator, or both, the goal of reading this book should be to learn how to do all types of testing well. Bad or mediocre testing is common, yet most language professionals recognize that such practices are irresponsible and eventually lead to bad or mediocre decisions being made about their students' lives. The tools necessary to do sound testing are provided in this book. Where statistics are involved, they are explained in a straightforward "recipe book" style so that readers can immediately understand and apply what they learn to their teaching or administrative situations. If this book makes a difference in the quality of decision making in even one language program, the time and effort that went into writing it will have been worthwhile.

I would like to thank Kathi Bailey, Lyle Bachman, Carol Chapelle, Graham Crookes, Grant Henning, Thom Hudson and two other anonymous readers for their perceptive and useful comments on earlier versions of this book. I would also like to thank the hundreds of graduate students who suffered patiently through manuscript versions of this book, for their countless questions, criticisms, and suggestions.

J.D.B.

CHAPTER 1

TYPES AND USES OF LANGUAGE TESTS: NORM-REFERENCED AND CRITERION-REFERENCED DECISIONS

Test results can serve a variety of different functions within a language program. In this chapter, I clarify how two categories of tests perform these different functions: one category that helps administrators and teachers to make program-level decisions (that is, proficiency and placement decisions), and another category that helps teachers to make classroom-level decisions (diagnostic and achievement decisions). In the technical jargon of testing, these two categories are labeled *norm-referenced tests* and *criterion-referenced tests*. I begin the chapter by making a detailed comparison of these two categories. Then I define and discuss the four primary functions that tests serve in language programs, two functions that are norm-referenced (proficiency and placement) and two that are criterion-referenced (diagnostic and achievement). I end the chapter by explaining how teachers can best approach the task of matching language tests to the purposes and decision-making needs of their own language courses and programs. As in all chapters of this book, I end with a summary checklist, a list of the new terms and symbols found in the chapter, a series of review questions, and a set of application exercises.

TWO FAMILIES OF LANGUAGE TESTS

The concepts underlying norm-referenced testing have been fully developed in educational measurement circles for most of the twentieth century, and many language teachers have been exposed to this category of testing. However, the idea of criterion-referenced testing did not surface in educational measurement circles until 1963, when Glaser first mentioned the idea (see Popham & Husek 1969; Popham 1978, 1981; and Berk 1980, 1984a, for much more on the background of criterion-referenced testing). The distinction between norm-referenced and criterion-referenced tests has only gradually entered the language testing literature (see Cartier 1968; Cziko 1983; Hudson & Lynch 1984; Bachman 1987; and Brown 1984a, 1988a, 1989a, 1990, 1993, 1995). In recent years, this distinction has increased in importance in educational and psychological measurement, and I hope that it will continue to do so in language testing as well, because an understanding of the fundamental differences and similarities between these two categories of tests can help language teachers to make much better decisions about their students.

Norm-Referenced Tests

In brief, a ***norm-referenced test*** (NRT) is designed to measure global language abilities (for instance, overall English language proficiency, academic listening ability, reading comprehension, and so on). Each student's score on such a test is interpreted relative to the scores of all other students who took the test. Such comparisons are usually done with reference to the concept of the normal distribution (familiarly known as the *bell curve*). The purpose of an NRT is to spread students out along a continuum of scores so that those with "low" abilities in a general area such as reading comprehension are at one end of the normal distribution, while those with "high" abilities are at the other end (with the bulk of the students falling near the middle). In addition, while students may know the general format of the questions on an NRT (for example, multiple-choice, true-false, dictation, or essay), they will typically not know what specific content or skills will be tested by those questions.

Criterion-Referenced Tests

In contrast, a ***criterion-referenced test*** (CRT) is usually produced to measure well-defined and fairly specific objectives. Often these objectives are specific to a particular course, program, school district, or state. The interpretation of scores on a CRT is considered absolute in the sense that each student's score is meaningful without reference to the other students' scores. In other words, a student's score on a particular objective indicates the percent of the knowledge or skill in that objective that the student has learned. Moreover, the distribution of scores on a CRT need not necessarily be normal. If all the students know 100% of the material on all the objectives, then all the students should receive the same score with no variation at all. The purpose of a CRT is to measure the amount of learning that a student has accomplished on each objective. In most cases, the students would know in advance what types of questions, tasks, and content to expect for each objective because the question content would be implied (if not explicitly stated) in the objectives of the course.

Comparing Norm-referenced and Criterion-referenced Approaches

A more detailed step-by-step comparison of norm-referenced and criterion-referenced tests will help to clarify the distinction. The six characteristics listed in the first column of Table 1.1 indicate that norm-

Table 1.1: Differences Between Norm-Referenced and Criterion-Referenced Tests*

Characteristic	Norm-Referenced	Criterion-Referenced
Type of Interpretation	Relative (A student's performance is compared to that of all other students in percentile terms.)	Absolute (A student's performance is compared only to the amount, or percentage, of material learned.)
Type of Measurement	To measure general language abilities or proficiencies	To measure specific objectives-based language points
Purpose of Testing	Spread students out along a continuum of general abilities or proficiencies	Assess the amount of material known, or learned, by each student
Distribution of Scores	Normal distribution of scores around a mean	Varies, usually nonnormal (students who know all of the material should all score 100%)
Test Structure	A few relatively long subtests with a variety of question contents	A series of short, well-defined subtests with similar question contents
Knowledge of Questions	Students have little or no idea what content to expect in questions	Students know exactly what content to expect in test questions

*Adapted from Brown 1984a

referenced and criterion-referenced tests contrast in: (a) the ways that scores are interpreted, (b) the kinds of things that they are used to measure, (c) the purposes for testing, (d) the ways that scores are distributed, (e) the structures of the tests, and (f) the students' knowledge of test question content.

Type of interpretation. One essential difference between these two categories of tests is that each student's performance on a CRT is compared to a particular criterion in absolute terms. Some confusion has developed over the years about what the *criterion* in criterion-referenced testing refers to. This confusion is understandable, because two definitions have evolved for criterion. For some authors, the material that the student is supposed to learn in a course is the criterion against which he or she is being measured. For other authors, the term *criterion* refers to the standard, called a *criterion level*, against which each student's performance is judged (for instance, if the cut-point for passing a CRT is set at 70%, that is the criterion level).

Regardless of which version of the term is being applied in a given situation, the primary focus in interpreting CRT scores is on how much of the material each student has learned in absolute terms. For example, the following would be a characteristic CRT score interpretation: A student scored 85%, which means that the student knew 85% of the material. Notice that there is no need for any reference to the performances of other students.

On an NRT, testers interpret each student's performance in relationship to the performances of the other students in the norm group in relative terms. In fact, NRT scores are sometimes expressed with no reference to the actual number of test questions answered correctly. For example, the following would be a typical NRT score interpretation: A student scored in the 84th percentile, which means that the student scored better than 84 out of 100 students in the group as a whole. How many questions did the student answer correctly? We have no way of knowing because a percentile score only expresses the student's position relative to the other students.

The key to understanding the difference between NRT and CRT score interpretations is captured in the terms *percentage* and *percentile*. On CRTs, teachers are primarily concerned with how much of the material the students know; that is, the focus is on the **percentage** of material known. The teachers really only care about the percentage of questions the students answered correctly (or percentage of tasks the students correctly completed) in connection with the material at hand and perhaps in relationship to a previously established criterion level. The percentages are interpreted directly without reference to the students' positions vis-à-vis each other. Hence, a high percentage score means that the test was easy for the students, which may in turn mean that the students knew the material being tested or that the test questions were written at too low a level. Similarly, a low percentage score means that the test was difficult for the students, which may in turn mean that the students did not know the material being tested or that the test questions were written at too high a level of difficulty.

On NRTs, the concern is entirely different. Teachers focus instead on how each student's performance relates to the performances of all other students. Thus, in one way or another, they are interested in the student's **percentile** score, which tells them the proportion of students who scored above and below the student in question. For instance, a student with a percentile score of 70 performed better than 70 out of 100 students but worse than 30 out of 100. If another NRT were administered to the same students but had much more difficult questions on it, the percentage of correct answers would be lower for all students, but their positions relative to each other in terms of percentile scores might be virtually the same. Similarly, if another NRT had easy questions on it, the percentage of correct answers would be high for all students, but their positions relative to each other in terms of percentile scores would probably be very similar.

In short, CRTs look at the amount of material known by the students in percentage terms, while NRTs examine the relationship of a given student's performance to that of all other students in percentile terms.

Type of measurement. Typically, NRTs are most suitable for measuring general abilities; such as reading ability in French, listening comprehension in Chinese, and overall English language proficiency. *The Test of English as a Foreign Language* (1994) (TOEFL) is a good example of such a test. While the TOEFL does have three subtests, these subtests are very general in nature, measuring listening comprehension, writing and analysis, and reading comprehension and vocabulary.

In contrast, CRTs are better suited to providing precise information about each individual's performance on well-defined learning points. For instance, if a language course focuses on a structural syllabus, the CRT for that course might contain subtests (of five questions each) on: (a) subject pronouns, (b) the *a/an* distinction, (c) the third person -*s*, (d) the use of present tense copula, and so forth. However, CRTs are not limited to grammar points. Subtests on a CRT for a notional–functional language course might consist of a short interview where ratings are made of the student's abilities to: (a) perform greetings, (b) agree or disagree, (c) express an opinion, and so on. The variety and types of test questions used on a CRT are limited only by the imagination of the test developer(s).

Purpose of the testing. Clearly, major differences exist in the way scores are interpreted on NRTs and CRTs. As mentioned above, NRT interpretations are relative (that is, a student's performance is compared to the performances of other students), while CRT interpretations are absolute (that is, a student's performance is compared to the amount, or percentage, of material known by that student). The purpose of an NRT is therefore to generate scores that spread the students out along a continuum of general abilities so that any existing differences among the individuals can be distinguished. Since the purpose of a CRT is to assess the amount of knowledge or skill learned by each student, the focus is on the individuals' knowledge or skills, not on distributions of scores. As a result, the distributions of scores for NRTs and CRTs can be quite different.

Distribution of scores. Since NRTs must be constructed to spread students out along a continuum or distribution of scores, the manner in which test questions for an NRT are generated, analyzed, selected, and refined (see Chapter 3) will usually lead to a test that produces scores which fall into a normal distribution, or bell curve. Such a distribution is desirable so that any existing differences among the students will be clearly revealed. In other words, if there is variation within the group with regard to the knowledge or skill being tested, any differences among students should be reflected in their scores.

In contrast, on a criterion-referenced final examination, all students who have learned all the course material should be able to score 100% on the final examination. Thus, very similar scores can occur on a CRT. As a corollary, in the first week of class, those students who do not know the material (because they have not learned it yet) should all score very low. Again, very similar scores might be produced in such a situation. Indeed, the ways that test questions are generated, analyzed, selected, and refined for a CRT will lead to these types of results. In short, very similar scores among students on a CRT may be perfectly logical, acceptable, and even desirable if the test is administered at the beginning or end of a course. In either situation, a normal distribution of scores may not appear. As I explain in later chapters, a normal distribution in CRT scores may even be a sign that something is wrong with the test, with the curriculum, or with the teaching.

Test structure. Popham and Husek (1969) contend that "it is not possible to tell [an] NRT from a CRT by looking at it." I argue instead that the strategies used to accomplish the differing NRT and CRT purposes and distributions most often result in NRTs and CRTs that are considerably different in structure. Typically, an NRT is relatively long and contains a wide variety of different types of question content. Indeed, the content can be so diverse that students find it difficult to know exactly what will be tested. Such a test is usually made up of a few subtests on rather general language skills like reading comprehension, listening comprehension, grammar, writing, and so forth, but close examination will reveal that each of these subtests is relatively long (30–50 questions) and covers a wide variety of different contents.

In contrast, CRTs usually consist of numerous, shorter subtests. Each subtest will typically represent a different instructional objective, and often, each objective will have its own subtest. If a course has twelve instructional objectives, the associated CRT will usually have twelve subtests, although sometimes only a subsample of the objectives will be tested. Because the subtests are often numerous, they must remain short for practical reasons (3–10 questions, as a rule of thumb).

Sometimes for economy of time and effort, subtests on a CRT will be collapsed together, which makes it difficult for an outsider to identify the subtests. For example, on a reading comprehension test, the students might be required to read five passages and answer four multiple-choice questions on each passage. If on each passage there is one fact question, one vocabulary question, one cohesive device question, and one inference question, the teachers will most likely consider the five fact questions together as one subtest, the five vocabulary questions together as another subtest, and so on. In other words, the teachers will be focusing on the question types as subtests, not the passages, and this fact might not be obvious to an outside observer.

Knowledge of questions. Students rarely know in any detail what content to expect on an NRT. In general, they might know what question formats to expect (for example, multiple-choice, true-false, and so forth), but seldom would the actual language points be predictable. This unpredictability of the question content results from the general nature of what NRTs are testing and the wide variety of question contents that are typically used.

On a CRT, good teaching practice is more likely to lead to a situation in which the students can predict not only the question formats on the test but also the language points that will be tested. If the instructional objectives for a course are clearly stated, if the students are given those objectives, if the objectives are addressed by the teacher, and if the language points involved are adequately practiced and learned, then the students should know exactly what to expect on the test unless for some reason the criterion-referenced test is not properly referenced to the criteria—the instructional objectives.

Such statements often lead to complaints that the development of CRTs will cause teachers to "teach to the test," to the exclusion of other more important ways of spending classroom time. While I acknowledge that not all elements of the teaching and learning process can be tested, I argue that teaching to the test should nevertheless be a major part of what teachers do. If the objectives of a language course are worthwhile and have been properly constructed to reflect the needs of the students, then the tests that are based on those objectives should reflect the important language points that are being taught. Teaching to such a test should help teachers and students stay on track, and the test results should provide useful feedback to both groups on the effectiveness of the teaching and learning processes. In short, CRTs, as I envision them, should help teachers and students rather than constrain them.

A very useful side effect of teaching to the test is the fact that the information gained can have what Oller (1979, p. 52) termed *instructional value*—that is, "to enhance the delivery of instruction in student populations." In other words, such CRT scores can provide useful information for evaluating the effectiveness of the needs analysis, the objectives, the tests themselves, the materials, the teaching, the students' study habits, and so forth. In short, CRTs can prove enlightening in the never ending evaluation process that I advocate in Chapter 9.

I am not arguing that teachers should only address a very restricted set of objectives in a language course. Flexibility and time must be allowed in any curriculum for the teachers to address problems and learning points that arise along the way. Nevertheless, if a common core of objectives can be developed for a course, a CRT can then be developed to test those objectives, and a number of benefits will surely accrue to the teachers, the students, and the curriculum developers alike (see Chapter 9 for more on this topic).

I should also mention that I do not see CRTs as better than NRTs. Both test categories are very important for the decision-making processes in a language program—but for different types of decisions. In fact, the distinction between NRTs and CRTs can help teachers to match the correct type of test with any type of decision.

MATCHING TESTS TO DECISION PURPOSES

A variety of different types of decisions are made in almost any language program, and language tests of various kinds can help in making those decisions. In order to test appropriately, I argue that each teacher must be very clear about his/her purpose for making a given decision and then match the correct type of test to that purpose. If my purpose is to measure weight, I will use some sort of weighing device. If I want to measure linear distance, I will use a ruler or odometer. In this section, I summarize the main points that teachers must keep in mind when matching the appropriate measuring tool (NRT or CRT in this case) with the types of decisions they must make about their students. The main points to consider are shown in Table 1.2. As the discussion develops, I briefly cover each point as it applies to four types of decisions.

In administering language programs, I have found myself making basically just four kinds of decisions: proficiency, placement, achievement, and diagnostic. Since these are also the four types of tests identified in Alderson, Krahnke, and Stansfield (1987) as the most commonly used types of tests in our field, I call them the primary *language testing functions* and focus on them in the remainder of this chapter. These testing functions correspond neatly to the NRT and CRT categories as follows: NRTs aid in making program-level decisions (that is, proficiency and placement decisions), and CRTs are most effective in making classroom-level decisions (that is, diagnostic and achievement). As I will explain, these testing categories and functions provide a useful framework for thinking about decision making in language programs.

Of course, other categories of tests do exist. For instance, aptitude tests, intelligence tests, learning strategy tests, attitude tests, and so forth do not fit into these four language testing functions. Generally, these other types of tests are not administered in language programs so I do not discuss them in this book. Instead, proficiency, placement, achievement, and diagnostic testing will be my focus because a command of these testing

Table 1.2: Matching Tests to Decision Purposes

| | Type of Decision | | | |
| | Norm-Referenced | | Criterion-Referenced | |
Test Qualities	Proficiency	Placement	Achievement	Diagnostic
Detail of Information	Very General	General	Specific	Very Specific
Focus	Usually, general skills prerequisite to entry	Learning points all levels and skills of program	Terminal objectives of course or program	Terminal and enabling objectives of courses
Purpose of Decision	To compare individual overall with other groups/ individuals	To find each student's appropriate level	To determine the degree of learning for advancement or graduation	To inform students and teachers of objectives needing more work
Relationship to program	Comparisons with other institutions	Comparisons within program	Directly related to objectives of program	Directly related to objectives still needing work
When Administered	Before entry and sometimes at exit	Beginning of program	End of courses	Beginning and/or middle of courses
Interpretation of Scores	Spread of scores	Spread of scores	Number and amount of objectives learned	Number and amount of objectives learned

functions will provide all the tools needed for decision making in most language programs. This approach should not only help teachers to learn about language testing but also should help them to make responsible proficiency decisions, placement decisions, achievement decisions, and diagnostic decisions about their students.

Program-Level Decisions

Proficiency decisions. Sometimes, teachers and administrators need to make decisions based on the students' general levels of language proficiency. The focus of such decisions is usually on the general knowledge or skills prerequisite to entry or exit from some type of institution, for example, American universities. Such *proficiency decisions* are necessary in setting up entrance and exit standards for a curriculum, in adjusting the level of program objectives to the students' abilities, or in making comparisons between programs. In other words, teachers and administrators must make a variety of curricular and administrative decisions on the basis of overall proficiency information.

Proficiency decisions are often based on proficiency tests specifically designed for such decisions. By definition, then, a *proficiency test* assesses the general knowledge or skills commonly required or prerequisite to entry into (or exemption from) a group of similar institutions. One example is the *Test of English as a Foreign Language* (TOEFL), which is used by many American universities that have English language proficiency prerequisites in common (see Educational Testing Service 1992, 1994). Understandably, such tests are very general in nature and cannot be related to the goals and objectives of any particular language program. Another example of the general nature of proficiency tests is the *ACTFL Proficiency Guidelines* (American Council on the Teaching of Foreign Languages 1986). Although proficiency tests may contain subtests for each skill, the testing of the skills remains very general, and the resulting scores can only serve as overall indicators of proficiency.

Since proficiency decisions require knowing the general level of proficiency of language students in comparison to other students, the test must provide scores that form a wide distribution so that interpretations of the differences among students will be as fair as possible. Thus, I argue that proficiency decisions should be made on the basis of norm-referenced proficiency tests because NRTs have all the qualities desirable for such decisions (refer to Table 1.1). Proficiency decisions based on large-scale standardized tests may sometimes seem unfair to teachers because of the arbitrary way that they are handled in some settings, but like it or not, such proficiency decisions are often necessary: (a) to protect the integrity of the institutions involved, (b) to keep students from getting in over their heads, and (c) to prevent students from entering programs that they really do not need.

Proficiency decisions most often occur when a program must relate to the external world in some way. The students are arriving. How will they fit into the program? And when the students leave the program, is their level of proficiency high enough to enable them to succeed linguistically in other institutions?

Sometimes, comparisons are also made among different language programs. Since proficiency tests, by definition, are general in nature, rather than geared to any particular program, they could serve to compare regional branches of a particular language teaching delivery system. Consider what would happen if the central office for a nationwide chain of ESL business English schools wanted to compare the effectiveness of all its centers. To make such decisions about the relative merit of the various centers, the administrators in charge would probably want to use some form of business English proficiency test.

However, extreme care must be exercised in making comparisons among different language programs because of the very fact that such tests are not geared to any particular language program. By chance, the test could fit the teaching and content of one program relatively closely; as a consequence, the students in that program might score high on average. By chance, the test might not match the curriculum of another program quite so well; consequently, the students would score low on that particular proficiency test. The question is: Should one program be judged less effective than another simply because the teaching and learning that is going on in that program (though perfectly effective and useful) is not adequately assessed by the test? Of course not. Hence, great care must be used in making such comparisons with special attention to the validity and appropriateness of the tests to the decisions being made.

Because of the general nature of proficiency decisions, a proficiency test must be designed so that the general abilities or skills of students are reflected in a wide distribution of scores. Only with such a wide distribution can decision makers make fair comparisons among the students, or groups of students. This need for a wide spread of scores most often leads testers to create tests that produce normal distributions of scores. All of which is to argue that proficiency tests should usually be norm-referenced.

Proficiency decisions should never be undertaken lightly. Instead, these decisions must be based on the best obtainable proficiency test scores as well as other information about the students. Proficiency decisions can dramatically affect students' lives, so slipshod decision making in this area would be particularly unprofessional.

Placement decisions. *Placement decisions* usually have the goal of grouping together students of similar ability levels. Teachers benefit from placement decisions because their classes contain students with relatively homogeneous ability levels. As a result, teachers can focus on the problems and learning points appropriate for that level of student. To that end, placement tests are designed to help decide what each student's appropriate level will be within a specific program, skill area, or course. The purpose of such tests is to reveal which students have more of, or less of, a particular knowledge or skill so that students with similar levels of ability can be grouped together.

Examining the similarities and differences between proficiency and placement testing will help to clarify the role of placement tests. To begin with, a proficiency test and a placement test might at first glance look very similar because they are both testing fairly general material. However, a proficiency test tends to be very, very general in character, because it is designed to assess extremely wide bands of abilities. In contrast, a *placement test* must be more specifically related to a given program, particularly in terms of the relatively narrow range of abilities assessed and the content of the curriculum, so that it efficiently separates the students into level groupings within that program.

Put another way, a general proficiency test might be useful for determining which language program is most appropriate for a student; once in that program, a placement test would be necessary to determine the level of study from which the student would most benefit. Both proficiency and placement tests should be norm-referenced instruments because decisions must be made on the students' relative knowledge or skill levels. However, as demonstrated in Brown (1984b), the degree to which a test is effective in spreading students out is directly related to the degree to which that test fits the ability levels of the students. Hence, a proficiency test would typically be norm-referenced to a population of students with a very wide band of language abilities and a variety of purposes for using the language. In contrast, a placement test would typically be norm-referenced to a narrower band of abilities and purposes—usually the abilities and purposes of students at the beginning of studies in a particular language program.

Consider, for example, the English Language Institute (ELI) at the University of Hawaii at Manoa (UHM). All of the international students at UHM have been fully admitted by the time they arrive. In order to have been admitted, they must have taken the TOEFL and scored at least 500. From our point of view, language proficiency test scores are used to determine whether these students are eligible to study in the ELI and follow a few courses at UHM. Those students who score 600 or above on the TOEFL are told that they are completely exempt from ELI training. Thus, I can safely say that most of the ELI students at UHM have scored between 500 and 600 on the TOEFL.

Within the ELI, there are three tracks, each of which is focused on one skill (reading, writing, or listening) and also up to three levels within each track. As a result, the placement decisions and the tests upon which they are based must be much more focused than the information provided by TOEFL scores. The placement tests must provide information on each of the three skills involved as well as on the language needed by students in the relatively narrow proficiency range reflected in their TOEFL scores, which were between 500 and 600. I see a big difference between our general proficiency decisions and our placement decisions. While the contrasts between proficiency and placement decisions may not be quite so clear in all programs, my definitions and ways of distinguishing between proficiency and placement decisions should help teachers to think about the program-level decisions and testing in their own language programs.

If a particular program is designed with levels that include beginners as well as very advanced learners, a general proficiency test *might* adequately serve as a placement instrument. However, such a wide range of abilities is not common in the programs that I know about and, even when appropriately measuring such general abilities, each test must be examined in terms of how well it fits the abilities of the students and how well it matches what is actually taught in the classrooms.

If there is a mismatch between the placement test and what is taught in a program (as found in Brown 1981), the danger is that the groupings of similar ability levels will simply not occur. For instance, consider an elementary school ESL program in which a general grammar test is used for placement. If the focus of the program is on oral communication at three levels, and a pencil and paper test is used to place the children into those levels, numerous problems may arise. Such a test is placing the children into levels on the basis of their *written grammar* abilities. While grammar ability may be related to oral proficiency, other factors may be more important to successful oral communication. Such testing practices could result in the oral abilities of the children in all three of the (grammar-placed) levels being about the same in terms of average abilities as well as range of abilities.

Some form of oral placement procedure (for example, the oral proficiency scale of the American Council on the Teaching of Foreign Languages 1986) might more accurately separate the children into three ability-level groups for the purposes of teaching them oral communication skills. However, the ACTFL scale was designed for assessing overall language proficiency and therefore may be too general for making responsible placement decisions in this particular elementary school program. In addition, the ACTFL scale may only be tangentially related to the goals and purposes of this particular school. Most importantly, the ACTFL scale was designed with adult university students in mind, so it may not be at all appropriate for elementary school children. Clearly then, the purpose of a program, the range of abilities within the program, and the type of students involved are factors that may make a proficiency test inappropriate for purposes of testing placement. Typically, placement decisions should be based on placement tests that have either been designed with a specific program in mind or been seriously examined for their appropriateness for the program in question.

Classroom-Level Decisions

Achievement decisions. All language teachers are in the business of fostering achievement in the form of language learning. In fact, the purpose of most language programs is to maximize the possibilities for students to achieve a high degree of language learning. Hence, sooner or later, most language teachers will find themselves interested in making achievement decisions. *Achievement decisions* are decisions about the amount of learning that students have done. Such decisions may involve who will be advanced to the next level of study or which students should graduate. Teachers may find themselves wanting to make rational decisions that will help to improve achievement in their language programs. Or they may find a need to make and justify changes in curriculum design, staffing, facilities, materials, equipment, and so on. Such decisions should most often be made with the aid of achievement test scores.

Making decisions about the achievement of students and about ways to improve that achievement usually involves testing to find out how much each person has learned within the program. Thus, an *achievement test* must be designed with very specific reference to a particular course. This link with a specific program usually means that the achievement tests will be directly based on course objectives and will therefore be criterion-referenced. Such tests will typically be administered at the end of a course to determine how effectively students have mastered the instructional objectives.

Achievement tests must be not only very specifically designed to measure the objectives of a given course but also flexible enough to help teachers readily respond to what they learn from the test about the students' abilities, the students' needs, and the students' learning of the course objectives. In other words, a good achievement test can tell teachers a great deal about their students' achievements *and* about the adequacy of the course. Hence, while achievement tests should definitely be used to make decisions about students' levels of learning, they can also be used to affect curriculum changes and to test those changes continually against the program realities.

Diagnostic decisions. From time to time, teachers may also take an interest in assessing the strengths and weaknesses of each individual student vis-à-vis the instructional objectives for purposes of correcting an individual's deficiencies "before it is too late." *Diagnostic decisions* are aimed at fostering achievement by promoting strengths and eliminating the weaknesses of individual students. Naturally, the primary concern of the teacher must be the entire group of students collectively, but some attention can also be given to each individual student. Clearly, this last category of decision is concerned with diagnosing problems that students may be having in the learning process. While diagnostic decisions are definitely related to achievement, diagnostic testing often requires more detailed information about the very specific areas in which students have strengths and weaknesses. The purpose is to help students and their teachers to focus their efforts where they will be most effective.

As with an achievement test, a *diagnostic test* is designed to determine the degree to which the specific instructional objectives of the course have been accomplished. Hence, it should be criterion-referenced in nature. While achievement decisions are usually focused on the degree to which the objectives have been accomplished at the end of the program or course, diagnostic decisions are normally made along the way as the students are learning the language. As a result, diagnostic tests are typically administered at the beginning or in the middle of a language course. In fact, if constructed to reflect the instructional objectives, one CRT in three equivalent forms could serve as a diagnostic tool at the beginning and midpoints in a course and as an achievement test at the end (see Chapter 9 for more on the relationship between tests and curriculum). Perhaps the most effective use of a diagnostic test is to report the performance level on each objective (in a percentage) to each student so that he or she can decide how and where to invest time and energy most profitably.

SUMMARY

The following checklist should help you to select the correct type of test for each type of decision that you face.

☐ Have you decided the referencing of the test?

☐ If the following six characteristics apply, the test you need is probably an **NRT**.

☐ The interpretation will be relative (each student's performance will be compared primarily to the performances of the other students).

☐ The test will measure general language abilities or proficiencies.

☐ The purpose of testing will be to spread students out along a continuum of general abilities or proficiencies.

☐ The scores should be normally distributed around a mean.

☐ The test will have relatively few subtests with a wide variety of different test question contents.

☐ Students will have little or no idea what content to expect in questions.

☐ If the following six characteristics apply, the test you need is probably a **CRT**.

☐ Interpretation will be absolute (each student's performance will be compared primarily to the amount, or percentage, of material learned).

☐ The test will measure specific well-defined (perhaps objectives-based) language points.

☐ The purpose of the testing will be to assess the amount of material known, or learned, by each student.

☐ If all students know all the material, they should all be able to score 100%.

☐ The test will be made up of a series of short, well-defined subtests with fairly similar questions in each.

☐ Students will know exactly what content to expect in test questions.

☐ Have you decided the type of test that best matches the decision that you must make?

☐ (a.) If you check more of the qualities below (than in b.–d. below), the test you need is probably a **proficiency** test.

☐ The test is norm-referenced.

☐ The test provides very general information.

☐ The focus is on general skills, usually those prerequisite to program entry.

☐ The purpose of decision is to compare individual's overall performance with other groups/individuals.

☐ Comparisons with other institutions make sense.

☐ The test is administered before entry and sometimes at exit.

☐ (b.) If you check more of the qualities below (than in a. or c.–d.), the test you need is probably a **placement** test.

☐ The test is norm-referenced.

☐ The test provides general information.

☐ The focus is on learning points offered in all levels and skills of particular program.

☐ The purpose of decision is to find each student's appropriate level within the program.

☐ Comparisons within the program make sense.

☐ The test is usually administered at the beginning of the program.

☐ (c.) If you check more of the qualities below (than in a.–b. or d.), the test you need is probably an **achievement** test.

☐ The test is criterion-referenced.

☐ The test provides specific information.

☐ The focus is on the terminal objectives of the course or program.

☐ The purpose of the decision making is to determine the degree of learning vis-à-vis program objectives.

☐ Comparisons are directly related to the program objectives.

☐ The test is administered at the end of the course or program.

☐ (d.) If you check more of the qualities below (than in a.–c.), the test you need is probably a **diagnostic** test.

☐ The test is criterion-referenced.

☐ The test provides very specific information.

☐ The focus is on terminal and enabling objectives.

☐ The purpose of the decision is to inform students and teachers of the objectives needing more work.

☐ Comparisons are directly related to program objectives.

☐ The test is administered at the beginning of the program to test readiness or in the middle of courses to diagnose progress.

TERMS AND SYMBOLS

achievement decisions

achievement test

criterion

criterion-referenced test (CRT)

diagnostic decisions

diagnostic test

instructional value

language testing functions

norm-referenced test (NRT)

percentage

percentile

placement decisions

placement test

proficiency decisions

proficiency test

REVIEW QUESTIONS

1. For which type of test (NRT or CRT) would you expect the interpretation to be absolute? For which type would it be relative?

2. For which type of test (NRT or CRT) would you expect the scores to spread students out along a continuum of general abilities or proficiencies?

3. For which type of test (NRT or CRT) would you expect all the students to be able to score 100% if they knew all of what was taught?

4. For which type of test (NRT or CRT) would the students usually have little or no idea what content to expect in questions?

5. For which type of test (NRT or CRT) would you expect to find a series of short, well-defined subtests with fairly similar test questions in each?

6. For which type of decision (proficiency, placement, diagnostic, or achievement) would you use a test that is designed to find each student's appropriate level within a particular program?

7. For which type of decision (proficiency, placement, diagnostic, or achievement) would you use a test that is designed to inform students and teachers of objectives needing more work?

8. For which type of decision (proficiency, placement, diagnostic, or achievement) would you use a test that is designed to determine the degree of learning (with respect to the program objectives) that had taken place by the end of a course or program?

9. For which type of decision (proficiency, placement, diagnostic, or achievement) would you use a test that is designed to compare an individual's overall performance with that of groups/individuals at other institutions?

10. Do you think that the concepts behind CRTs and NRTs can be mixed into one test? If so, how and why?

APPLICATION EXERCISES

A. Consider some specific language teaching situation in an elementary school, a secondary school, a commercial language center, a university intensive program, or other language teaching setting. Think of one type of decision that administrators and teachers must make in that language program. Decide what type of decision it is (proficiency, placement, diagnostic, or achievement).

B. Now describe the test that you would recommend using to make the decision that you selected in part A. Decide what type of test you would use and what it should be like in terms of overall characteristics, as well as the skills tested, level of difficulty, length, administration time, scoring, and type of report given to teachers and students.

C. Best of all, if you have the opportunity, match a real test to a real decision in some language program; administer, score, interpret, and report the results of the test; and make or help others make the appropriate decisions so that they minimize any potential negative effects on the students' lives.

CHAPTER 2

ADOPTING, DEVELOPING, AND ADAPTING LANGUAGE TESTS

The first contact that many students have with a foreign or second language program is the relatively cold, detached, and "objective" experience of taking a placement examination. Placement tests are important in most programs because of the necessity for sorting students into relatively similar ability groups, sometimes within specific content or skill areas. Establishing homogeneous classes is often considered desirable because teachers can then focus their attention on a relatively narrow set of language learning goals in each class. Regardless of the benefits, many students tend to be apprehensive, even terrified, of placement tests.

Other tests are designed to monitor the students' learning, or achievement. These tests may also be high-anxiety experiences for some students. Like the placement procedures, achievement tests are necessary. In this case, they are necessary as periodic checks on the students' progress, as well as checks on the quality of the program of instruction being offered. Since students often dread going through placement and achievement tests, or the proficiency and diagnostic tests also discussed in Chapter 1, teachers should make every effort to see that they make responsible decisions based on the results.

When most teachers first think of a test, they think of a multiple-choice standardized test like the *Scholastic Aptitude Test, American College Testing Program, Graduate Record Examination*, or the equivalent in other countries. When North American teachers think of ESL testing, they probably think of the *Test of English as a Foreign Language* (Educational Testing Service 1994). These tests (more commonly known by their acronyms, SAT, ACT, GRE, and TOEFL, respectively) are important and influential tests, but they represent just one type of test, a type that comes from one testing tradition. Testing in general and language testing in particular are far more complex than that one tradition might indicate. In fact, numerous issues influence the kinds of choices that teachers must make if they want to develop an effective testing program at their institution. I explore these perspectives in this chapter as a series of testing *issues*, each of which can be described and thought about separately. Nonetheless, all these issues must be considered simultaneously when adopting, developing, or adapting proficiency, placement, achievement, and diagnostic tests for any language program. Each issue involves one way of characterizing language tests and, taken together, these issues must all be considered in classifying and describing language tests in a state of the art manner. Thus, thinking about these issues will help teachers to understand the central concerns of language testing and language test design.

Generally speaking, all these issues can be classified as either theoretical or practical. However, the distinction that I make here between theory and practice is not clear-cut with definite boundaries. The distinction is made primarily to organize the discussion of the issues involved. As I will explain, the theoretical and practical issues described here interact with each other in complex and unpredictable ways. Thus, labeling these issues as theoretical or practical may aid in discussing and remembering them, but it will not keep them separate in reality. Nevertheless, teachers will find it useful to consider all the issues discussed in this chapter whenever they are putting tests in place in their own language program.

THEORETICAL ISSUES

The *theoretical issues* that I address have to do with what tests should look like and what they should do. These issues have a great deal to do with how a group of teachers feels that their course or program fits pedagogically within the overall field of language teaching. Theoretical issues may include pedagogical beliefs in various language teaching methodologies ranging from grammar-translation to communicative language teaching, or beliefs in the relative importance of the skills that teachers will teach and test in their program (written or oral, productive or receptive, and various combinations of the four). Other theoretical issues may range from the linguistic distinction between competence and performance to the purely testing distinction among the various types of tests that are available in language teaching. These test types range from what are called discrete-point to integrative tests and various combinations of the two. I discuss each of these issues in turn and then look at some of the ways in which they may interact with each other. Remember, they are just theoretical viewpoints on what tests should look like and what they should do.

One problem that arises is that language teaching professionals often disagree on these issues. In addition, since tests are instruments developed by people to make decisions about other people, test development and test administration are inherently political activities. Thus, a program's position on the various issues should be decided, perhaps by consensus, or at least discussed whenever new tests are being put into place. Recognizing the political nature of testing early in the process can stave off many problems later.

The Language Teaching Methodology Issue

Since views of what constitutes good language teaching vary widely throughout the profession, ideas about what constitutes a good test will probably also differ. Taking just the language teaching methodology issue that I mentioned earlier, consider how a teacher like the mythical Miss Fiditch (of the granny glasses, hair-in-a-bun, ruler-in-hand, structuralist school of language teaching) might argue with the much more real, and realistic, Sandra Savignon, who was one of the early advocates of communicative testing (see Savignon 1972) and continues to be active on testing issues (Savignon 1985; Bachman & Savignon 1986). Miss Fiditch would tolerate only strict testing of knowledge of grammar rules probably through translation of a selection from the "great books" of the target language into the mother tongue. Savignon, on the other hand, advocated testing "the students' ability to communicate in four different communicative contexts: discussion, information-getting, reporting, and description" (1972, p. 41). How did language testing get from the extreme represented by Miss Fiditch to the more modern views of Savignon?

An exceptionally short history of language testing. Spolsky (1978) and Hinofotis (1981) both have pointed out that language testing can be broken into periods, or trends, of development. Hinofotis labeled them the prescientific period, the psychometric/structuralist period, and the integrative/sociolinguistic period. I use the term *movements* instead of periods to describe them because they overlap chronologically and can be said to co-exist today in different parts of the world.

The *prescientific movement* in language testing is associated with the grammar-translation approaches to language teaching. Since such approaches have existed for ages, the end of this movement is usually delimited rather than its beginning. I infer from Hinofotis's article that the prescientific movement ended with the onset of the psychometric-structuralist movement, but clearly such movements have no end in language teaching because, without a doubt, such teaching and testing practices are going on in many parts of the world at this very moment.

The prescientific movement is characterized by translation and free composition tests developed exclusively by the classroom teachers, who are on their own when it comes to developing tests. One problem that arises with these types of tests is that they are relatively difficult to score objectively. Thus, subjectivity becomes an important factor in the scoring of such tests. Perhaps, mercifully, there were no language testing specialists involved in the prescientific movement. Hence, there was little concern with the application of statistical techniques such as descriptive statistics, reliability coefficients, validity studies, and so forth. Some teachers may think back to such a situation with a certain nostalgia for its simplicity, but along with the lack of concern with statistics came an attendant lack of concern with concepts like objectivity, reliability, and validity—that is, a lack of concern with making fair, consistent, and correct decisions about the lives of the students involved. Teachers today would definitely not advocate such unfair practices with regard to their students (and would complain even more vigorously if such lax practices were applied to themselves as students in a teacher training course).

With the onset of the *psychometric-structuralist movement* of language testing, worries about the objectivity, reliability, and validity of tests began to arise. Largely because of an interaction between linguists and specialists in psychological and educational measurement, language tests became increasingly scientific, reliable, and precise. Psychometric-structuralist tests typically set out to measure the discrete structure points (Carroll 1972) being taught in audio-lingual and related teaching methods of the time. As with the language teaching methods, these tests were influenced by behavioral psychology. The psychometric-structuralist movement saw the rise of the first carefully designed and standardized tests like the *Test of English as a Foreign Language* (first introduced in 1963), the *Michigan Test of English Language Proficiency: Form A* (University of Michigan 1961), *Modern Language Association Foreign Language Proficiency Tests for Teachers and Advanced Students* (Educational Testing Service 1968), *Comprehensive English Language Test for Speakers of English as a Second Language* (Harris & Palmer 1970), and many others. Such tests, usually in multiple-choice format, are easy to administer and score and are carefully constructed to be objective, reliable, and valid. Thus, they are an improvement on the testing practices of the prescientific movement.

The psychometric-structuralist movement is important because for the first time language test development follows scientific principles. In addition, psychometric-structuralist test development is squarely in the hands of trained linguists and language testers. As a result, statistical analyzes are used for the first time. Psychometric-structuralist tests are still very much in evidence around the world, but they have been supplemented (and in some cases, supplanted) by what Carroll (1972) labeled integrative tests.

The *integrative-sociolinguistic movement* has its roots in the argument that language is creative. More precisely, language professionals began to believe that language is more than the sum of the discrete parts being tested during the psychometric-structuralist movement. Beginning with the work of sociolinguists like Hymes (1967), it was felt that the development of communicative competence depended on more than simple grammatical control of the language; communicative competence also hinged on knowledge of the language appropriate for different situations. Tests typical of this movement were the cloze test and dictation, both of which assess the student's ability to manipulate language within a context of extended text rather than in a collection of discrete-point questions. The possibility of testing language in context led to further arguments (Oller 1979) for the benefits of integrative tests with regard to pragmatics (that is, the ways that linguistic and extra-linguistic elements of language are interrelated and relevant to human experience). The integrative-sociolinguistic movement is probably most important because it questions the linguistic assumptions of the previous structuralist movement yet uses the psychometric tools made available by that movement to explore language testing techniques designed to assess contextualized language.

Hinofotis, in her discussion of trends for the 1980s, suggests that the influence of notional-functional syllabuses and English for specific purposes have added new elements to language testing, including new attempts to define communicative competence. She refers to Brière 1979) and Canale and Swain (1981). Other useful references might include Canale and Swain (1980), Canale (1983), and Bachman (1990). Perhaps there will be a trend toward performance-based tests—that is, tests that require the students to use the language to perform a task. Such a task, if well-designed, might in turn dictate that the student do something (for instance, solve a problem) by means of the language. Such a test might be oriented toward unpredictable data in the same way that real-life interactions between speakers are unpredictable. Maybe the tests of the future will focus on authentic and purposeful language situations where the student is attempting to communicate some real message. This may necessarily lead to a partial shift away from objective and seemingly dispassionate measures of language ability to more subjective ratings of students' language performance. No one really knows what directions language teaching and testing will take, but it seems clear that, beginning with Savignon (1972), there has been a new direction in language testing which might usefully be labeled the *communicative movement*.

The methodology issue, initially described in terms of language teaching practices ranging from those advocated by teachers from "Miss Fiditch" to Sandra Savignon (that is, structuralist to communicative), has serious implications in thinking about historical movements within language testing, as well as important ramifications for the decisions that teachers make about which types of tests to use in their language programs.

For instance, different theoretical views on linguistics and language teaching may exist in any program. These views might vary from teachers who still believe in a structural approach to others who passionately argue for communicative language teaching—with the bulk of the teachers falling somewhere in between. The degree to which different teachers believe in various language teaching theories (even if they do not know what they are called) can strongly influence the teaching in a program and also the choices made in testing. Thus, a program will have to come to grips with such differences before any serious efforts can be made to implement tests of one type or another.

Two Skills-based Issues

The subtests on language tests are often separated into skill areas like reading, writing, listening, and speaking. An example of such skills-based subtests is the TOEFL, which currently reports subtest scores for (a) Listening Comprehension, (b) Structure and Written Expression, and (c) Vocabulary and Reading Comprehension (see Educational Testing Service 1994). In the English Language Institute at the University of Hawaii, where the core courses consist of levels within the listening, reading, and writing skills, we also organize our placement testing around skill areas with a placement battery that includes two subtests each for listening, reading, and writing, as well as a placement interview.

The channel issue. Language teachers and testers can benefit from thinking about such subtests in terms of the channel used for communication—that is, written or oral. For instance, reading and writing subtests can be lumped together and referred to as *written channel* subtests because they both involve language written on paper. Listening and speaking subtests, on the other hand, would more properly be labeled *oral channel* subtests because they involve the use of sound to communicate. Examples of tests that primarily assess the students' abilities to use the written channel would include a range from reading comprehension tests to compositions; examples of tests that primarily assess the students' abilities to function in the oral channel might range from a test of how well they can follow directions in the language to a public-speaking task that they must perform for a grade.

The mode issue. Some tests also necessitate the simultaneous use of two skills within a single channel. For instance, an oral interview procedure like the *Interagency Language Roundtable Oral Interview* (ILR 1982) may require the students to understand and produce spoken language. While the raters consider each skill separately, the net result is a single score that probably reflects some combined rating of both the listening and speaking skills. In such situations, a distinction between productive and receptive modes of communication can be useful. The *productive mode* includes those skills used to send information to others in the form of sound or light waves, or, put another way, those skills used to create the outward manifestations of language by writing or speaking. The ***receptive mode*** includes those skills that involve receiving and understanding the message from others—that is, reading and listening.

Examples of tests that primarily assess the students' abilities to use the productive mode would include a range of tasks from composition assignments to graded public speeches. Examples of tests that primarily assess the students' abilities to function in the receptive mode would range from tests of reading comprehension to tests of how well spoken directions in the language can be followed.

In language testing, teachers must realize that certain types of test questions are more closely related to testing the receptive skills and others are more closely associated with productive skills. Consider what is involved in answering true-false, multiple-choice, or matching tests. The activities are predominantly receptive, right? The student looks at a question and selects the correct answer, both of which are receptive activities. The only productive action a student must do is to mark the answer, which is an activity that, in itself, has little to do with language. Conversely, consider what is going on when a student answers a fill-in, short-response, or essay test. With the fill-in type of question, both receptive mode (reading the question) and productive mode (writing a word or phrase in a blank) are about equally involved. However, as the responses lengthen, as on an essay examination, the productive mode becomes more and more important to answering each question correctly. Teachers should keep these distinctions in mind when deciding what types of questions to use in testing the various skills.

Interactions of skills-based issues. In the previous section, the same example tests were used to explain channels *and* modes. This is possible because a test necessarily taps at least one channel and one mode at any given time. Thus, reading comprehension tests are typically viewed as receptive mode tests of the written channel. Composition tests also involve the written channel, but they are in the productive mode. Figure 2.1 shows how these two channels and two modes can co-exist. Notice that the channels are labeled across the top of the figure while the modes are labeled to the left. Inside the boxes, examples of each possible combination of channel and mode have been provided.

Sometimes tests become even more complex, assessing two modes at the same time, or two channels simultaneously. The possible combinations are obviously numerous. Consider a composition test where students are required to read a two-page academic passage and then analyze it in their written composition. One part of the campus-wide writing test for all incoming freshmen at the University of Hawaii takes this form, which

CHANNELS

	Written	Oral
Receptive	Reading Comprehension	Listening Comprehension
Productive	Composition	Speaking

MODES

Figure 2.1: Skills-Based Issues

combines the reading and writing skills. What channel(s) are they being required to use? Written only, right? And what mode(s)? The students must first read the passage (receptive) and then write a composition based on it (productive).

Consider also the commonly used dictation task. Dictation is sometimes used in language programs to test listening ability. Given the nature of the distinctions discussed above, what channel(s) are involved in taking a dictation? And what mode(s)? The student must understand what is being dictated, thus utilizing the oral channel, but must also be able to write it down, which is tapping the written channel. The student must receive the message, which is receptive mode, and must put it on paper, which is productive mode. After considering the dictation as it relates to these different issues, is it still logical to view it as a test of listening ability, or is it perhaps something more complex?

Thus, thinking about what is actually happening in language tests can be enhanced by thinking in terms of the productive and receptive modes and the written and oral channels. Remember, however, that various combinations are possible. For instance, a test like dictation is best described as partially written channel and partially oral channel, as well as partially receptive mode and partially productive mode. Hopefully, knowing about these issues will help teachers to better understand what they are testing.

The Competence/Performance Issue

Much elaboration has been made in linguistics on the distinction originally proposed by Chomsky between competence and performance. Chomsky (1965, p. 4) differentiates between the two as follows: "*competence* (the speaker-hearer's knowledge of his language) and *performance* (the actual use of language in concrete situations)." This distinction has some interesting ramifications for language testing. If linguistic performance is viewed as imperfect and full of flaws, even in native speakers, such performance can only be taken as an outward manifestation of the underlying but unobservable linguistic competence. If such a difference exists for native speakers of a language, the difference may be even more pronounced in non-native speakers.

This distinction can help teachers to realize that tests are at best fairly artificial observations of a student's performance, and performance is only an imperfect reflection of the underlying competence. Since both competence and performance are of interest to language teachers, they must be very careful in their interpretation of test results to remember that performance is only part of the picture—a part that is a second-hand observation of competence.

In testing circles, the underlying competence is more often described in terms of a *psychological construct* (see Chapter 7 for much more on this concept). An example of a construct in our field is the notion of overall English as a foreign language proficiency. Thus, a student's competence in EFL might more readily be discussed as overall EFL proficiency, which is a psychological construct. However, even a relatively successful attempt to test this construct, as with the TOEFL, only provides an estimate of the student's performance, which is only a reflection of the underlying construct, or competence. The important thing to remember, in my view, is that language testing can provide an estimate of a student's performance (sometimes from various angles as in listening, reading, and grammar subtests) but never provides a direct measure of the actual competence that underlies the performance.

The Discrete-point/Integrative Issue

Another issue that concerns language testers has to do with the different types of tests, which can range from discrete-point tests to integrative tests. Various combinations of these two types are possible as well (see Farhady 1979 for a discussion of this issue).

Discrete-point tests are those which measure the small bits and pieces of a language, as in a multiple-choice test made up of questions constructed to measure students' knowledge of different structures. One question on such an ESL test might be written to measure whether the students know the distinction between *a* and *an* in English. A major assumption that underlies the use of questions like this is that a collection of such discrete-point questions covering different structures (or other language learning points), if taken together as a single score, will produce a measure of some more global aspect of language ability. In other words, a teacher who believes in discrete-point tests would argue that scores based on the administration of fifty narrowly defined discrete-point, multiple-choice questions covering a variety of English grammatical structures will reveal something about the students' overall proficiency in grammar. Anyone holding the psychometric-structuralist view of language teaching and testing would probably be comfortable developing a test along these lines. A corollary to this general view would be that the individual skills (reading, writing, listening, and speaking) can be tested separately and that different aspects of these skills (pronunciation, grammar, vocabulary, culture, and so forth) can also be assessed as isolated phenomena.

As noted above, however, not all testers and teachers are comfortable with the discrete-point view of testing. *Integrative tests* are those designed to use several skills at one time, or more precisely, to employ different channels and/or modes of the language simultaneously and in the context of extended text or discourse. Consider dictation as a test type. The student is usually asked to listen carefully and write down a short prose passage as it is read aloud three times (with or without pauses) by the teacher or played on a tape. The skills involved are at least listening comprehension and writing, but different aspects of these two skills come into play as well. Sometimes handwriting is a factor; certainly distinguishing between phonemes is important as is grammatical ability. In short, dictation is testing many different things at the same time (including the receptive and productive modes in the oral and written channels) and does so in the context of extended text. Advocates of the integrative-sociolinguistic movement would argue that such a test is complex, as actual language use is complex. They would also argue that the language in integrative procedures like dictation, cloze test, and writing samples is being tested in the more natural, or at least larger, context of extended text (see Oller 1979).

Along the continuum between the most discrete-point types of tests and the most integrative, other kinds of tests are in a sense both integrative and discrete-point in nature. Consider a typical reading test in which the student is asked to read a passage and then answer multiple-choice fact, vocabulary, and inference questions about the passage. Viewing this task as a combination of reading a passage and integrating that reading into answering questions at different conceptual levels (that is, fact, vocabulary, and inference) might lead a teacher to conclude that reading comprehension is an integrative test. Yet looking at the very focused nature of the fact and vocabulary questions, a discrete-point label would come to mind. The point is that the sometimes useful distinction between discrete-point and integrative tests is not always clear.

PRACTICAL ISSUES

The *practical issues* that I address have to do with physically putting tests into place in a program. Teachers may find themselves concerned with the degree to which tests are fair in terms of objectivity. Or they may have to decide whether to keep the tests cheap or fight for the resources necessary to do a quality job of testing. Teachers may also be concerned about the logistics of testing. For instance, they may be worried about the relative difficulty of constructing, administering, and scoring different types of tests. In discussing each of these practical issues, I illustrate how each works and how it interrelates with the other practical issues.

The Fairness Issue

Fairness can be defined as the degree to which a test treats every student the same or the degree to which it is impartial. Teachers would generally like to ensure that their personal feelings do not interfere with fair assessment of the students or bias the assignment of scores. The aim in maximizing objectivity is to give each student an equal chance to do well. So teachers and testers often do everything in their power to find test questions, administration procedures, scoring methods, and reporting policies that optimize the chances that each student will receive equal and fair treatment. This tendency to seek objectivity has led to the proliferation of "objective" tests, which is to say tests, usually multiple-choice, which minimize the possibility of varying treatment for different students. Since such tests can and often are scored by machine, the process is maximally dispassionate and therefore objective.

However, many of the elements of any language course may not be testable in the most objective test types, such as multiple-choice, true-false, and matching. Whether teachers like it or not, one day they will have to recognize that they are not able to measure everything impartially and objectively. Consider what would happen if a group of adult education ESL teachers decided to test their students' communicative abilities. In thinking through such a test, they would probably decide that a multiple-choice format is not appropriate and that, instead, they need to set up situations, probably role plays, in which the students would use the spoken language in interactions with other students (or with native speakers if they can convince some to help out). Having set up the testing situations, they would then have to decide how the performance of each student would be scored and compared to the performances of all other students.

They might begin by designing some sort of scale, which includes descriptions of what they are looking for in the language use of their adult education students—that is, whether they want to score for grammatical accuracy, fluency, clear pronunciation, ability to use specific functions, or any of the myriad other possible focuses. The teachers might then have to further analyze and describe each area of focus in order to provide descriptive categories that would help them to assign so many points for excellent performance, fewer points for mediocre performance, and no points for poor performance. All this is possible and even admirable if their methodological perspective is communicative. The problem is not with the scale itself but rather with the person who would inevitably assign the scores on such a test. Can any person ever be completely objective when assigning such ratings? Of course not.

There are a number of test types that necessitate rater judgments like that just described. These tend to be toward the integrative end of the discrete-point to integrative continuum and include tests like oral interviews, translations, and compositions. Such tests ultimately require someone to use some scale to rate the written or spoken language that the students produce. The results must eventually be rated by some scorer, and there is always a threat to objectivity when these types of tests are used. The problem is not whether the test is objective but rather the degree of subjectivity that the teachers are willing to accept. For example, the University of Hawaii ELI placement test mixes relatively objective subtests like multiple-choice reading, multiple-choice proofreading, and multiple-choice academic listening subtests with a fairly judgmental, and therefore relatively subjective, composition subtest. We also have cloze and dictation subtests, which cannot be classed as entirely objective (because some judgments must be made) nor completely subjective (because the range of possibilities for those judgments is fairly restricted).

Thus, teachers may find that their thinking about this issue cannot be framed in absolutes but instead must center on the trade-offs that are sometimes necessary in testing theoretically desirable elements of student production while trying to maintain a relatively high degree of objectivity.

The Cost Issue

In the best of all possible worlds, unlimited time and funds would be available for teaching and testing languages. Unfortunately, this is rarely true. Most teachers are to some degree underpaid and overworked and must constantly make decisions that are based on how expensive some aspect of teaching, or testing, may turn out to be. This issue affects all the other issues covered in this chapter, so it cannot be ignored even if it seems self-evident. Lack of funds can cause the abandonment of otherwise well thought out theoretical and practical positions that teachers have taken (and cause them to do things that they would previously have found detestable). Consider the example of the adult education ESL communicative test that I just discussed. The teachers might have decided, for sound and defensible theoretical reasons, to include such a test in their placement battery. They could also have agreed to tolerate a certain amount of subjectivity in order to achieve their collective theoretical ends. They develop a scale and procedures for administering the test and take them proudly to the department head who says that it is absolutely impossible to conduct these interviews because of the time (and therefore cost) involved in paying teachers to do the ratings.

Something happens to teachers when they become administrators. I know that this is true because I watched it happen to me. When I first became a language teacher, I staunchly detested multiple-choice tests because I could not see how they represented students' abilities to actually use language in real situations. After all, people rarely communicate in real life with four optional answers provided. However, when I became an administrator, I found myself arguing for large-scale placement testing in machine-scorable, multiple-choice formats—a position based on the fact that such testing is relatively easy and cheap to administer and score. While testing each student individually may sometimes be desirable, teachers must recognize that it is very expensive in terms of both time and money. Nevertheless, if a group of teachers decides that interviews or role plays are worth doing, they must somehow find enough funding so that the testing can be done well.

Logistical Issues

Other logistical concerns must also be addressed in any language testing situation, especially the relative degree to which a particular test or subtest is easy to construct, administer, and score. As I will explain, certain trade-offs are often necessary among these issues.

Ease of test construction. Special considerations with regard to test construction can range from deciding how long the test should be to considering what types of questions to use. All things being equal, a long test of say 100 questions is likely to be better than a short test in terms of the consistency and accuracy of what is being measured. This is logical given that a one-question, multiple-choice test is not likely to be as accurate in assessing students' performance as a two-question test, or a ten-question test, or a fifty-question test. In which test should teachers have the most confidence? The fifty-question test, right? The problem is that this characteristic of tests is in direct conflict with the fact that short tests are easier to write than long ones. One goal of many test development projects is to find the "happy medium"—that is, the shortest test length that does a consistent and accurate job of testing the students (see Chapter 7 for more on the relationship between test length and reliability).

Another test construction issue involves the degree to which different types of tests are easy or difficult to produce. Some test types (for instance, a composition test) are relatively easy to construct. A teacher needs only to think of a good topic for the students to write on and make up some test directions that specify how long the students will have to write and perhaps the types of things that the teacher will be looking for in scoring the writing samples. Dictation tests are also easy to construct: just find an appropriate passage, provide paper, read the passage aloud (perhaps once straight through, a second time in phrases with pauses so that students can write, and a third time straight through for proofreading), and have the students write the passage down. Short-answer questions and translations are also relatively easy to construct. Constructing a cloze test is somewhat more difficult: find an appropriate passage, and type it up replacing every tenth word (or every seventh word, or every thirteenth word, etc.) with a numbered blank (for evidence that this process is not quite as easy as it seems, see Brown 1984b).

Writing fill-in, matching, true-false, and multiple-choice questions is more difficult, as I explain in the next chapter. Most language testers find that writing sound multiple-choice questions is the most difficult of these. Anyone who does not find that to be the case might want to look very carefully at his or her questions to see if they are indeed sound and effective. With these more restricted and receptive types of test questions, questions must be carefully constructed so that the correct answers are truly correct and incorrect answers are really wrong. Any teacher who has ever tried this will verify that the process of writing such questions can quickly become time-consuming.

Ease of test administration. My experience also indicates that ease of administration is a very important issue because testing is a human activity that is very prone to mix-ups and confusion. Perhaps this problem results from the fact that students are often nervous during a test and teachers are under pressure. The degree to which a test is easy to administer will depend on the amount of time it takes, the number of subtests involved, the amount of equipment and materials required to administer it, and the amount of guidance that the students need during the test. A short thirty-question, 15-minute, one-page cloze test with clear directions is relatively easy to administer. A one-hour, lecture-listening test based on a video tape that requires the students to write an essay will probably be relatively difficult to administer. Like so many of the issues discussed here, ease of administration must be considered in the trade-offs that seem to plague the choices that teachers must make in testing language.

Ease of test scoring. Ease of scoring is an important issue because a test that is easy to score is cheaper and is less likely to result in scorers making simple tallying, counting, and copying mistakes that might affect the students' scores. Most teachers will agree that such scoring mistakes are undesirable because they are not fair to the students, but I am willing to wager that any teacher who has served as a scorer in a pressure-filled testing situation has made such scoring mistakes. In one composition scoring situation, I found that ten language teachers made numerous mistakes in adding five two-digit subscores to find each student's total score. These mistakes affected 20% of the compositions, and no teacher (myself included) was immune. The best that teachers can hope to do is to minimize mistakes in scoring by making the processes as simple and clear as humanly possible and by double- and triple-checking those parts of the process that are error prone.

Ease of scoring seems to be inversely related to the ease of constructing a test type. In other words, the easiest types of tests to construct initially (composition, dictation, translation, and so forth) are usually the most difficult to score (and least objective), while those test types that are more difficult to construct initially (multiple-choice, true-false, matching, and so forth) are usually the easiest to score (and most objective).

INTERACTIONS OF THEORETICAL AND PRACTICAL ISSUES

While it may seem redundant, I must stress the importance of recognizing that each of the theoretical and practical issues discussed above can and will interact with all the others—sometimes in predictable patterns and at other times in unpredictable ways. For instance, if a group of high-school language teachers want to develop a test that, from a theoretical point of view, is communicative yet integrative and measures productive skills, they may have to accept that the test will be relatively subjective, expensive, and hard to administer and score. If, on the other hand, they decide they want a test that is very objective and easy to administer and score, they may have to accept the fact that the questions must be relatively discrete-point (and therefore difficult to write) so that the answer sheets can be machine-scorable. This decision will naturally result in a test that is less communicative and that focuses mostly on receptive skills. I am not arguing for one type of test or the other. I am, however, arguing that trade-offs are linked to the many testing issues discussed in this chapter.

ADOPT, DEVELOP, OR ADAPT?

In adopting, developing, or adapting language tests for a particular situation, teachers may be surprised at the diversity of opinion that exists about what a good test should include. Some teachers may have naive views of what a test should be, while others hold very sophisticated, very idealistic, or impractical views. For instance, those teachers who studied languages in the audio-lingual tradition often think of a language test as a longer and more varied form of the transformation drill, while colleagues who have recently graduated from M.A. or Ph.D. programs may be talking about communicative, task-based procedures that take two teachers 20 minutes per student to administer.

The appropriate managerial strategies for developing tests must, of course, be tailored to each situation. But every management strategy falls somewhere along a continuum that ranges from authoritarian to democratic. Since most language teachers of my acquaintance do not take well to dictatorial administrative practices, I find that the best strategies to employ are those which involve the teachers in the process of adopting, developing, or adapting tests. An additional benefit, of course, is the fact that they can usually be drawn into contributing more than just their ideas and opinions. Since testing sometimes involves long hours of work (often with no extra pay), any help that colleagues can give will help.

Once a consensus has been achieved as to the purpose and type of test to employ, a strategy must be worked out that will maximize the quality and effectiveness of the test that is eventually put into place. In the best of all possible worlds, each program would have a resident testing expert, whose entire job is to develop tests especially tailored for that program. But even in the worst of all possible worlds, rational decisions can be made in selecting commercially available tests if certain guidelines are followed. In many cases, any rational approach to testing will be a vast improvement over the existing conditions. Between these two extremes (developing tests from scratch or adopting them from commercial sources on pure faith) is the notion of adapting existing tests and materials so that they better serve the purposes of the program.

The main point I am making is that tests are, or should be, situation-specific. Since a test can be very effective in one situation with one particular group of students and be virtually useless in another, teachers cannot simply go out and buy a commercial test and automatically expect it to work with all their students. That commercial test may have been developed for an entirely different type of student and for entirely different purposes. The goal of this section is to provide teachers with rational bases for adopting, developing, or adapting language tests so that the tests will be maximally useful in their specific language programs.

Adopting Language Tests

The tests that are used in language programs are often adopted from sources outside of the program. This may mean that the tests are bought from commercial publishing houses, adopted from other language programs, or pulled straight from the current textbook. Given differences that exist among the participants in the various language programs around the world (for instance, differences in sex, number of languages previously studied, type of educational background, educational level, levels of proficiency, and so forth), it is probable that many of the tests acquired from external sources are being used with students quite different from those envisioned when the tests were originally developed and standardized. Using tests with the wrong types of students can result in mismatches between the tests and the abilities of the students as well as mismatches between the tests and the purposes of the program. For instance, many placement decisions, ones that dramatically affect the lives of the students (in terms of tuition costs, time, and effort), may be based on test questions quite unrelated to the needs of the particular students in a given language program or questions unrelated to the curriculum being taught in that program. Such practices are irresponsible and should be corrected.

Selecting good tests to match the purposes of a particular language program is therefore very important. However, properly making these matches is often difficult because of the technical aspects of testing that many language teachers find intimidating. In searching for tests that are suitable for a program, teachers and administrators may therefore wish to begin by looking for test reviews. These are usually written by testing specialists and are useful in the same way that book reviews are. Test reviews sometimes appear in the review sections of language teaching journals along with reviews of textbooks and professional volumes. Naturally, testing is not the focus of these journals, so such reviews tend to appear infrequently. *Language Testing* is a journal that specializes in articles on testing and therefore is more likely to provide test reviews. These reviews are sometimes fairly technical because the intended audience is testing specialists. For teachers of ESL/EFL, Alderson, Krahnke, and Stansfield (1987) offer a book that provides a collection of practical and useful test reviews. Most of the major tests available for ESL in 1987 are reviewed.

Other approaches that teachers might want to use to improve their abilities to select quality tests for their programs would include: (a) informing themselves about language testing through taking a course or reading up on it, (b) hiring a new teacher, who also happens to have an interest in, or already knows about, the subject of testing, and (c) giving one member of the faculty release time to become informed on the topic. In all cases, the checklist provided in Table 2.1 should (with some background in testing) aid in selecting tests that more or less match the purposes of a language program.

In using the checklist, teachers should look at the test manual provided by the publisher and begin by considering the general facts about the test. What is the title? Who wrote it? Where and when was it published? As shown in Table 2.1, the theoretical orientation of the test should probably be reviewed next. Is it in the correct family of tests (NRT or CRT) for the program's purposes? Is it designed for the type of decisions involved? Does it match the methodological orientation of the teachers and the goals of the curriculum? What about the skills tested? Are they productive or receptive modes? Are they written or oral channels? What combinations of modes and channels are required of the students? And how are they likely to interact? What types of subtests are involved? Are they discrete-point or integrative, or some combination of the two?

In terms of practical orientation, a number of issues must also be considered. For instance, to what degree is the test objective? Will allowances have to be made for subjectivity? What about cost? Is the test too expensive for the program, or just about right? What about logistics? Is the test going to be easy to put together, administer, and score?

In terms of test characteristics, the nature of the test questions must be considered. What are the students confronted with in the receptive mode? And what are they expected to do in the productive mode? If the test is designed for norm-referenced decisions, is information about norms and standardized scores provided? Does the test seem to be aimed at the correct group of students and organized to test the skills that are taught in the program? How many parts and separate scores will there be, and are they all necessary? Do the types of test questions reflect the productive and receptive types of techniques and exercises that are used in the program? Is the test described clearly, and does the description make sense? Is the test reliable and valid? If the test is a commercial product, it is the publisher's responsibility to convince the test user that the test is worth

Table 2.1: Test Evaluation Checklist

A. General background information
   1. Title
   2. Author(s)
   3. Publisher and date of publication
   4. Published reviews available
B. Your theoretical orientation
   1. Test family: norm-referenced or criterion-referenced (see Chapter 1)
   2. Purpose of decision: placement, proficiency, achievement, diagnostic (see Chapter 1)
   3. Language methodology orientation—structural <—> communicative
   4. Skills Tested
      a. Productive <—> receptive (*receptive:* true-false, multiple-choice, matching; *productive:* fill-in, short-response, task)
      b. Channel: written <—> oral
      c. Mode: productive <—> receptive
   5. Type of test: discrete-point <—> integrative
C. Your practical orientation
   1. Objective <—> subjective
   2. Expensive <—> inexpensive
   3. Logistical issues: easy <—> difficult
      a. Test construction
      b. Test administration
      c. Test scoring
D. Test characteristics
   1. Item description
      a. Receptive mode (written, picture, cassette tape, and so on)
      b. Productive mode (marking choice, speaking, writing, and so on)
   2. Norms (see Chapter 5)
      a. Standardization sample (nature, size, method of selection, generalizability of results, availability of established norms for subgroups based on nationality, native language, sex, academic status, and so on)
      b. Number of subtests and separate scores
      c. Type of standardized scores (percentiles, and so on)
   3. Descriptive information (see Chapter 4)
      a. Central tendency (mean, mode, median, and midpoint)
      b. Dispersion (low–high scores, range, and standard deviation)
      c. Item characteristics (facility, discrimination, and so on)
   4. Reliability (see Chapter 7)
      a. Types of reliability procedures used (test–retest, equivalent forms, internal consistency, interrater, intrarater, and so on)
      b. Degree of reliability for each procedure in a.
      c. Standard error of measurement
   5. Validity (see Chapter 8)
      a. Types of validity procedures used (content, construct, and/or predictive/concurrent criterion-related validity)
      b. Degree to which you find convincing the validity statistics and argument(s) referred to above
   6. Actual practicality of the test
      a. Cost of test booklets, cassette tapes, manual, answer sheets, scoring templates, scoring services, and any other necessary test components
      b. Quality of items listed in a. above (paper, printing, audio clarity, durability, and so on)
      c. Ease of administration (time required, proctor/student ratio, proctor qualifications, equipment necessary, availability and quality of directions for administration, and so on)
      d. Ease of scoring (method of scoring, amount of training necessary, time per test, score conversion information, and so on)
      e. Ease of interpretation (quality of guidelines for the interpretation of scores in terms of norms or other criteria)

adopting. The user should therefore expect to find sound arguments supporting the quality of the test.

Other practical considerations are also important. What are the initial and ongoing costs of the test? What is the quality of the tapes, test booklets, answer sheets, and so forth? Are there preview booklets or other sorts of preparatory materials available to give out to the students? Is the test easy to administer? Is the scoring reasonably easy relative to the types of test questions being used? Is the interpretation of scores explained with guidelines for reporting and clarifying the scores to the students and teachers involved?

In short, there are many factors that must be considered even in adopting an already published test for a particular program. Many of these issues can be addressed by any thoughtful language teacher, but others, such as examining the degree to which the test is reliable and valid, will take more knowledge and experience with language tests. (For a quick idea of the scope of what a teacher must know to decide about the relative reliability and validity of a test, take a brief glance through Chapters 7 and 8.)

Developing Language Tests

In an ideal situation, teachers will have enough resources and expertise available in their program that proficiency, placement, achievement, and diagnostic tests can be developed and fitted to the goals of the program and to the ability levels and needs of the students. The guidelines offered in this book should help with that process.

If a group of teachers decides to develop their own tests, they will need to begin by deciding which tests to develop first. Perhaps those tests that were identified as most program-specific in the previous chapter should be developed first.That would mean developing tests of achievement and diagnosis first because they will tend to be based entirely and exclusively on the objectives of the particular program. In the interim, while developing these achievement and diagnostic tests, previously published proficiency and placement tests could be adopted as needed. Later, these teachers may wish to develop their own placement test so that the test questions being used to separate students into levels of study are related to the objectives of the courses and to what the students are learning in the program. However, because of their pan-programmatic nature, proficiency tests may necessarily always be adopted from outside sources so that comparisons between and among various institutions will make sense.

Somewhere in the process of developing tests, teachers may want to stop and evaluate them on the basis of the checklist provided in Table 2.1. Teachers should always be willing to be just as critical of their own tests as they are of commercial tests. The fact that a test is developed by and for a specific program does not necessarily make it a good test. So evaluation of test quality should be an integral part of the test development process.

Adapting Language Tests

A newly developed test may work fairly well in a program, but perhaps not as well as was originally hoped. Such a situation would call for further adapting of the test until it better fits the needs and purposes of the particular language program. The strategies described in the next chapter will help teachers to use qualitative and statistical analyzes of test results to revise and improve tests. Generally, however, the process of adapting a test to specific situations involves some variant of the following steps:

1. Administer the test in the particular program, using the appropriate teachers and their students;

2. Select those test questions that work well at spreading out the students (for NRTs) or that are efficient at measuring the learning of the objectives (for CRTs) in the particular program;

3. Develop a shorter, more efficient revision of the test—one that fits the program's purposes and works well with its students (some new questions may be necessary, ones similar to those that worked well, in order to have a long enough test); and

4. Evaluate the quality of the newly revised test (see Table 2.1).

With the basic knowledge provided in this book, any language teacher can accomplish all these steps. In fact, following the guidelines given in Chapter 3 will enable any teacher to adapt a test to a specific set of program goals and decision-making purposes. However, in the interest of fair advertising, I must provide the warning that test development is hard work and can be time-consuming. However, in the end, I have always felt that the hard work was worthwhile because of the useful information that is gained and the satisfaction that is derived from making responsible decisions about my students' lives. The point is that before teachers begin a test revision project, they should make sure that they will have enough time and help to do the job well.

PUTTING SOUND TESTS IN PLACE

Once teachers have decided to adopt, develop, or adapt tests, they are ready to put them into effect in order to help with decision making. The checklist shown in Table 2.2 should help put tests into place successfully. To begin with, make sure that the purposes for administering the various tests are clear to the curriculum developers and to the teachers (and eventually to the students). This presupposes that these purposes are already clearly defined in both theoretical and practical terms that are understood and agreed to by a majority of the staff. Then check the quality of the test itself, using the checklist in Table 2.1 as a guide.

The next step is to ensure that all the necessary physical conditions for the test have been met, such as making sure that there is a well-ventilated and quiet place to give the test, with enough time in that space for some flexibility and clear scheduling. Also make sure that the students have been properly notified and/or have signed up in advance for the test. Perhaps students should be given precise written information that answers their most pressing questions. Where and when will the test be administered? What should they do to prepare for the test? What should they bring with them? Should they bring picture identification? This type of information prepared in advance in the form of a handout or pamphlet may save answering the same questions hundreds of times.

Before actually administering the test, check that there are adequate materials on hand, perhaps with a few extras of everything. All necessary equipment should be ready and checked to see that it works (with backups if that is appropriate). Proctors must be trained in their duties and have sufficient information to do a professional job of test administration.

After the test has been administered, provision must be made for scoring. Again, adequate space and scheduling are important so that qualified staff can be properly trained and carry out the scoring of the test(s). Equally important is the interpretation of results. The purpose of the results must be clear, and provision must be made for helping teachers to use the scores and explain the scores to the students. Ideally, a well-defined purpose for the results will also exist in overall curriculum planning.

Record keeping is often forgotten in the process of test giving. Nevertheless, all necessary resources must be marshaled for keeping track of scores, including sufficient clerical staff, computers and software, or just some type of ledger book. In all cases, staff members should have ready access to the records. Provision must also be made for the eventual destruction or long-term storage of these records. Last but not least, an ongoing plan for research should be developed to utilize the information generated by test scores. Such research should take full advantage of the test results so that the new information can be effectively incorporated into the overall curriculum development process (see Chapter 9 for more on the relationship between testing and curriculum development).

Table 2.2: A Testing Program Checklist

A. Establishing purposes of test
   1. Clearly defined (from both theoretical and practical orientations)
   2. Understood and agreed upon by staff

B. Evaluating the test itself (see Table 2.1)

C. Arranging the physical needs
   1. Adequate, well-ventilated, and quiet space
   2. Enough time in that space for some flexibility
   3. Clear scheduling

D. Making pre-administration arrangements
   1. Students properly notified of test
   2. Students signed up for test
   3. Students given precise information (where and when test will be, as well as what they should do to prepare and what they should bring with them, especially identification if required)

E. Administering the test
   1. Adequate materials in hand (test booklets, answer sheets, cassette tapes, pencils, scoring templates, and so on) plus extras
   2. All necessary equipment in hand and tested (cassette players, microphones, public address system, video tape players, blackboard, chalk, and so on) with backups where appropriate
   3. Proctors trained in their duties
   4. All necessary information distributed to proctors (test directions, answers to obvious questions, schedule of who is to be where and when, and so on)

F. Scoring
   1. Adequate space for all scoring to take place
   2. Clear scheduling of scoring and notification of results
   3. Sufficient qualified staff for all scoring activities
   4. Staff adequately trained in all scoring procedures

G. Interpreting
   1. Clearly defined purpose for results
   2. Provision for helping teachers use scores and explain them to students
   3. A well-defined place for the results in the overall curriculum

H. Record keeping
   1. All necessary resources for keeping track of scores
   2. Ready access to the records for administrators and staff
   3. Provision for eventual systematic termination of records

I. Ongoing research
   1. Results used to full advantage for research
   2. Results incorporated into overall program evaluation plan

SUMMARY

The two checklists in Tables 2.1 and 2.2 summarize large chunks of the information contained in this chapter. Nevertheless, there are several global issues covered in the chapter but not in the checklists; I would now like to briefly review these in order to help pull together the various threads that have been developed in the first two chapters. For economy of space, I will summarize these various strands in the form of a checklist. Remember to ensure that you choose the correct test for a given decision, that each test is a good one, and that you are ready to incorporate it properly into your language program. To those ends, you may want to use the following checklist whenever making decisions about tests:

☐ Have you decided on the type of interpretation you need? (see Table 1.1)
  ☐ Criterion-referenced?
  ☐ Norm-referenced?
☐ Have you identified the type of decision you must make with the test scores?
  ☐ Proficiency?
  ☐ Placement?
  ☐ Achievement?
  ☐ Diagnostic?
☐ Does your test match your decision type? (see Table 1.2)
☐ Have you checked the quality of the test? (see Table 2.1)
☐ Are you adequately prepared to create an environment that makes the testing successful? (see Table 2.2)

TERMS

communicative movement

competence

discrete-point tests

fairness

integrative-sociolinguistic movement

integrative tests

movements

oral channel

performance

practical issues

prescientific movement

productive mode

psychological construct

psychometric-structuralist movement

receptive mode

theoretical issues

written channel

REVIEW QUESTIONS

1. What are the theoretical and practical issues that must be considered in developing language tests? How are the theoretical issues different in general from those classified as practical?

2. On a continuum of methodological choices that ranges from structural language teaching to communicative, where would your philosophy of teaching fit? What about your philosophy of testing? Are you prescientific? Are you a psychometric-structuralist? An integrative-sociolinguist? Or are you part of the communicative wave of the future? How so?

3. What are the differences between the written channel and the oral one? Under what conditions might these two channels interact?

4. What is the difference between the receptive mode and the productive mode? Under what conditions might they interact? What is the difference between a channel and a mode? Under what conditions might you expect both modes and/or both channels to be involved in a testing situation?

5. What is the difference between competence and performance as discussed by Chomsky? And why might this distinction be important to think about with regard to language testing?

6. What is the fundamental difference between a discrete-point test and an integrative one? Can you think of at least one example of each? Would you prefer to use discrete-point or integrative tests for purposes of placing students into the levels of a language program? Why?

7. Why is objectivity important to language testers? Under what conditions could you justify sacrificing some degree of objectivity? Why?

8. What are some of the logistical conditions that you should consider in any testing project? Which of the three discussed in this book (ease of construction, administration, and scoring) do you think is the most important? How are ease of test construction and ease of scoring inversely related?

9. What are the factors that you must consider in looking at the quality of a test? Which do you think are the most important?

10. What are the factors that you must keep in mind in putting together a successful testing program? Which factors do you think are the most important?

APPLICATION EXERCISES

A. Locate a test that you think might be useful in a language program in which you are now working, or if you have never taught, find a test for a hypothetical elementary, secondary, adult education, commercial, or university language program. Examine the test very carefully using Table 2.1. Perhaps you should consult with several colleagues and find out what they think of it. What differences do you have with your colleagues in your views on testing?

B. What issues would be of particular importance for implementing the test that you selected for part A (see Table 2.2)?

CHAPTER 3

DEVELOPING AND IMPROVING TEST ITEMS

In the first chapter, I covered the different types of decisions that teachers have to make in their language programs. In the second chapter, I discussed the different theoretical and practical issues that may affect teachers' choices in adopting, developing, and adapting language tests for use in making decisions about their students. In this chapter, I look much more closely at the elements that make up a good test. The basic unit of any test is the test *item*, so I begin the chapter with a broad definition of this crucial term. Then I turn to the procedures involved in item analyses, showing how item analysis procedures are quite different for the two basic categories of tests. For NRTs, the techniques for developing, analyzing, selecting, and refining items include item format analysis, item facility indices, item discrimination indices, and distractor efficiency analysis. For CRTs, some of the same analyses are typically used plus item quality analysis (for content), the difference index, and the B-index. The purpose of both sets of analyses is to decide which items to keep in revised and improved versions of a test and which to discard. I describe these revision processes step-by-step for both the NRT and CRT types of test development projects. In short, the information supplied in this chapter will enable teachers to develop, analyze, select, and refine those items most suitable for testing their students—whether their purpose is to develop an NRT for proficiency or placement decisions or a CRT for diagnostic or achievement decisions.

WHAT IS AN ITEM?

In the same sense that the phoneme is a basic unit in phonology and the morpheme is a basic unit in syntax, an item is the basic unit of language testing. Like the linguistic units above, the item is sometimes difficult to define. Some types of items, like multiple-choice or true-false items, are relatively easy to identify as the individual test questions that anyone can recognize as discrete units. For other more integrative types of language tests, such as dictations, interviews, role plays, or compositions, the individual item units may prove more difficult to identify. To accommodate the variety of discrete-point and integrative item types found in language testing, I will define the term *item* very broadly as the smallest unit that produces distinctive and meaningful information on a test or rating scale.

Since the item is the basic unit, or building block, in testing, one way to improve a test is to examine the individual items and revise the test so that only those items that are performing well remain in the revised version of the test. Teachers often look at the total scores of their students on a test, but careful examination of the individual items that contributed to the total scores can also prove very illuminating. This process of carefully inspecting individual test items is called *item analysis*.

More formally, **item analysis** is the systematic evaluation of the effectiveness of the individual items on a test. This is usually done for purposes of selecting the "best" items that will remain on a revised and improved version of the test. Sometimes however, item analysis is performed simply to investigate how well the items on a test are working with a particular group of students. Item analysis can take numerous forms, but when testing for norm-referenced purposes, four types of analyses are typically applied: item format analysis, item facility analysis, item discrimination analysis, and distractor efficiency analysis. In developing CRTs, three other concerns become paramount: item quality analysis, the item difference index, and the *B*-index for each item.

DEVELOPING NORM-REFERENCED LANGUAGE TESTS

Item Format Analysis

In **item format analysis**, testers focus on the degree to which each item is properly written so that it measures all and only the desired content. Such analyses often involve making judgments about the adequacy of item formats. The guidelines provided in this chapter are designed to help teachers make well-informed and relatively objective judgments about how well items are formatted. The first set of guidelines is a very general set that teachers can apply to virtually all types of items. A second set helps to guide analysis of receptive response item formats (true-false, multiple-choice, and matching items). The third set helps with the different types of productive response item formats (fill-in, short-response, and task). In all cases, the purpose is to help teachers to improve the formatting of the items that they use in their language tests.

General guidelines. Table 3.1 shows some general guidelines, which are applicable to most language testing formats. They are in the form of questions that teachers can ask themselves when writing or critiquing any type of item format. In most cases, the purpose of asking these questions is to ensure that the students answer the items correctly or incorrectly for the right reasons. In other words, the students should answer the items correctly only if they know the concept being tested or have the skill involved. By extension, the students should answer incorrectly only if they

Table 3.1: General Guidelines for Most Item Formats

Checklist Questions	YES	NO
1. Is the item format correctly matched to the purpose and content of the item?	☐	☐
2. Is there only one correct answer?	☐	☐
3. Is the item written at the students' level of proficiency?	☐	☐
4. Have ambiguous terms and statements been avoided?	☐	☐
5. Have negatives and double negatives been avoided?	☐	☐
6. Does the item avoid giving clues that could be used in answering other items?	☐	☐
7. Are all parts of the item on the same page?	☐	☐
8. Is only relevant information presented?	☐	☐
9. Have race, gender, and nationality bias been avoided?	☐	☐
10. Has at least one other colleague looked over the items?	☐	☐

do not know the material or lack the skill being tested. Let's consider each question in Table 3.1 in turn.

1. Teachers will of course want their item formats to match the purpose and content of the item. In part, this means matching the right type of item to what is being tested in terms of channels and modes. For instance, teachers may want to avoid using a multiple-choice format, which is basically receptive (students read and select, but they produce nothing), for testing productive skills like writing and speaking. Similarly, it would make little sense to require the students to read aloud (productive) the letters of the words in a book in order to test the receptive skill of reading comprehension. Such a task would be senseless, in part because the students would be using both receptive and productive modes mixed with both oral and written channels when the purpose of the test, reading comprehension, is essentially receptive mode and written channel. A second problem would arise because the students would be too narrowly focused in terms of content on reading the letters of the words. To avoid mixing modes and channels and to focus the content at the comprehension level of the reading skill, teachers might more profitably have the students read a written passage and use receptive-response items in the form of multiple-choice comprehension questions. In short, teachers must think about what they are trying to test in terms of all the dimensions discussed in the previous chapter and try to match their purpose with the item format that most closely resembles it.

2. The issue of making sure that each question has only one correct answer is not as obvious as it might at first seem. Correctness is often a matter of degrees rather than an absolute. An option that is correct to one person may be less so to another, and an option that seems incorrect to the teacher may appear to be correct to some of the students. Such differences may occur

due to differing points of view or to the differing contexts that people can mentally supply in answering a given question. Every teacher has probably disagreed with the "correct" answer on some test that he or she has taken or given. Such problems arise because the item writer was unable to take into account every possible point of view. One way that test writers attempt to circumvent this problem is by having the examinees select the *best* answer. Such wording does ultimately leave the judgment as to which is the "best" answer in the hands of the test writer, but how ethical is such a stance? I feel that the *best* course of action is to try to write items for which there is clearly only one correct answer. The statistics discussed in *Distractor Efficiency Analysis* (p. 70) help teachers to spot cases where the results indicate that two answers are possible, or that a second answer is very close to correct.

3. Each item should be written at approximately the level of proficiency of the students who will take the test. Since a given language program may include students with a wide range of abilities, teachers should think in terms of using items that are at about the *average* ability level for the group. To begin with, teachers may have to gauge this average level by intuition, but later, using the item statistics provided in this chapter, they will be able to identify more rationally those items that are at the appropriate average level for their students.

4. Ambiguous terms and tricky language should be avoided unless the purpose of the item is to test ambiguity. The problem is that ambiguous language may cause students to answer incorrectly even though they know the correct answer. Such an outcome is always undesirable.

5. Likewise, the use of negatives and double negatives may be needlessly confusing and should be avoided unless the purpose of the item is to test negatives. If negatives must be tested, wise test writers emphasize the negative elements (by underlining them, typing them in CAPITAL letters, or putting them in **boldfaced** type) so the students are sure to notice what is being tested. Students should *not* miss an item because they did not notice a negative marker, if indeed they know the answer.

6. Teachers should also avoid giving clues in one item that will help students to answer another item. For instance, a clear example of a grammatical structure may appear in one item that will help some students to answer a question about that structure later in the test. Students should answer the latter question correctly only if they know the concept or skill involved, not because they were clever enough to remember and look back to an example or model of it in a previous item.

7. All the parts of each item should be on one page. Students, who know the concept or skill being tested, should not respond incorrectly

simply because they did not realize that the correct answer was on the next page. This issue is easily checked but sometimes forgotten.

8. Teachers should also avoid including extra information that is irrelevant to the concept or skill being tested. Since most teachers will probably want their tests to be relatively efficient, any extra information not related to the material being tested should be avoided because it will just take extra time for the students to read and will add nothing to the test. Such extra information may also inadvertently provide the students with clues that they can use in answering other items.

9. All teachers should also be on the alert for bias that may have crept into their test items. Race, gender, religion, nationality, and other biases must be avoided at all costs, not only because they are morally wrong and illegal in many countries but also because they affect the fairness and objectivity of the test. The problem is that a biased item is testing something in addition to what it was originally designed to test. Hence, such an item cannot provide clear and easily interpretable information. The only practical way to avoid bias in most situations is to examine the items carefully and have other language professionals also examine them. Preferably these colleagues will be both male and female and will be drawn from different racial, religious, nationality, and ethnic groupings. Since the potential for bias differs from situation to situation, individual teachers will have to determine what is appropriate for avoiding bias in the items administered to their particular populations of students. Statistical techniques can also help teachers to spot and avoid bias in items; however, these statistics are still controversial and well beyond the scope of this book.

10. Regardless of any problems that teachers may find and correct in their items, they should always have at least one or more colleagues (who are native speakers of the language being tested) look over and perhaps take the test so that any additional problems may be spotted before the test is actually used to make decisions about students' lives. As Lado (1961, p. 323) put it, "if the test is administered to native speakers of the language they should make very high marks on it or we will suspect that factors other than the basic ones of language have been introduced into the items."

Receptive response items. Table 3.2 includes other questions that are specifically designed for *receptive response items*. A receptive response item requires the student to select a response rather than actually produce one. In other words, the responses involve receptive language in the sense that the item responses from which students must select are heard or read, receptively. Receptive response item formats include true-false, multiple-choice, and matching items.

Table 3.2: Guidelines for Receptive Item Formats

Checklist Questions	YES	NO
True-False		
1. Is the statement worded carefully enough that it can be judged without ambiguity?	☐	☐
2. Have "absoluteness" clues been avoided?	☐	☐
Multiple-Choice		
1. Have all unintentional clues been avoided?	☐	☐
2. Are all of the distractors plausible?	☐	☐
3. Has needless redundancy been avoided in the options?	☐	☐
4. Has the ordering of the options been carefully considered? Or are the correct answers randomly assigned?	☐	☐
5. Have distractors such as "none of the above" and "*a.* and *b.* only" been avoided?	☐	☐
Matching		
1. Are there more options than premises?	☐	☐
2. Are options shorter than premises to reduce reading?	☐	☐
3. Are the option and premise lists related to one central theme?	☐	☐

True-false items are typically written as statements, and students must decide whether the statements are true or false. There are two potential problems shown in Table 3.2 that teachers should consider in developing items in this format.

1. The statement should be carefully worded to avoid any ambiguities that might cause the students to miss it for the wrong reasons. The wording of true-false items is particularly difficult and important. Teachers are often tempted to make such items "tricky" so that the items will be difficult enough for intermediate or advanced language students. Such trickiness should be avoided: Students should miss an item because they do not know the concept or have the skill being tested rather than because the item is tricky.

2. Teachers should also avoid absoluteness clues. Absoluteness clues allow students to answer correctly without knowing the correct response. Absoluteness clues include terms like *all, always, absolutely, never, rarely, most often,* and so forth. True-false items that include such terms are very easy to answer regardless of the concept or skill being tested because the answer is inevitably *false.* For example: (True or False?) This book is always crystal clear in all its explanations.

Multiple-choice items are made up of an *item stem*, or the main part of the item at the top, a *correct answer*, which is obviously the choice (usually, *a., b., c.,* or *d.*) that will be counted correct, and the *distractors*, which are those choices that will be counted as incorrect. These incorrect choices are called distractors because they should distract, or divert, the students' attention away from the correct answer if the students really do not know which is correct. The term *options* refers collectively to all the alternative choices presented to the students and includes the correct answer and the distractors. All these terms are necessary for understanding how multiple-choice items function. Five potential pitfalls for multiple-choice items appear in Table 3.2.

1. Teachers should avoid unintentional clues (grammatical, phonological, morphological, and so forth) that help students to answer an item without having the knowledge or skill being tested. To avoid such clues, teachers should write multiple-choice items so that they clearly test only one concept or skill at a time. Consider the following item:

The fruit that Adam ate in the Bible was an _____ .

a. pear

b. banana

c. apple

d. papaya

The purpose of this item is neither clear nor straightforward. If the purpose of the item is to test cultural or biblical knowledge, an unintentional grammatical clue (in that the article *an* must be followed by a word that begins with a vowel) is interfering with that purpose. Hence, a student who knows the article system in English can answer the item correctly without ever having heard of Adam. If, on the other hand, the purpose of the item is to test knowledge of this grammatical point, why confuse the issue with the cultural/biblical reference? In short, teachers should avoid items that are not straightforward and clear in intent. Otherwise, unintentional clues may creep into their items.

2. Teachers should also make sure that all the distractors are plausible. If one distractor is ridiculous, that distractor is not helping to test the students. Instead, those students who are guessing will be able to dismiss that distractor and improve their chances of answering the item correctly without really knowing the correct answer. Why would any teacher write an item that has ridiculous distractors? Brown's law may help to explain this phenomenon: When writing four-option, multiple-choice items, the stem and correct option are easy to write, and the next two distractors are relatively easy to make up as well, but the last distractor is absolutely impossible. The only way to understand Brown's law is to try writing a few four-option, multiple-choice items. The point is that teachers are often tempted to put something ridiculous for that last distractor because they

are having trouble thinking of an effective distractor. So always check to see that all the distractors in a multiple-choice item are truly distracting. The section on *Distractor Efficiency Analysis* (p. 70) provides statistical tools that can help with this process.

3. In order to make a test reasonably efficient, teachers should double-check that items contain no needless redundancy. For example, consider the following item designed to test the past tense of the verb *to fall*:

The boy was on his way to the store, walking down the street, when he stepped on a piece of cold wet ice and _____ .

a. fell flat on his face.

b. fall flat on his face.

c. felled flat on his face.

d. falled flat on his face.

In addition, to the problem of providing needless words and phrases throughout the stem, the phrase "flat on his face" is repeated four times in the options, when it could just as easily have been written once in the stem. Thus, the item could have been far shorter to read and less redundant, yet equally effective, if it had been written as follows:

The boy stepped on a piece of ice and _____ flat on his face.

a. fell

b. fall

c. felled

d. falled

4. Any test writer may unconsciously introduce a pattern into the test that will help the students who are guessing to increase the probability of answering an item correctly. A teacher might decide that the correct answer for the first item should be *c*. For the second item, that teacher might decide on *d*., and for the third item *a*. Having already picked *c.*, *d.*, and *a.* to be correct answers in the first three items, the teacher will very likely pick *b*. as the correct answer in the next item. Human beings seem to have a need to balance things out like this, and such patterns can be used by clever test takers to help them guess at better than chance levels without actually knowing the answers. Since testers want to maximize the likelihood that students answer items correctly because they know the concepts being tested, they generally avoid patterns that can help students to guess.

A number of strategies can be used to avoid creating patterns. If the options are always ordered from the shortest to longest or alphabetically, the choice of which option is correct is out of the test writer's hands, so the human tendency to create patterns will be avoided. Another strategy that can be used is to select randomly which option will be correct. Selection can be done with a table of random numbers or with the aces, twos, threes, and fours taken from a deck of cards. In all cases, the purpose is to eliminate patterns that may help students to guess the correct answers if they do not know the answers.

5. Teachers can also be tempted (often due to Brown's law, mentioned above) to use options like "all of the above," "none of the above," and "*a.* and *b.* only." I normally advise against this type of option unless the specific purpose of the item is to test two things at a time and students' abilities to interpret such combinations. For the reasons discussed in numbers 1 and 2 above, such items are usually inadvisable.

Matching items present the students with two columns of information; the students must then find and identify matches between the two sets of information. For the sake of discussion, the information given in the left-hand column will be called the *premises* and that shown in the right-hand column will be labeled *options*. Thus, in a matching test, students must match the correct option to each premise. There are three guidelines that teachers should apply to matching items.

1. More options should be supplied than premises so that students cannot narrow down the choices as they go along by simply keeping track of the options that they have already used. For example, in matching ten definitions (premises) to a list of ten vocabulary words (options), a student who knows nine will be assured of getting the tenth one correct by the process of elimination. If, on the other hand, there are ten premises and fifteen options, this problem is minimized.

2. The options should usually be shorter than the premises because most students will read a premise and then search through the options for the correct match. By controlling the length of the options, the amount of reading will be minimized. Teachers often do exactly the opposite in creating vocabulary matching items by using the vocabulary words as the premises, and using the definitions (which are much longer) as the options.

3. The premises and options should be logically related to one central theme that is obvious to the students. Mixing different themes in one set of matching items is not a good idea because it may confuse the students and cause them to miss items that they would otherwise answer correctly. For example, lining up definitions and the related vocabulary items is a good idea, but also mixing in matches between graphemic and phonemic representations of words would only cause confusion. The two different themes could be much more clearly and effectively tested as separate sets of matching items.

Table 3.3: Guidelines for Productive Item Formats

Checklist Questions	YES	NO
Fill-In		
1. Is the required response concise?	☐	☐
2. Is there sufficient context to convey the intent of the question to the students?	☐	☐
3. Are the blanks of standard length?	☐	☐
4. Does the main body of the question precede the blank?	☐	☐
5. Has a list of acceptable responses been developed?	☐	☐
Short-Response		
1. Is the item formatted so that only one relatively concise answer is possible?	☐	☐
2. Is the item framed as a clear and direct question?	☐	☐
Task		
1. Is the student's task clearly defined?	☐	☐
2. Is the task sufficiently narrow (and/or broad) for the time available?	☐	☐
3. Have scoring procedures been worked out in advance with regard to the approach that will be used?	☐	☐
4. Have scoring procedures been worked out in advance with regard to the categories of language that will be rated?	☐	☐
5. Have scoring procedures been clearly defined in terms of what each score within each category means?	☐	☐
6. Is scoring to be as anonymous as possible?	☐	☐

Productive response items. Table 3.3 includes additional questions that should be applied to *productive response items*. Productive response items require the students actually to produce responses rather than just select them receptively. In other words, the responses involve productive language in the sense that the answers must either be written or spoken. Productive item formats include fill-in, short-response, and task types of items.

Fill-in items are those wherein a word or phrase is replaced by a blank in a sentence or longer text, and the student's job is to fill in that missing word or phrase. There are five sets of issues that teachers should consider when using fill-in items.

1. In answering fill-in items, students will often write alternative correct answers that the teacher did not anticipate when the items were written. To guard against this possibility, teachers should check to make sure that each item has one very concise correct answer. Alternatively, the teacher can develop a glossary of acceptable answers for each blank. Obviously, as the number of alternative possibilities rises for each item, the longer and more difficult the scoring becomes. One goal should be to create an answer key that will help the teacher to make clear-cut decisions as to whether each item is correct. Another goal should be to create an answer key that is so

complete that no modifications will be necessary during the scoring process itself; such modifications necessitate backtracking and rescoring tests that have already been scored.

2. In deciding how much context to provide for each blank (that is, how many words or phrases should surround each item), teachers should make sure that enough context has been provided that the purpose, or intent, of the item is clear to those students who know the answer. At the same time, avoid giving too much extra context. Extra context will burden students with extraneous material to read (see Table 3.1, #8) and may inadvertently provide students with extraneous clues (see Table 3.1, #6).

3. Generally speaking, all the blanks in a fill-in test should be the same length—that is, if the first blank is twelve spaces long, then all the items should have blanks with twelve spaces. Blanks of uniform length do not provide extraneous clues about the relative length of the answers. Obviously, this stricture would not apply if a teacher purposely wants to indicate the length of each word or the number of words in each blank.

4. Teachers should also consider putting the main body of the item before the blank in most of the items so that the students have the information necessary to answer the item once they encounter the blank. Such a strategy helps to make the test a bit more efficient. Of course, situations do exist in language testing wherein the blank must be early in the item (for instance, when trying to test for the head noun in a sentence), but as a general rule, the blank should occur relatively late in the item.

5. In situations where the blanks may be very difficult and frustrating for the students, teachers might consider supplying a list of responses from which the students can choose in filling in the blanks. This list will not only make answering the items easier for the students but will also make the correction of the items easier for the teacher because the students will have a limited set of possible answers from which to draw. However, even a minor modification like this one can dramatically change the nature of the items. In this case, the modification would change them from productive response items to receptive response items.

Short-response items are usually questions that the students can answer in a few phrases or sentences. This type of question should conform to at least the following two guidelines.

1. Teachers should make sure that the item is formatted so that there is one, and only one, concise answer or set of answers that they are looking for in the responses to each item. The parameters for what will be considered an acceptable answer must be thought through carefully and clearly delineated before correcting such questions. As in number 1 above for fill-in items, the goal in short-response items is to ensure that the

answer key will help the teacher to make clear-cut decisions as to whether each item is correct, without making modifications as the scoring progresses. Thus, the teacher's expectations should be thought out in advance, recognizing that subjectivity may become a problem because he or she will necessarily be making judgments about the relative quality of the student's answers. Thus, partial credit often becomes an issue with this type of item. *Partial credit* entails giving some credit for answers that are not 100% correct. For instance, on one short-response item, a student might get two points for an answer with correct spelling and correct grammar, but only one point if either grammar or spelling were wrong, and no points if both grammar and spelling were wrong. As with all the other aspects of scoring short-response items, any partial credit scheme must be clearly thought out and delineated before scoring starts so that backtracking and rescoring will not be necessary.

2. Short-response items should generally be phrased as clear and direct questions. Unnecessary wordiness should particularly be avoided with this type of item so that the range of expected answers will stay narrow enough to be scored with relative ease and objectivity.

Task items are defined here as any of a group of fairly open-ended item types that require students to perform a task in the language that is being tested. A task test (or what one colleague accidentally called a *tesk*) might include a series of communicative tasks, a set of problem-solving tasks, and a writing task. In another alternative that has become increasingly popular in the last decade, students are asked to perform a series of writing tasks and revisions during a course and put them together into a portfolio (see Belanoff & Dickson 1991, Fusco, Quinn, & Hauck 1993, or Hewitt 1995 for much more on evaluating portfolios).

While task items are appealing to many language teachers, a number of complications may arise in trying to use them. To avoid such difficulties, consider at least the following points.

1. The directions for the task should be so clear that both the tester and the student know exactly what the student must do. The task may be anything that people have to do with language. Thus, task items might require students to solve written word puzzles, to give oral directions to the library, to explain to another student how to draw a particular geometric shape, to write a composition on a specific topic, and so forth. The possibilities are only limited by the degree of imagination among the teachers involved. However, the point to remember is that the directions for the task must be concisely explained so the student knows exactly what is expected of him or her and thus cannot stray too far away from the intended purpose of the item.

2. The task should be sufficiently narrow in scope so that it fits logistically into the time allotted for its performance and yet broad enough so that an adequate sample of the student's language use is obtained for scoring the item properly.

3. Teachers must carefully work out the scoring procedures for task items for the same reasons listed in discussing the other types of productive response items. However, such planning is particularly crucial for task items because teachers have less control over the range of possible responses in such open-ended items.

Two entirely different approaches are possible in scoring tasks. A task can be scored using an ***analytic approach***, in which the teachers rate various aspects of each student's language production separately, or a task can be scored using a ***holistic approach***, in which the teachers use a single general scale to give a single global rating for each student's language production. The very nature of the item(s) will depend on how the teachers choose to score the task. If teachers choose to use an analytic approach, the task may have three, four, five, or even six individual bits of information, each of which must be treated as a separate item. A decision for a holistic approach will produce results that must be treated differently—that is, more like a single item. Thus, teachers must decide early on whether they will score the task items using an analytic approach or a holistic one.

4. If teachers decide to use an analytic approach, they must then decide which categories of language to judge in rating the students' performances. Naturally, these decisions must also occur before the scoring process actually begins. For example, when I was teaching ESL at UCLA, we felt that compositions should be rated analytically, with separate scores for organization, logic, grammar, mechanics, and style, as shown in Table 3.4 (see Brown & Bailey 1984 for more on this scale). Thus, five categories of language were important to us, but these categories are not the only possible ones. In contrast, at UHM, we presently use an analytic scale that helps us to rate content, organization, vocabulary, language use, and mechanics (see Jacobs, Zinkgraf, Wormuth, Hartfiel, & Hughey 1981). Thus, the teachers at UHM prefer to rate five categories of language that are different from the five categories used at UCLA. Because such decisions are often very different from course to course and program to program, decisions about which categories of language to rate should most often rest with the teachers who are involved in the teaching process.

5. Having worked out the approach and categories of language to rate, it is still necessary to define clearly the points on the scales for each category. Written descriptions of the kinds of language that would be expected at each score level will help. The descriptors shown in Table 3.4

Table 3.4: Analytic Scale for Rating Composition Tasks (Brown & Bailey 1984, pp. 39–41)

	20–18 Excellent to Good	17–15 Good to Adequate	14–12 Adequate to Fair	11–6 Unacceptable—not college-level work	5–1
I. Organization: Introduction, Body, and Conclusion	Appropriate title, effective introductory paragraph, topic is stated, leads to body; transitional expressions used; arrangement of material shows plan (could be outlined by reader); supporting evidence given for generalizations; conclusion logical and complete	Adequate title, introduction, and conclusion; body of essay is acceptable but some evidence may be lacking, some ideas aren't fully developed; sequence is logical but transitional expressions may be absent or misused	Mediocre or scant introduction or conclusion; problems with the order of ideas in body; the generalizations may not be fully supported by the evidence given; problems of organization interfere	Shaky or minimally recognizable introduction; organization can barely be seen; severe problems with ordering of ideas; lack of supporting evidence; conclusion weak or illogical; inadequate effort at organization	Absence of introduction or conclusion; no apparent organization of body; severe lack of supporting evidence; writer has not made any effort to organize the composition (could not be outlined by reader)
II. Logical development of ideas: Content	Essay addresses the assigned topic; the ideas are concrete and thoroughly developed; no extraneous material; essay reflects thought	Essay addresses the issues but misses some points; ideas could be more fully developed; some extraneous material is present	Development of ideas not complete or essay is somewhat off the topic; paragraphs aren't divided exactly right	Ideas incomplete; essay does not reflect careful thinking or was hurriedly written; inadequate effort in area of content	Essay is completely inadequate and does not reflect college-level work; no apparent effort to consider the topic carefully

III. Grammar	Native-like fluency in English grammar; correct use of relative clauses, prepositions, modals, articles, verb forms, and tense sequencing; no fragments or run-on sentences	Advanced proficiency in English grammar; some grammar problems don't influence communication, although the reader is aware of them; no fragments or run-on sentences	Ideas are getting through to the reader, but grammar problems are apparent and have a negative effect on communication; run-on sentences or fragments present	Numerous serious grammar problems interfere with communication of the writer's ideas; grammar review of some areas clearly needed; difficult to read sentences	Severe grammar problems interfere greatly with the message; reader can't understand what the writer was trying to say; unintelligible sentence structure
IV. Punctuation, spelling, and mechanics	Correct use of English writing conventions: left and right margins, all needed capitals, paragraphs indented, punctuation and spelling; very neat	Some problems with writing conventions or punctuation; occasional spelling errors; left margin correct; paper is neat and legible	Uses general writing conventions but has errors; spelling problems distract reader; punctuation errors interfere with ideas	Serious problems with format of paper; parts of essay not legible; errors in sentence-final punctuation; unacceptable to educated readers	Complete disregard for English writing conventions; paper illegible; obvious capitals missing, no margins, severe spelling problems
V. Style and quality of expression	Precise vocabulary usage; use of parallel structures; concise; register good	Attempts variety; good vocabulary; not wordy; register OK; style fairly concise	Some vocabulary misused; lacks awareness of register; may be too wordy	Poor expression of ideas; problems in vocabulary; lacks variety of structure	Inappropriate use of vocabulary; no concept of register or sentence variety

are examples of one way to go about delineating such language behaviors. Regardless of the form that they take, such descriptions will help to ensure that the judgments of the scorers are all relatively consistent within and across categories and that the scores will be relatively easy to assign and interpret. Sometimes training workshops will be necessary for the raters so that they can agree upon the definitions within each scale and develop consistency in the ways that they assign scores (more on this point in Chapter 7 under "Reliability of Rater Judgments," p. 203).

6. Another strategy that can help to make the scoring as objective as possible is to assign the scores anonymously. A few changes in testing procedures may be necessary to ensure anonymous ratings. For instance, students may have to put their names on the back of the first page of a writing task so that the raters do not know whose test they are rating. Or, if the task is audiotaped in a face-to-face interview, teachers other than the student's teachers may have to be assigned to rate the tape without knowing who they are hearing on the cassette. Such precautions will differ from task to task and situation to situation. The important thing is that teachers consider using anonymity as a way of increasing objectivity.

In sum, item format analysis involves asking those questions in Tables 3.1–3.3 that are appropriate for a specific set of items and making sure that the items conform to the guidelines insofar as they apply to the particular teaching situation. Clearly, this type of item analysis relies heavily on common sense. Nevertheless, item format analysis is important because an item that is badly constructed is not likely to be effective or fair, even if the item looks like it is testing the appropriate content. In other words, good format would seem to be a precondition for effective testing of any content.

NORM-REFERENCED ITEM STATISTICS

Two statistical analyses can help in analyzing a set of norm-referenced items: item facility analysis and item discrimination analysis. I would like to stress at the outset that these statistical analyses are only useful insofar as they help teachers to understand and improve the effectiveness of item formats and content. Teachers must be careful to keep these statistical techniques in perspective, remembering that the statistics are only tools for improving actual test items and are not an end in themselves.

Item Facility Analysis

Item facility (IF) (also called *item difficulty* or *item easiness*) is a statistical index used to examine the percentage of students who correctly answer a given item. To calculate the IF index, add up the number of students who correctly answered a particular item, and divide that sum by the total number of students who took the test. As a formula, it looks like this:

$$IF = \frac{N_{correct}}{N_{total}}$$

where $N_{correct}$ = number of students answering correctly

N_{total} = number of students taking the test

The formula is just a shorthand way of expressing the same thing that was explained in prose. (Note that this formula assumes that items left blank are incorrect answers.)

The result of this formula is an item facility value that can range from 0.00 to 1.00 for different items. Teachers can interpret this value as the percentage of correct answers for a given item (by moving the decimal point two places to the right). For example, the correct interpretation for an IF index of .27 would be that 27% of the students correctly answered the item. In most cases, an item with an IF of .27 would be a very difficult question because many more students missed it than answered it correctly. On the other hand, an IF of .96 would indicate that 96% of the students answered correctly—a very easy item because almost everyone responded accurately.

Table 3.5: Item Analysis Data (First Ten Items Only)

Students	1	2	3	4	5	6	7	8	9	10	Total
					Item Number						
Robert	1	1	1	1	1	1	0	1	1	0	77
Millie	1	0	1	1	1	1	0	1	0	0	75
Dean	1	0	0	1	1	1	0	1	0	0	72
Shenan	1	1	0	1	1	1	0	0	0	0	72
Cuny	1	1	1	1	1	0	0	1	0	0	70
Bill	1	1	0	1	1	0	1	1	1	0	70
Corky	1	0	1	1	1	1	0	1	0	0	69
Randy	1	1	0	1	1	0	0	1	0	0	69
Monique	1	0	1	0	1	0	1	1	0	0	69
Wendy	1	1	0	0	1	1	0	0	1	0	69
Henk	1	0	1	0	1	0	1	0	0	0	68
Elisabeth	1	1	0	0	1	1	1	1	1	0	68
Jeanne	1	1	0	0	1	0	1	0	1	0	67
Iliana	1	1	1	0	1	0	1	0	0	0	64
Archie	1	0	0	0	1	0	1	0	1	0	64
Lindsey	0	0	0	0	1	0	1	1	0	0	61

Such seemingly simple information can be very useful. For example, consider the item response pattern shown in Table 3.5. As with all testing statistics, the first thing that teachers must do is to arrange the data so that they can be easily examined and manipulated. (Yes, I still love the stuffy notion that data *ARE* plural.) In Table 3.5, the students' names have been listed in the left-hand column, and the item numbers for the first ten items and the total scores are labeled across the top.

The actual responses are recorded with a *1* for each correct answer and *0* for a wrong answer. Notice that Robert answered the first item correctly—indeed, so did everyone else except poor Lindsey. This item must have been very easy. Note, though, that item one is not the easiest item. Another item was answered correctly by every student. Which one? Item 5, right? And, which item was the most difficult in these data? Item 10 was clearly the most difficult because every student missed it (as indicated by the zeros straight down that column).

The calculation of IF for any item will follow a consistent pattern. Consider item 3. Count up the number of students who answered item three correctly (seven); then count the number of people who took the test (sixteen), fill in the formula, and do the calculations:

$$IF = \frac{N_{correct}}{N_{total}}$$

$$= \frac{7}{16}$$

$$= .4375 \approx .44$$

With this simple IF index in hand, the teacher knows that about 44% of the students answered item 3 correctly. Try calculating the IF for a few of the other items shown in Table 3.5. (The answers are shown in Table 3.6, on p. 68.)

Arranging the data in a matrix like this can help you to clearly calculate IFs. As you will see next, other item statistics can also be used for ferreting out other kinds of information and patterns from such data. With these other item statistics, it is easiest if you first sort and arrange the data in a matrix like that shown in Table 3.5.

Item Discrimination Analysis

Item discrimination (ID) indicates the degree to which an item separates the students who performed well from those who performed poorly. These two groups are sometimes referred to as the high and low scorers or upper-

and lower-proficiency students. The reason for identifying these two groups is that ID allows teachers to contrast the performance of the upper-group students on the test with that of the lower-group students. The process begins by determining which students had scores in the top group on the whole test and which had scores in the bottom group. To do this, begin by lining up the students' names, their individual item responses, and total scores in descending order based on the total scores. Notice that the order of the listings in Table 3.5 is from high to low based on total scores. Such a high-to-low arrangement allows for quick determination of which students fall into the high- and low-scoring groups.

The upper and lower groups are sometimes defined as the upper and lower third, or 33%. Some test developers will use the upper and lower 27%. I also know of instances where 25% was used in calculating ID. Like so many things in the seemingly "scientific" area of language testing, the decision as to which way to define the upper and lower groups is often a practical matter. In Table 3.5, for instance (where the three groups are separated by blank rows), five students each have been assigned to the top and bottom groups and six to the middle group. Rather than using thirds, the groupings here are based on the upper and lower 31.25% ($5 \div 16 =$ .3125). Such decisions result from the fact that groups of people do not always come in nice neat numbers that are divisible by three. The solution is often like that found in Table 3.5—that is, the upper and lower groups are defined as some whole number that is roughly 33%.

Once the data are sorted into groups of students, calculation of the discrimination indexes is easy. To do this, calculate the item facility (the IF discussed above) for the upper and lower groups separately for each item. This is done by dividing the number of students who answered correctly in the upper group by the total number of students in the upper group; then divide the number who answered correctly in the lower group by the total number of students in the lower group. Finally, to calculate the ID index, the IF for the lower group is subtracted from the IF for the upper group on each item as follows:

$$ID = IF_{upper} - IF_{lower}$$

where ID = item discrimination for an individual item

          IF_{upper} = item facility for the upper group on the whole test

          IF_{lower} = item facility for the lower group on the whole test

For example, in Table 3.5, the IF for the upper group on item 4 is 1.00, because everyone in that group answered it correctly. At the same time, the IF for the lower group on that item is .00 because everyone in the lower group answered it incorrectly. I calculated the item discrimination index for this item by subtracting the IF for the lower group from the IF for the upper group and got an index of the contrasting performance of those students who scored high on the whole test with those who scored low. In this case, it turned out to be 1.00 (ID = $IF_{upper} - IF_{lower}$ = 1.00 − .00 = 1.00), as is reported in Table 3.6. An item discrimination index of 1.00 is very good because it indicates the maximum contrast between the upper and lower groups of students—that is, all the high-scoring students answered correctly, and all the low-scoring students answered incorrectly.

The theory is that the scores on the whole test are the best single estimate of ability for each student. In fact, these whole test scores must be more accurate than any single item because a relatively large number of observations, when taken together, will logically give a better measurement than any of the single observations. Consider, for instance, the accuracy of one observation of your pulse rate as compared to the average of twenty such observations over a period of hours. The average of the multiple observations would clearly be more accurate than any of the single observations. Analogously, since each item is only one observation of the students' performances and the whole test is a collection of such observations, the whole total test scores are more accurate estimates of the students' performances than any given item.

One implication of this conclusion is that those norm-referenced items which separate students into upper and lower groups in similar manner to the whole test scores are the items which should be kept in any revised versions of the test. An item with an ID of 1.00 is indicating that the item separates the upper and lower groups in the same manner as the whole test scores. Such an item is therefore a good candidate for retention in any revised version of the test, although the adequacy of the item format and the suitability of the item facility index must also be considered for each and every decision. ID indexes can range from 1.00 (if all the upper-group students answer correctly and all the lower-group students answer incorrectly, as with item 4 in Tables 3.5 and 3.6) to −1.00 (if all the lower-group students answer correctly and all the upper-group students answer

Table 3.6: Item Statistics

Item Statistic	Item Number									
	1	2	3	4	5	6	7	8	9	10
IF_{total}	.94	.56	.44	.50	1.00	.44	.50	.63	.38	.00
IF_{upper}	1.00	.60	.60	1.00	1.00	.80	.00	.80	.20	.00
IF_{lower}	.80	.60	.20	.00	1.00	.20	1.00	.40	.60	.00
ID	.20	.00	.40	1.00	.00	.60	−1.00	.40	−.40	.00

incorrectly, as with item 7 in these tables). Naturally, ID indexes can take on all the values between +1.00 and −1.00, as well.

Consider several other items in Table 3.6. In item 6, the students in the upper group have an IF of .80, and those in the lower group have an IF of .20, so the item discrimination index for item 6 is .60 (.80−.20 = .60). This ID index indicates that the item is "discriminating," or distinguishing, fairly well between the high-scoring students and low-scoring students on the whole test. On the other hand, item 9, for which the upper group had an IF of .20 and the lower group an IF of .60, would have an ID of −.40 (.20−.60 = −.40). This ID index indicates that the item is somehow testing something quite different from the rest of the test because those who scored low on the whole test managed to answer this item correctly more often than those who scored high on the total test. Since the multiple observations of the whole test are logically a better estimate of the students' actual knowledge or skills than any single item, good reasons exist for doubting the value of the contribution being made to a norm-referenced test by items that have low or negative ID indexes.

Another statistic that is often used for the same purpose as the ID is the point biserial correlation coefficient. This statistic is usually lower in magnitude when compared directly with the ID for a given item but is analogous in interpretation. Because ID is easier to calculate and understand conceptually, teachers are much more likely to use it in most language programs. Hence, I can safely delay the discussion of the point biserial correlation coefficient until Chapter 6.

NRT Development and Improvement Projects

The development or improvement of a norm-referenced language test is a major undertaking like many other aspects of language curriculum development. Such projects are usually designed to:

1. pilot a relatively large number of test items on a group of students similar to the group that will ultimately be assessed with the test,

2. analyze the items using format analysis and statistical techniques, and

3. select the best items to make up a shorter, more effective revised version of the test. (See Brown 1988c for an example of such a test revision project.)

Ideal items in an NRT development project have an average IF of .50 and the highest available ID. These ideal items would be considered well-centered—that is, 50% answer correctly and 50% incorrectly. In reality, however, items rarely have an IF of exactly .50, so those that fall in a range between .30 and .70 are usually considered acceptable. Once those items that fall within the allowable range of IFs are identified, the items among them that have the highest ID indexes would be further selected for retention in the revised test. This process can help the teacher to retain only those items that are well-centered and discriminate well between the low- and the high-scoring students. Ebel (1979, p. 267) has suggested the following guidelines for making decisions based on ID:

.40 and up	Very good items
.30 to .39	Reasonably good but possibly subject to improvement
.20 to .29	Marginal items, usually needing and being subject to improvement
Below .19	Poor items, to be rejected or improved by revision

Of course, Ebel's guidelines should not be used as hard and fast rules but rather as aids in making decisions about which items to keep and which to discard until a sufficient number of items has been found to make up whatever norm-referenced test is under development. This process is usually far less scientific than many novice test developers would like.

Consider the items in Table 3.6. Which three items from the ten shown in the table would be best to select for a new revised version of the test? Items 4 and 6 seem like good candidates for retention in a revised version of the test because they both have IFs that are close to .50 and have the highest IDs in this set of items. But which other item should be kept? Items 3 and 8 both seem like possibilities because they have IFs within the .30 to .70 range of acceptability and have the highest available IDs of those items that remain. But such decisions are not always clear-cut. For instance, a test developer might decide to keep both items 3 and 8 because they are effective, or to reject both items because they do not discriminate above .40, or to keep both items but revise them to make the distractors more efficient.

Distractor Efficiency Analysis

Even after careful selection of the items to be used in a revised and improved version of a test, the job of improving the test may not be finished, particularly for multiple-choice items. Further statistical analysis of the different parts of each item may help to ensure that they are all functioning well. Recall that the parts of a multiple-choice item include the *item stem*, or the main part of the item at the top, the *options*, which are the alternative choices presented to the student, the *correct answer*, which is the option that will be counted as correct, and the *distractors*, which are the options that will be counted as incorrect. Also recall that these incorrect options are called distractors because they should divert, or pull away, the students from the correct answer if they do not know which is correct. The primary goal of **distractor efficiency analysis** is to examine the degree to which the distractors are attracting students who do not know the correct answer. To do this for an item, the percentages of students who chose each option are analyzed. If this analysis can also give the percentages choosing each option in the upper, middle, and lower groups, the information will be even more interesting and useful. In any case, the goal is to investigate the degree to which the distractors are functioning efficiently.

Consider the distractor efficiency analysis results (for the same items previously shown in Table 3.6) that are given in Table 3.7 for items 1 through 10 (listed down the left side of the table). Notice that the table also provides the same item facility and discrimination indexes that were previously shown in Table 3.6. In addition, Table 3.7 gives information about the proportion of students in the high, middle, and low groups who chose each of the options. For example, in item 1, nearly everyone chose option *a*. In fact, the figures for item 1 indicate that 100% of the students in the high and middle groups chose *a.*, while 80% of the students in the low group chose *a*. The other 20% of the low students apparently chose option *b*. Since the asterisk indicates which of the options was correct, this item appears to have been fairly easy, with the majority of the students in the low group answering it correctly. This is confirmed by the IF value of .94, which also indicates that the item was easy because, overall, 94% of the students answered correctly. Notice that subtracting the percentage of students in the lower group who correctly answered from the same figure for the upper group confirms the ID reported for this first item (ID = IF_{upper} $-\text{IF}_{lower} = 1.00 - .80 = .20$). I might consider this item too easy for the group of students involved and, since it is not discriminating well, might choose to eliminate it from future versions of the test. On the other hand, from a humanitarian point of view, an easy first item is sometimes a good idea—just so the students can get off to a good start. As with all item analyses, the decision is up to the teacher involved, but the IF, ID, and distractor efficiency analyses can certainly help in making such decisions.

A number of other insights can be gained from distractor efficiency statistics which might never have been perceived without them. In item 2, for instance, option *c.* is the correct answer, with the majority (60%) of the high group choosing that answer. Oddly, the other 40% of the high group selected a wrong answer, option *a*. In a situation like this, it is important to go back to the original item and examine it carefully from both format and content points of view. The high group may be attracted to both *a.* and *c.*

Table 3.7: Distractor Efficiency

Item Number	IF	ID	Group	Options a.	b.	c.	d.
1.	.94	.20	High	1.00*	.00	.00	.00
			Middle	1.00*	.00	.00	.00
			Low	.80*	.20	.00	.00
2.	.56	.00	High	.40	.00	.60*	.00
			Middle	.35	.05	.50*	.10
			Low	.13	.07	.60*	.20
3.	.44	.40	High	.12	.60*	.13	.15
			Middle	.17	.50*	.12	.21
			Low	.21	.20*	.27	.32
4.	.50	1.00	High	1.00*	.00	.00	.00
			Middle	.50*	.12	.23	.15
			Low	.00*	.34	.32	.34
5.	1.00	.00	High	.00	.00	.00	1.00*
			Middle	.00	.00	.00	1.00*
			Low	.00	.00	.00	1.00*
6.	.44	.60	High	.06	.00	.80*	.11
			Middle	.20	.00	.33*	.47
			Low	.49	.00	.20*	.31
7.	.50	-1.00	High	.00*	.80	.08	.12
			Middle	.50*	.40	.07	.03
			Low	1.00*	.00	.00	.00
8.	.63	.40	High	.08	.12	.80*	.00
			Middle	.09	.09	.67*	.15
			Low	.20	.19	.40*	.21
9.	.38	-.40	High	.72	.08	.00	.20*
			Middle	.22	.13	.32	.33*
			Low	.13	.13	.14	.60*
10.	.00	.00	High	.84	.00*	.13	.03
			Middle	.52	.00*	.31	.17
			Low	.17	.00*	.37	.46

*Correct option.

because they are both correct answers (or both very nearly correct). If this is the case, the best strategy would be to change option a. so that it is more clearly wrong, and/or revise c. so that it is more clearly correct. Doing either will help to strengthen the item and perhaps increase its ID on future administrations.

Items 3 and 4 look like good items with well-centered IF and relatively high ID. The high group is answering both of these items correctly, with the middle group doing less well and the low group doing poorly. Thus, these items appear to be functioning well—at least for an NRT. If they continue to look good in terms of content and format, then they should probably appear in the revised version of the test.

Note also in items 3 and 4 that all three distractors seem to be about equally attractive to those students who did not answer correctly. Item 5, on the other hand, appears to be doing nothing to discriminate between the high, middle, and low groups as indicated by the ID of zero. This low ID is caused by the fact that everyone is answering the item correctly. Item 5 might be improved by making the distractors more attractive. Careful examination might reveal that the distractors are so ridiculous that even students who do not know the content select the correct answer. By making those distractors less ridiculous, the item might be salvaged. On the other hand, if I had enough good items without this one, I might just eliminate it.

Item 6 provides an example of an item with one distractor that is not attracting any of the students. In other words, distractor *b.* is not carrying its weight in the process of testing the students. Since the item is otherwise fairly good from an NRT perspective (IF = .44; ID = .60), I might decide to revise option *b.* so that it will be more attractive to students who do not know the content of the item. Alternatively, I might decide to leave the item alone and continue to use it on the theory that tampering with an item that is working is foolhardy. As always, the decision is up to the individual test developer.

Item 7 presents an entirely different picture. This item appears to be doing everything backwards from the other items on the test. Notice that the low students are all answering this question correctly, while only 50% of the middle group is getting it right, and none of the high group. The ID index of −1.00 also indicates that the item is discriminating in exactly the opposite way from the way the rest of the test spreads students out. Look at option *b.* to figure out what might be wrong with this item. The pattern of statistics indicates to me that the item might be miskeyed. Option *b.* is *behaving* more like the correct answer, although *a.* appears to be the correct answer. If examination of the item itself confirms that it is miskeyed, a quick change of the answer key and reanalysis of the item will probably revealthat the item is functioning fairly well.

Item 8 looks like a reasonably sound item, but whether or not I will decide to keep it depends on how high the IDs are for all the other items and on how many items I need in the revised version. If many other items have IDs that are higher than this one, I may decide to throw it out (even though it is not such a bad item) simply because it would be adding very little other than length to the test. Again, the content and format analysis should figure into this decision.

Items 9 and 10 are similar to item 7 in that they seem to be miskeyed. I should check the original items for the correct answer and then change the answer key, if appropriate, and reanalyze these items. In the end, they may turn out to be good items. The point is that I might never have noticed this repairable problem if I had not done distractor efficiency analysis.

Admittedly, my examples are designed to exemplify the types of problems that distractor efficiency analysis can help teachers to solve. And, as a result, most of the items are not functioning very well. Typically, in the real world, when a set of items is carefully developed to suit a particular group of students in a particular situation, a much higher percentage of the items will be sound and can therefore be retained in the revised version of the test. However, the problems exemplified here can arise. Based on my experience in developing tests, I generally like to have enough items in the development stage that I can throw out one-third to half of the items and still have a good test of the length that I want. For example, I recently developed some multiple-choice tests of business English proficiency for Sony to use in their adult education schools throughout Japan (Brown forthcoming a). I wanted to end up with four 70-item tests (with a total of 280 items), so I started out with 600 items, which permitted me to throw out more than half of the items after pilot testing them and still end up with the test lengths that I wanted. Unfortunately, no hard and fast rule exists for how many items will be necessary for all types of tests in all types of situations, but starting with lots of extra items is always a good idea.

I should also point out that the organization of the distractor efficiency information displayed in Table 3.7 is only one way of presenting such information. Individual testers and different computer programs may arrange the results quite differently. The important things to look for in the statistics for each item are the IF, some form of ID, and the percentages of the high and low groups selecting each of the options.

DEVELOPING CRITERION-REFERENCED LANGUAGE TESTS

Recall that a central difference between NRTs and CRTs is that NRTs typically produce normal distributions, while CRTs do not necessarily do so. In addition, the item selection process for developing NRTs is designed to retain items that are well-centered (with IFs of .30 to .70) and spread students out efficiently (the highest IDs are retained, and distractors are analyzed for efficiency). Such items, once selected for a revised version of a test, will generally work together to provide a normal distribution of scores.

In contrast, CRTs may not necessarily produce scores that are normally distributed. In fact, a CRT that is designed to measure student achievement might produce scores that are predominantly high. If all the students learned all the material because they were perfect students and the teacher was marvelous, the students would all score 100% on any end-of-course achievement test that was criterion-referenced to measuring that material. Of course, a teacher could create the same effect (that is, everyone scoring 100%) by writing a final examination that is far too easy for the students. To check for this possibility, the teacher may want to administer the test (or an equivalent form of the test) at the beginning of the course as a kind of diagnostic test. If the students perform poorly on the beginning-of-course diagnostic test (pretest) and score well on the end-of-course achievement test (posttest), then the teacher can interpret the high scores at the end of the course as legitimate reflections of the students' knowledge or skills rather than as reflections of a test that is too easy for the students.

In fact, the distributions of scores on a CRT may not be normal for either the pretest or the posttest. On an ideal CRT designed to test course objectives, all the students would score 0% at the beginning of the course (indicating that they need to learn the material) and 100% at the end of the course (indicating that they have all learned the material). However, in reality, human beings are never perfectly ignorant at the beginning of a course nor perfectly knowledgeable at the end. Such distributions are, nonetheless, ideals that teachers can aim for in CRT development in much the same sense that they should aim for the normal distribution when they are developing NRTs.

One consequence of this fundamental difference in score distributions between the NRT and CRT categories of tests is that many of the statistics used for analyzing NRTs, which assume that the test scores are normally distributed, do not work very well for analyzing CRTs. Consider the item discrimination statistic. If all the students were to answer all the items wrong at the beginning of a course and answer all the items correctly at the end of the course, the teacher should be delighted from a CRT perspective. However, the ID for each and every item would be zero. Statistics that depend on a spread of scores, like the ID does in comparing the upper and lower groups of students, become meaningless if the test does not create a spread of scores. Such a spread occurs naturally in developing NRTs. However, in developing CRTs, other item analysis strategies must be used, especially item quality analysis and attendant item statistics that reflect the degree to which an item is measuring learning.

Item Quality Analysis

As with NRTs, the quality of a CRT can only be as good as the items that are on it. Remember that the CRT category of tests is commonly used for testing achievement and diagnosis, both of which are fairly specific to a particular program (see Chapter 1). One result of the program-specific nature of CRTs is that the analysis of individual item quality is often crucial.

Item quality analysis for CRTs ultimately means that judgments must be made about the degree to which the items are valid for the purposes and content of the course or program involved. The first concern in analyzing CRT item quality is with the content of each item. A second consideration is whether the form of each item adequately assesses the desired content.

Because of the program-specific nature of CRT items, item quality analysis must often be much more rigorous than it is for NRTs. In developing or revising an NRT, the purposes are general in nature, and the test developer's main concern is to find items that discriminate well between students in their overall performances. Hence, the tester can rely fairly heavily on item facility and discrimination statistics to help guide the choices of which items to keep and which to discard in revising the test. In developing CRTs, the test developer must rely less on statistics and more on common sense to create a revised version of the test that measures what the students know, or can do, with regard to the program's objectives.

A criterion-referenced test developer should be concerned primarily with the degree to which a test, and therefore the items within the test, is testing whatever content is desired. This content may turn out to be as narrow, objective, receptive, and discrete-point as a test of each student's ability to distinguish between phonemes, or as broad, subjective, productive, and integrative as a test of the students' overall proficiency in terms of strategic competence. These choices and others are up to the teachers who must develop and use the test. Regardless of what is decided, the goal of *item content analysis* for a CRT is to determine the degree to which each item is measuring the content that it was designed to measure, as well as the degree to which that content should be measured at all.

In the end, content analysis inevitably involves some "expert" (for example, the language teacher or a colleague) who must judge the items. Typically, even in ideal situations, this involves each teacher looking at the test and having some input as to which items should be kept in the revised version of the test and which should be reworked or thrown out. In some situations, strategies similar to those advocated by Popham (1981) are employed. These strategies include the writing of item specifications based on clearly defined objectives that are judged by teachers as well as by outside and independent reviewers and by examinees.

Item specifications, in Popham's (1981) terms, are clear item descriptions that include a general description, a sample item, stimulus attributes, response attributes, and specification supplements, which will be defined here (adapting liberally from Popham 1981, pp. 121–122) as follows:

1. *General description:* A brief general description of the knowledge or skills being measured by the item.

2. *Sample item:* An example item that demonstrates the desirable item characteristics (further delimited by the stimulus and response attributes below).

3. *Stimulus attributes:* A clear description of the stimulus material—that is, the material that will be encountered by the student—or the material to which they will be expected to react through the response attributes below.

4. *Response attributes:* A clear description of the types of (a) options from which students will be expected to select their receptive language choices (responses), or (b) standards by which their productive language responses will be judged.

5. *Specification supplement:* For some items, supplemental material will be necessary for clarifying the four previous elements; for example, the specification supplement might include a list of vocabulary items from which the item writer should draw, or a list of grammatical forms, or a list of functions of the language.

The goal of such item specifications is to provide a clear enough description so that any trained item writer using them will be able to generate items very similar to those written by any other item writer. However, Popham admits that "some people using the specifications, particularly busy individuals, may find their need for test description satisfied with the general description statement and the illustrative item alone."

At the University of Hawaii, we have been using rating scales to judge item content in our CRT development projects. (We do not yet use item specifications, although plans are underway to take this next step in further developing our criterion-referenced tests.) An example rating scale is shown in Table 3.8. Notice how the scale is broken into two categories: *content congruence* (to judge the degree to which an item is measuring what it was designed to assess) and *content applicability* (to judge the degree to which the content is appropriate for a given course or program).

From an administrative perspective, certain advantages can be gained from having all the teachers who teach a specific course judge the quality of the items on the test for that course. Consider, for instance, an elementary-school ESL program in which the children must pass an achievement test at the end of each of three levels of ESL study. If all five of the program's teachers are asked to judge the quality of the items on these achievement tests, they would be much more likely to feel a vested interest in the tests and would probably be much more cooperative in the testing process. Where conflicting views arise among the teachers in making these quality judgments, compromise will be necessary. However, even this process of compromise can be healthy for the test because not only will the teachers have to agree on what test content means; they will also have

Table 3.8: Item Content Congruence and Applicability

Directions: Look at the test questions and objectives that they are designed to test. For each item, circle the number of the rating that you give for each criterion described at the left.

Criteria for Judgement	Rating Scale				
	Very Poor		Moderate		Very Good
Content Congruence					
Overall match between the item and the objective which it is meant to test. *Comment:*	1	2	3	4	5
Proficiency level match. *Comment:*	1	2	3	4	5
Content Applicability					
Match between the objective and a related material that you teach. *Comment:*	1	2	3	4	5
Match between the item and related material that you teach. *Comment:*	1	2	3	4	5

to think about the link between what is tested and what is taught in the course. Remember, such teacher activities should always focus on ensuring that each item makes sense for assessing the specific content of the course or program and that the content is worth measuring given the context of language teaching that exists.

Item format analysis is as important in developing CRTs as it was in writing or assessing the quality of NRT items. All the comments made in and about Tables 3.1, 3.2, and 3.3 are applicable for CRTs. One big difference with CRT item format analysis is that program politics may necessitate drawing all the teachers who will ultimately use and score the tests into the process of doing the item format analysis.

CRT Development and Improvement Projects

The revision process for NRTs was described earlier as being based on a single administration of the test, which is fine because the purpose of an NRT is usually a one-shot determination of the proficiency or placement of the students in a single population. The piloting of items in a CRT development project is quite different because the purpose of selecting those items is fundamentally different. Since a central purpose of a CRT is to assess how much of an objective or set of objectives has been learned by each student, CRT assessment has to occur before and after instruction in the concepts or skills being taught in order to determine whether there was any gain in scores. As a result, the piloting of a CRT often involves administering it as a pretest and posttest and comparing results. To limit the "practice effect" of taking the same test twice, two forms can be developed, with each half of the students taking one form on the pretest and the other form on the posttest.

Role of Item Facility

Once teachers have selected those items judged to have high item quality, the resulting CRTs can be administered, and statistical item analysis can proceed. As in NRT item analysis, *item facility* plays an important role; however, two possible item facilities exist for each item—one for the pretest and one for the posttest. In CRT development, the goal is to find items that reflect what is being learned, if anything. Hence, an ideal item for CRT purposes is one that has an IF (for the whole group) of .00 at the beginning of instruction and an IF of 1.00 at the end of instruction. Such pretest and posttest IFs indicate that everyone missed the item at the beginning of instruction (that is, they needed to study the content or skill embodied in the item) and everyone answered it correctly at the end of instruction (that is, they had completely absorbed whatever was being taught). Of course, this example is an ideal item, in an ideal world, with ideal students, and an infallible teacher.

Reality may be quite a bit different. Students arrive in most teaching situations with differing amounts of knowledge. Thus, an IF of .00 for any CRT item that measures a realistic objective seems unlikely, even at the very beginning of instruction. Similarly, students differ in ability and in the speed with which they learn, so they will probably not learn each and every objective to an equal degree. Thus, CRT items with IFs of 1.00 are unlikely, even at the end of instruction.

Nevertheless, much can be learned about each item on a CRT from comparing the performance on the item of those students who have studied the content (posttest) with those who have not (pretest). Two different strategies can be used to make such a comparison. The first approach, which I call an *intervention strategy*, begins by testing the students before instruction in a pretest. At this stage, the students are *uninstructed*. The next step is to intervene with whatever instruction is appropriate and then test the *instructed* students on a posttest. This strategy puts the test developer in a position to do an item-by-item comparison of the two sets of IF results.

The second approach is the **differential groups strategy**. This strategy begins by finding two groups of students: one group that has the knowledge or skills that are assessed on the test and another group that lacks them. The test developer can then compare the item facility indexes of the first group, sometimes termed **masters**, with the item facility indexes for the second group, called **non-masters**. Whether test developers use the intervention strategy or differential groups strategy depends on what is most convenient and logical in a given teaching situation (see Chapter 8 *Construct Validity* for other uses of these strategies). In either case, the item statistic that the tester calculates to estimate the degree of contrast between the two administrations of the test is called the *difference index*.

Difference Index

The **difference index** (DI, not to be confused with ID) indicates the degree to which an item is reflecting gain in knowledge or skill. In contrast to item discrimination, which shows the degree to which an NRT item separates the upper third from the lower third of the students on a given test administration, the difference index indicates the degree to which a CRT item is distinguishing between the students who know the material or have the skill being taught and those who do not. To calculate the difference index, the IF for the pretest results (or non-masters) is subtracted from the IF for posttest results (or masters). For example, if the posttest IF for item 10 on a test was .77 and the pretest IF was .22, the teacher would know that only 22% knew the concept or skill at the beginning of instruction while 77% knew it by the end. The relatively high DI for that item of .77 − .22 = .55 would indicate 55% gain. DIs can range from −1.00 (indicating that students knew but somehow unlearned the knowledge or skill in question) to +1.00 (showing that the students went from knowing nothing about the knowledge or skill to knowing it completely)—and everything in between as well.

Other examples of calculations for the DI are shown in Table 3.9. The statistics in the table are derived from pretest and posttest results in the ESL academic reading course at the University of Hawaii (from a study reported in Brown 1989a). Notice that only the results for items 41 to 60 are presented. Clearly, the DI is relatively easy to calculate. Yet this simple statistic is also very useful because teachers can use it to identify those items which are most highly related to the material being taught in their courses. The teachers can then keep those items in revised versions of their CRTs and eliminate items that are not related to the curriculum. More importantly, teachers can study those items which have low DIs and try to figure out why the material is apparently not being learned by many students. Is it being taught poorly? Are the materials confusing the

Table 3.9: Calculating the Difference Index

Item Number	Posttest IF	–	Prestest IF	=	Difference Index (DI)
41	.770	–	.574	=	.196
42	.623	–	.492	=	.131
43	.836	–	.689	=	.147
44	.787	–	.639	=	.148
45	.738	–	.656	=	.082
46	.328	–	.246	=	.082
47	.869	–	.574	=	.295
48	.689	–	.344	=	.345
49	.623	–	.311	=	.312
50	.557	–	.262	=	.295
51	.821	–	.640	=	.181
52	.262	–	.246	=	.016
53	.754	–	.623	=	.131
54	.639	–	.508	=	.131
55	.689	–	.541	=	.148
56	.508	–	.426	=	.082
57	.656	–	.492	=	.164
58	.426	–	.361	=	.065
59	.492	–	.311	=	.181
60	.639	–	.443	=	.196

students? Is the test item poorly constructed? Do the students resist learning the material for some cultural reason? And so forth.

The B-index

One problem that may crop up in using the difference index is that two administrations of the CRT are necessary. To solve this problem, other methods for assessing the sensitivity of CRT items to differences in knowledge or skill have been developed (see Shannon & Cliver 1987 for more on these statistics). The most straightforward of these indexes is called the *B*-index. The **B-index** is an item statistic that compares the IFs of those students who passed a test with the IFs of those who failed it. In other words, the masters and non-masters on the test are identified by whether or not they passed the test, and then the *B*-index indicates the degree to which the masters (students who passed the test in this case) outperformed the non-masters (students who failed the test) on each item. The first step in calculating this statistic is determining the cut-point for passing the test.

Table 3.10 shows hypothetical item-by-item performance results on a CRT posttest at the end of a high-school ESL course. Notice that the cut-point is 70% and that, at the bottom of the table, the IFs for those students who passed and those who failed are given separately for each item. To calculate the *B*-index for each item, I subtracted the item facility for those students who failed from that for those who passed. This can be expressed in the following simple formula:

$$B\text{-index} = IF_{pass} - IF_{fail}$$

where   *B*-index = difference in IF between students who passed and failed a test

    IF_{pass} = item facility for students who passed the test

    IF_{fail} = item facility for students who failed the test

Notice in Table 3.10 that all the students who passed the test answered the first item correctly and all those who failed the test missed item 1. Notice also that the *B*-index, based on an item facility of 1.00 for the students who passed and 0.00 for those who failed, would be:

$$B\text{-index} = IF_{pass} - IF_{fail}$$
$$= 1.00 - 0.00$$
$$= 1.00$$

Thus, item 1 maximally separates the students who passed the test from the students who failed it, and its *B*-index is as high as the statistic can go. Item 2 shows the opposite situation: All the students who passed the test missed this item, and all those who failed the test answered the item correctly. The resulting *B*-index is −1.00, which is as low as this statistic can go (0.00 − 1.00 = −1.00). Fifty-seven percent answered item 3 correctly in the pass group and fifty percent in the fail group, with the result that the *B*-index is 0.07 (0.57 − 0.50 = 0.07), indicating that item 3 does not distinguish very well between students who have passed the test and others who have failed it. Item 4 illustrates very well the result obtained if everyone answers an item correctly (1.00 − 1.00 = 0.00). The same would be true if everyone answered the item incorrectly. The other items show somewhat more realistic results in between the extremes just explained.

Interpretation of the *B*-index is similar to that for the difference index (DI). However, the *B*-index indicates the degree to which an item distinguishes between the students who passed the test and those who failed rather than contrasting the performances of students before and after instruction, as is the case with the difference index. Nevertheless, the *B*-index does have the advantage of requiring only one administration of a CRT and therefore may prove useful.

Table 3.10: Calculating the *B*-index

Student ID	Item Number										Total	Percent
	1	2	3	4	5	6	7	8	9	10		
R	1	0	1	1	1	1	1	1	1	1	9	90%
Q	1	0	1	1	1	1	1	1	1	1	9	90%
G	1	0	1	1	1	1	1	1	1	1	9	90%
I	1	0	1	1	1	1	1	1	1	1	9	90%
B	1	0	1	1	1	1	1	1	0	1	8	80%
F	1	0	1	1	1	0	1	1	1	1	8	80% **PASS**
E	1	0	0	1	1	1	1	1	1	1	8	80%
T	1	0	0	1	1	1	1	1	1	1	8	80%
S	1	0	0	1	1	1	1	1	1	1	8	80%
C	1	0	1	1	1	1	1	1	1	0	8	80%
K	1	0	1	1	1	1	1	0	0	1	7	70%
M	1	0	0	1	0	1	1	1	1	1	7	70%
O	1	0	0	1	1	1	0	1	1	1	7	70%
A	1	0	0	1	1	1	1	1	0	1	7	70%
												70% **cut-point**
D	0	1	1	1	0	0	1	1	0	1	6	60%
N	0	1	0	1	0	1	1	0	1	1	6	60%
H	0	1	0	1	1	1	0	0	1	1	6	60% **FAIL**
L	0	1	1	1	1	1	0	0	0	0	5	50%
J	0	1	1	1	0	0	1	0	0	0	4	40%
P	0	1	0	1	0	0	0	0	0	0	2	20%
IF_{pass}	1.00	0.00	0.57	1.00	0.93	0.93	0.93	0.93	0.79	0.93	8.01	80% $MEAN_{pass}$
IF_{fail}	0.00	1.00	0.50	1.00	0.33	0.50	0.50	0.17	0.33	0.50	4.83	48% $MEAN_{fail}$
B-index	1.00	−1.00	0.07	0.00	0.60	0.43	0.43	0.76	0.46	0.43	3.18	32% PASS–FAIL

CRT Item Selection

Having analyzed the items on a CRT, teachers will ultimately want to revise the tests by selecting and keeping those items that are functioning well for achievement or diagnostic decisions. The item quality analysis can help with this selection process by providing information about how well each item fits the objective being measured and the degree to which that objective fits the course or program involved. Calculating difference indexes (comparing pretest and posttest results) provides additional information about how sensitive each item was to instruction. Calculating *B*-indexes (for the posttest results) provides information about how effective each item was in making the decision about who passed the test and who failed.

In other words, teachers must use multiple sources of information, including the DI, the *B*-index, as well as item quality analysis and item format analysis, to make decisions about which items to keep and which to discard in the CRT revision process. Consider Table 3.9 once again. Which of the items should the teacher select if only the five best were needed? Numbers 47 through 50 would be attractive and obvious choices for the four best items. But what about the fifth best item? Should the teacher keep item 41 or item 60 (both of which have DIs of .196), or should the teacher keep item 51 or item 59 (which are not far behind with DIs of .181)? These last choices would no doubt involve looking at the items in terms of their other qualities, particularly item quality and item format analyses. Also consider what you would do if you had the *B*-indexes on the posttest and the one for number 47 turned out to be only .02.

In short, the difference index and *B*-index can help teachers to select that subset of CRT items that are most closely related to the instruction and learning in a course and/or that subset most closely related to the distinction between students who passed or failed the test. With sound CRTs in place, teachers can indeed judge the performance of their students. However, equally important, teachers can also examine the fit between what they think they are teaching and what the students are actually absorbing. Oddly enough, some teachers may be examining this important issue for the first time in their careers.

SUMMARY

The following checklist summarizes everything covered in this chapter. I provide it so that you can quickly and easily recall the steps to take in using information about the individual items on your tests. As always, your purpose is to improve the quality of your tests through selecting those items that are functioning well and throwing out those that are doing no good. Notice that the checklist is separated into two main parts, one for NRT development and one for CRTs.

- ☐ Have you identified what it is that you wish to treat as an item (smallest unit of distinctive test information)?
- ☐ Are you developing an NRT (proficiency or placement)?
  - ☐ Have you done item format analysis?
    - ☐ Checked the general guidelines (Table 3.1)?
    - ☐ Checked the receptive item guidelines (Table 3.2)?
    - ☐ Checked the productive item guidelines (Table 3.3)?
  - ☐ Have you done an item facility analysis?
  - ☐ Have you done an item discrimination analysis?
  - ☐ Have you followed all NRT development steps?
    - ☐ Piloted a relatively large number of items?
    - ☐ Analyzed items?
    - ☐ Selected the best items on the basis of item format, item facility, item discrimination, as well as on the basis of your knowledge of linguistics and language teaching?
    - ☐ Put together a new revised and more efficient test?
  - ☐ Have you used distractor efficiency analysis to help improve ailing items?
- ☐ Are you developing a CRT (achievement or diagnosis)?
  - ☐ Have you used item quality analysis?
    - ☐ Item content analysis?
      - ☐ Content congruence?
      - ☐ Content applicability?
  - ☐ Have you considered item facility (for pretest and posttest, or for masters and non-masters)?
  - ☐ Have you calculated and used the difference index (and/or B-index) for each item?
  - ☐ Have you followed all CRT development steps?
    - ☐ Piloted a relatively large number of items both before and after instruction?
    - ☐ Analyzed items?
    - ☐ Selected the best items on the basis of item content and format, item facility, and difference indexes, (and/or B-indexes) as well as on the basis of your knowledge of linguistics and language teaching?
    - ☐ Put together a new revised and more efficient test?

TERMS AND SYMBOLS

analytic approach

B-index

content applicability

content congruence

correct answer

difference index (DI)

differential groups strategy

distractor efficiency analysis

distractors

fill-in items

general description (in item specifications)

holistic approach

instructed

intervention strategy

item

item analysis

item content analysis

item discrimination (ID)

item facility (IF)

item format analysis

item quality analysis

item specifications

item stem

masters

matching items

multiple-choice items

non-masters

options

partial credit

premises

productive response items

receptive response items

response attributes (in item specifications)
sample item (in item specifications)
short-response items
specification supplement (in item specifications)
stimulus attributes (in item specifications)
task items
true-false items
uninstructed

REVIEW QUESTIONS

1. What is an item? What is the difference between an item and a test? What is an item on a cloze test? A dictation? A composition?

2. What characteristics of items are commonly considered for both NRT and CRT development? Which are specific to NRTs? Which are exclusively used in CRT improvement projects?

3. Why is item format analysis so important? And why was it mentioned as an important consideration for developing both NRTs and CRTs?

4. What is the item facility index? How do you calculate it? How do you interpret the results of your calculations?

5. What is the item discrimination index? How do you calculate it? How do you interpret the results of your calculations?

6. What are basic steps that you should follow in developing an NRT? How are they different and similar to the steps involved in CRT development?

7. What is distractor efficiency analysis? How do you do it? What can you learn from it in terms of improving your test items?

8. What is item quality analysis? Should you be more interested in content congruence or content applicability?

9. What is the item difference index? What role does item facility play in the calculation of item difference indices? How are the pretest–posttest strategies, used to calculate the item difference, different from the pass–fail strategies used to calculate the *B*-index? Once you have your data using one or the other of these strategies, how do you calculate the difference index, or *B*-index, for each of the items? How do you interpret the results of your calculations? Lastly, how can you use both statistics in combination in selecting CRT items?

10. What are the fundamental differences between the strategies used to revise NRTs and those used for CRTs? Do you now think that careful examination of the items on a test can help you to adapt it for your language program? What general steps would you follow in such a process?

APPLICATION EXERCISES

A. Consider the results presented in Table 3.11. Notice that items are coded *1* for correct answers and *0* for incorrect for thirty students (rows labeled with student numbers in the left column) on thirty different items (columns labeled with numbers across the top). Note also that the students' answers are listed in descending order (from high to low) according to their total scores in the right column. These item data (used in the analysis for Premaratne 1987) are real results of the cloze test performance of a group of high-school students in Sri Lanka. The table provides all the information that you will need to go ahead and calculate the IF and ID for each item in this norm-referenced test. In calculating the ID, use the top ten students for the upper group and the bottom ten for the lower group. (See the *Answer Key* for answers.)

B. Examine the computer output shown in Table 3.12 for an NRT in terms of IF, ID, and distractor efficiency. These results are real data from a pilot version of the Reading Comprehension subtest of the English Language Institute Placement Test at UHM. If you were responsible for choosing five of the fifteen items for a revised version of the test, which five would you choose? Why? Would you make any changes in the distractors of those you chose? (See the *Answer Key* for my choices.)

C. Look at Table 3.9 (p. 81). If your task was to select the best fifteen CRT items out of the twenty shown in the table, which would you choose, and why? (See the *Answer Key* for my choices.)

D. Examine Table 3.13. You will note that Table 3.13 is exactly the same as Table 3.10 (p. 83) except that the cut-point for passing or failing the test has been changed to 60%. Recalculate the *B*-index for each item. How would you interpret these new indexes, and how do they compare to the results when the cut-point was 70%? (See the *Answer Key*.)

Table 3.11: Example NRT Item Data from Sri Lankan High-School Students on a Cloze Test

Student Number	\multicolumn{30}{c}{Item Number}	Total Score

Student Number	1	2	3	4	5	6	7	8	9	10	11	12	13	14	15	16	17	18	19	20	21	22	23	24	25	26	27	28	29	30	Total Score
1	1	1	1	1	1	1	1	1	1	1	1	1	1	1	0	0	1	1	1	1	1	0	1	1	1	1	1	1	0	1	27
2	0	1	1	1	1	1	1	1	1	1	1	1	1	1	0	1	1	1	1	1	1	1	1	1	1	1	1	1	0	1	27
20	0	1	1	1	1	1	1	1	1	1	1	1	1	1	0	1	1	0	1	1	1	1	1	0	1	1	1	1	0	1	26
29	1	1	1	1	1	1	1	1	1	1	1	1	0	0	1	1	1	0	1	1	1	0	1	1	0	1	1	1	0	1	26
12	1	1	1	1	1	1	1	1	1	1	1	0	0	0	1	0	1	0	1	1	1	1	1	1	1	1	1	1	0	1	24
5	1	1	0	1	1	1	1	1	1	1	1	1	1	0	1	1	1	1	1	1	1	0	1	0	0	1	1	1	1	1	21
4	1	1	0	1	1	1	1	1	1	1	1	0	0	0	1	0	0	0	1	1	1	0	1	0	1	1	1	1	0	1	21
3	1	1	1	1	1	1	1	1	1	1	1	0	0	0	0	1	0	1	1	1	1	0	1	1	0	1	1	1	0	1	20
16	1	1	1	1	1	0	1	1	1	1	1	0	0	0	1	0	0	0	1	1	1	0	0	0	0	0	1	1	0	0	19
30	1	1	1	1	1	1	1	1	1	1	1	1	1	0	0	0	1	0	1	1	1	0	1	0	1	1	0	0	0	1	18
17	0	1	1	1	1	1	1	1	1	1	1	0	0	1	1	0	1	0	1	1	1	0	1	0	0	0	1	0	0	0	18
6	1	1	1	1	1	1	1	1	1	1	1	0	0	0	0	0	0	0	1	1	1	0	1	0	1	1	1	1	0	1	18
27	0	0	0	1	1	1	1	1	1	1	1	0	0	0	1	0	1	0	1	1	1	0	0	0	0	1	0	1	0	0	18
18	1	1	1	1	1	1	1	1	1	1	1	1	1	1	0	1	0	0	1	1	1	0	1	0	0	1	1	0	0	1	18
19	0	0	0	1	1	1	1	1	1	1	1	0	0	0	1	0	0	0	1	1	1	0	1	0	0	1	0	1	0	0	17
9	0	0	1	1	1	0	1	1	1	0	1	1	1	1	1	0	0	0	1	1	1	0	1	0	0	1	1	1	0	1	17
22	0	1	1	1	1	1	1	1	1	1	0	1	1	0	1	0	1	0	1	1	1	0	1	0	0	1	1	0	0	0	16
8	1	0	1	1	1	1	1	1	1	1	0	0	1	0	0	0	0	0	1	1	1	0	0	0	0	1	1	0	0	0	16
24	0	1	0	1	1	1	0	1	1	1	0	0	0	1	1	0	0	0	1	1	1	0	1	0	0	1	1	0	0	1	16
21	0	0	0	1	1	1	1	0	1	1	1	1	1	0	0	0	0	0	1	1	1	0	0	0	0	1	1	0	0	0	15
14	0	1	0	1	1	0	0	1	1	1	0	0	0	0	0	0	0	0	1	1	0	0	1	0	0	1	1	0	0	0	14
10	1	1	0	0	1	1	1	0	1	1	0	0	0	1	1	0	0	0	1	1	1	0	0	0	0	1	1	0	0	0	14
25	1	0	0	1	1	0	0	0	1	1	1	0	1	0	0	0	0	0	1	0	0	0	1	0	0	0	0	0	0	0	14
15	1	1	1	1	0	1	1	1	1	1	0	0	0	0	0	0	0	0	0	1	1	0	0	0	0	1	1	1	0	0	13
26	1	1	0	0	1	0	0	0	1	1	0	0	1	0	1	0	0	0	1	1	0	0	0	0	0	0	1	0	0	0	13
23	1	0	1	1	0	1	0	0	0	1	1	0	0	1	1	0	1	0	1	0	1	0	1	0	1	0	0	1	0	0	12
11	1	1	0	0	1	0	1	0	1	0	0	0	0	0	1	0	0	0	1	1	0	0	0	0	0	1	1	0	0	0	12
7	0	0	0	0	0	1	0	1	0	1	0	1	0	0	0	0	0	0	1	0	1	0	1	0	1	1	0	1	0	0	11
13	0	1	0	0	0	1	1	1	1	0	1	0	0	0	0	0	1	0	0	1	0	0	1	0	0	1	0	0	0	0	10
28	0	0	0	0	0	1	1	0	0	0	1	1	0	0	0	0	1	0	0	0	1	0	1	0	0	0	0	1	0	0	8

90

Table 3.12: Computer Analysis of 15 Items

Item Number	Group	Difficulty	Options					Correlation
			a.	b.	c.	d.	e.	
1	High	(93.0)	284*	1	2	5	0	(0.153)
	Low		260	1	18	13	0	
2	High	(65.6)	11	9	229*	43	0	(0.295)
	Low		39	18	154	81	0	
3	High	(88.2)	18	5	5	263*	0	(0.122)
	Low		13	13	12	252	2	
4	High	(73.8)	237*	12	40	3	0	(0.189)
	Low		195	13	76	5	0	
5	High	(45.5)	19	4	98	169*	0	(0.310)
	Low		39	14	143	96	0	
6	High	(83.8)	5	10	273*	3	0	(0.394)
	Low		23	42	216	11	0	
7	High	(68.4)	10	251*	11	20	0	(0.469)
	Low		14	148	29	100	0	
8	High	(55.2)	84	6	13	189*	0	(0.231)
	Low		102	19	37	134	0	
9	High	(58.1)	15	5	52	220*	0	(0.375)
	Low		29	7	136	120	0	
10	High	(39.8)	25	166*	46	55	0	(0.399)
	Low		51	67	91	83	0	
11	High	(92.6)	4	0	286*	2	0	(0.468)
	Low		10	15	255	12	0	
12	High	(77.4)	268*	6	10	9	0	(0.468)
	Low		184	13	57	37	0	
13	High	(66.3)	1	9	246*	36	0	(0.414)
	Low		9	48	141	92	0	
14	High	(86.2)	271*	0	2	19	0	(0.276)
	Low		233	17	18	24	0	
15	High	(62.4)	39	5	46	202*	0	(0.205)
	Low		75	15	40	162	0	

*Correct option.

Table 3.13: Example Item Data for *B*-index Calculations

Student ID	1	2	3	4	5	6	7	8	9	10	Score	Percent	
						Item Number							
R	1	0	1	1	1	1	1	1	1	1	9	90%	
Q	1	0	1	1	1	1	1	1	1	1	9	90%	
G	1	0	1	1	1	1	1	1	1	1	9	90%	
I	1	0	1	1	1	1	1	1	1	1	9	90%	
B	1	0	1	1	1	1	1	1	0	1	8	80%	
F	1	0	1	1	1	0	1	1	1	1	8	80%	**PASS**
E	1	0	0	1	1	1	1	1	1	1	8	80%	
T	1	0	0	1	1	1	1	1	1	1	8	80%	
S	1	0	0	1	1	1	1	1	1	1	8	80%	
C	1	0	1	1	1	1	1	1	1	0	8	80%	
K	1	0	1	1	1	1	1	0	0	1	7	70%	
M	1	0	0	1	0	1	1	1	1	1	7	70%	
O	1	0	0	1	1	1	0	1	1	1	7	70%	
A	1	0	0	1	1	1	1	1	0	1	7	70%	
D	0	1	1	1	0	0	1	1	0	1	6	60%	
N	0	1	0	1	0	1	1	0	1	1	6	60%	
H	0	1	0	1	1	1	0	0	1	1	6	60%	
												60% cut-point	
L	0	1	1	1	1	1	0	0	0	0	5	50%	
J	0	1	1	1	0	0	1	0	0	0	4	40%	**FAIL**
P	0	1	0	1	0	0	0	0	0	0	2	20%	
IF_{pass}												$Mean_{pass}$	
IF_{fail}												$Mean_{fail}$	
B-index												Pass–Fail	

CHAPTER 4

DESCRIBING TEST RESULTS

The purpose of describing the results of a test is to provide test developers and test users with a picture of how the students performed on it. In order to show how testers graphically and statistically describe test results, I first explain four different types of scales that can be used to organize numerical information. Then I illustrate several useful ways of visually displaying sets of numbers (also known as *data*) with reference to the frequency of occurrence of each score. Such graphs help testers, teachers, and students to understand the results on the test more easily. Descriptive statistics provide another useful set of tools for describing sets of data. In this chapter, I cover statistics for describing the central tendency of a set of numbers, as well as for characterizing the dispersion of numbers away from the central tendency. I end the chapter with a discussion of how best to go about describing test results, whether the results are for an NRT or CRT decision.

SCALES OF MEASUREMENT

All quantifiable data are by definition countable or measurable in some way. However, various types of data must be handled in different ways. For example, German as a foreign language proficiency could be measured on a test that would produce scores spread along a very wide continuum. The scores might be quite different for the various nationalities studying German. If I was interested in learning more about such patterns of behavior, I might ask the students for information about their nationalities. These nationality data would not, of course, be scores but rather categories within which individual students would fall. The next step might be to sort through the various sets of scores produced by these groups and use descriptive statistics to summarize their performances on the test, but this time, for each nationality separately. The difference between German language proficiency and students' nationality in this discussion is a difference in the ways that the data are organized and treated. German language proficiency is observed as a set of test scores, while nationality is observed as a set of categories. Such differences will be reflected in the different kinds of scales used to measure various types of language behavior.

Typically, four types of *scales* appear in the language teaching literature. The four scales, all useful in one way or another, represent four different ways of observing, organizing, and quantifying language data. The four

Table 4.1: Four Scales of Measurement

	Names Categories	Shows Ranking	Gives Distances	Ratios Make Sense
Nominal				
Ordinal				
Interval				
Ratio				

scales are the nominal, ordinal, interval, and ratio scales. Although the scales organize data in different ways, they should be thought of as supplying varying amounts of information. In fact, the amounts of information can be arranged hierarchically from least to most information, as shown in Table 4.1. This is why they are sometimes termed *levels of measurement* (Bachman 1990). I start by discussing the scale that provides the least information, the nominal scale, and then gradually move down the table toward the scale that provides the most information, the ratio scale.

Nominal Scales

A ***nominal scale*** is used for categorizing and naming groups. Most language teaching professionals will, at one time or another, be interested in identifying groups into which language students might fall. Some of the most common categories or groupings are according to gender, nationality, native language, educational background, socioeconomic status, level of language study, membership in a particular language class, and even whether or not the students say that they enjoy language study. However, nominal scales are by no means restricted to people. Rocks, molecules, photons, dinosaurs, birds, flowers, trees, smells, algae, or almost anything that the human mind can conceptualize can be categorized, grouped, and counted on nominal scales. The list of possible nominal scales is unlimited. However, in order to be a nominal scale, one condition must always be met: Each observation on the scale must be independent—that is, each observation must fall into one, and only one, category. The ensuing observations can be in different categories, but they too must each fall into one, and only one, category. The essence of the nominal scale is that it names independent categories into which people (or other living things or objects) can be classified. One source of confusion with this type of scale is that it is sometimes called a ***categorical scale*** or, in the case of two categories like female/male, a ***dichotomous scale***. Regardless of what it is called, such a scale identifies and gives a name to the categories involved.

Ordinal Scales

Like the nominal scale, an *ordinal scale* names a group of observations, but, as its label implies, an ordinal scale also orders, or ranks, the data. For instance, if I wanted to rank my students from best to worst in some ability based on a test that I have administered to them, I would arrange the student's scores from high to low and then simply rank the students, using ordinal numbers. The highest student would be first, the next student second, then third, fourth, and so on. This would be an ordinal scale for my group of students. In fact, my high-school French teacher did just that each time she administered a unit test. She then seated us based on the rankings from the front left seat (the worst score on the test) systematically from left to right all the way back to the back right seat (the best score). I often had the bad luck of being assigned to the front left seat; as a result, I still find ordinal scales a bit oppressive.

Other ordinal scales may also be of interest to language teachers. For instance, ordinal scales might be used to quantify the salary or seniority rankings of teachers within a language program, or to quantify the rankings for the relative difficulty of morphemes or structures like those measured on structure tests. If the data are arranged in order and labeled in ordinal numbers (first, second, third, and so forth), the data are on an ordinal scale. More exactly, an ordinal scale orders, or ranks, people (or other living things or objects) such that each point on the scale is a position that is "more than" and "less than" the other points on the scale.

Interval Scales

An *interval scale* also represents the ordering of a named group of data, but it provides additional information. As its name implies, an interval scale also shows the intervals, or distances, between the points in the rankings. For instance, language test scores are usually on interval scales. Consider the scores shown in Table 4.2. Notice, in the last column, that the students can be categorized into four groups (top, upper middle, lower middle, and lower groups) on a nominal scale and that the students can also be ranked on an ordinal scale, as shown in the third column. However, the scores themselves provide much more information than either of the other two scales because interval scale scores indicate the interval, or distance, between the students' scores on the test. For example, Robert scored 12 points higher than Millie, but Millie was only 3 points higher than Iliana. In addition, the distances between some of the middle scores are only one point each. In short, interval scales contain information about the distances between students' scores, which is missing on ordinal and nominal scales. Hence, interval scales provide more information than

Table 4.2: Three Example Scales

Students	Test Scores (Interval)	Rankings (Ordinal)		Frequencies (Nominal)	
Robert	97	1	/	1	"Top
Millie	85	2	/	1	Group"
Iliana	82	3	/	1	
Dean	71	4	/	1	
Cuny	70	5.5	//	2	"Upper
Bill	70	5.5			Middle
Corky	69	7	/	1	Group"
Randy	68	8	/	1	
Monique	67	10	///	3	"Lower
Wendy	67	10			Middle
Henk	67	10			Group"
Shenan	66	12	/	1	
Jeanne	62	13	/	1	"Lower
Elisabeth	59	14	/	1	Group"
Archie	40	15	/	1	
Lindsey	31	16	/	1	

either ordinal or nominal scales. Examples of interval scales include virtually all language tests, whether for placement, proficiency, achievement, or diagnosis, as well as other scales used to measure attitudes, learning styles, and so forth.

One problem arises among statisticians due to the fact that the intervals between points on the scale are assumed to be equal. On the test shown in the second column of Table 4.2, the distance between scores of 25 and 27, which is 2 points, is assumed to be the same as the distance between 96 and 98, which is also 2 points. The problem is that some items on a language test may be much more difficult than others, so the distances between intervals may not, in fact, be equal. Items that make a difference between high scores like 96 and 98 might be considerably more difficult than items at the other end of the scale that make the difference between scores of 25 and 27. The assumption of equal intervals is one that language testers worry about but also learn to live with.

Ratio Scales

A *ratio scale* also represents the ordering of a named group of data and shows the distances between the points in the rankings, but it provides additional information. First, a ratio scale has a zero value; and second, as the name implies, the points on the scale are precise multiples, or ratios, of other points on the scale. For instance, if the lights in a room are turned off, there is zero electricity flowing through the wires. If I turn on a 50-watt bulb, a certain amount of electricity is flowing through the wires. If I then switch on another bulb that uses 100 watts, two times as much electricity is flowing through the wires. Thus, electricity can be measured on a ratio scale; zero electricity makes sense as do multiples or ratios along the scale.

However, arguing that any person knows zero, or no part, of any foreign language would be a difficult position to take. Even a person who has never studied a foreign language knows certain lexical, phonological, and syntactic facts about language in general from learning a native language. This information, in addition to providing cognates and other links between any two languages, can be brought to bear on the task of learning a foreign language. Hence, the position that a person knows zero Japanese (or any other foreign language) is theoretically untenable.

Another shaky position would be to state that a student who scores 100 on a Russian proficiency test knows twice as much Russian as another student who scored 50, or that the student who scored 50 knows five times as much as a student who scored 10. Ratio scales of concern to language teachers include things like the students' ages, the number of years of schooling that they have had, their years of language study, the number of languages they speak, and so forth.

Relationships among Scales

The relationships among the four types of scales is hierarchical in the sense shown in Table 4.1. The table shows that nominal scales name and categorize only, while ordinal scales use categories but also give the ranking, or ordering of points within the categories. Interval scales provide information about the categories and ordering but also give additional details about the distances, or intervals, between points in that ranking. Finally, ratio scales give the intervals between points in the ordering of certain categories, but with even more information, because the ratio scales have a zero, and points along the scale make sense as multiples or ratios of other points on the scale.

Another characteristic of scales is that they can sometimes be converted into other scales, but this is a one-way street in the sense that any of the scales can only be changed into those scales above it in the hierarchy shown in Table 4.1. For instance, the interval scale shown in Table 4.2 can easily be changed into an ordinal scale by going through the scores and ranking the students first, second, third, fourth, and so on. Likewise, either the interval scale scores or the ordinal scale ranks can be changed into a nominal scale by grouping the scores into "top group," "upper middle group," "lower middle group," and "lower group," as shown in the right column of Table 4.2. The result is a nominal scale with all students falling into one of the four groups.

However, once data are recorded at the nominal level without any indication of order or intervals, the information is not available that would be necessary to convert a scale in the other direction. In other words, a set of data recorded on a nominal scale cannot be converted into an ordinal or interval scale because in a nominal scale, the necessary information about the order of scores or about the distances between points is missing. Similarly, data recorded as an ordinal scale cannot magically become an interval scale. To check these statements, try converting each of the scales shown in Table 4.2 to the others, but with the other scales covered. You will see that you can only convert in one direction.

In virtually all cases, the tests that teachers design for their language programs produce scores that can be treated as interval scales, and so it should be. Nevertheless, knowing about the different types of scales is important because a number of the analyses presented later in the book assume an understanding of the differences between ratio, interval, ordinal, and nominal data. In addition, teachers should realize when they are recording data that they should keep the data on the highest level of measurement that they can, preferably on interval or ratio scale, so that information is not lost. A teacher can always convert a ratio scale into an interval scale, or an interval scale into a nominal or ordinal scale, but the reverse is never true. So teachers should keep records in the most precise scale possible.

DISPLAYING DATA

If I were to ask a neighbor how frequently people in our neighborhood read their mail, she would probably answer something like once per day. If I were to ask how frequent a score of 69 is in Table 4.3, the answer would clearly be "four people received 69." *Frequency* is the term that is used to describe this very common-sense sort of tallying procedure. Frequency can be used to indicate how many people did the same thing on a certain task, or how many people have a certain characteristic, or how many people fall into a certain set of categories. Thus, frequency is particularly useful when dealing with a nominal scale. However, it is not restricted to looking at nominal scales, since other scales can easily be converted to nominal data. For instance, to figure out the frequency of students receiving a score of 69 in Table 4.3, just count up the number of 69s in the score column. To calculate the frequency at each score level on the test, just tally the number of students who got each score and record the results as shown in the last

Table 4.3: Score Frequencies

Students	Score	Tally	Frequency
Robert	77	/	1
Millie	75	/	1
Dean	72	//	2
Shenan	72		
Cuny	70	//	2
Bill	70		
Corky	69	////	4
Randy	69		
Monique	69		
Wendy	69		
Henk	68	//	2
Elisabeth	68		
Jeanne	67	/	1
Iliana	64	//	2
Archie	64		
Lindsey	61	/	1

two columns of Table 4.3. Thus, frequency is one numerical tool for re-organizing the data in an interval scale into a nominal scale. But why bother going to all this trouble?

Frequencies are valuable because they can summarize data and thereby reveal patterns that might not otherwise be noticed. For instance, Table 4.4 displays the frequency of each score value arranged from high to low scores in what is called a *frequency distribution*. Table 4.4 shows the score values from 60 to 77, the frequency at each score level (that is, the number of students), the cumulative frequency, and the cumulative percentage. Each *cumulative frequency* can be viewed as the number of students who scored at or below the score in question. The *cumulative percentage* is the same thing but expressed as a percentage of the total number of students. Thus, in the example, four people scored 69 (frequency), which made a cumulative total of ten students at or below 69 on the test (cumulative frequency). These ten students amounted to 63% of the group (cumulative percentage). Or put another way, 63% of the students scored at or below a score of 69 on the test. The concept of cumulative percentage is particularly important for interpreting NRT results, as described in Chapter 5, because knowing the percent of other examinees falling below or above each student is an integral part of interpreting NRT scores.

Graphic Display of Frequencies

However, frequency data can be displayed in far more graphic and appealing ways than the plain, ordinary frequency distribution shown in

Table 4.4: Frequency Distribution

Score Value	Frequency	Cumulative Frequency	Cumulative Percentage
77	1	16	100%
76	0	15	94%
75	1	15	94%
74	0	14	88%
73	0	14	88%
72	2	14	88%
71	0	12	75%
70	2	12	75%
69	4	10	63%
68	2	6	40%
67	1	4	25%
66	0	3	19%
65	0	3	19%
64	2	3	19%
63	0	1	6%
62	0	1	6%
61	1	1	6%
60	0	0	0%

Table 4.4. Such graphic displays of scores generally come in one of three forms: a histogram, a bar graph, or a frequency polygon. All three are drawn on two axes: a horizontal line (also called the *abscissa*, or *x* axis) and a vertical line (or *ordinate*, or *y* axis). These are shown in Figure 4.1.

A *histogram* of the frequencies of a set of scores is normally displayed by assigning score values to the horizontal line (abscissa), and putting the possible frequency values on the vertical line. An "X," asterisk, dot, or other symbol is then marked to represent each student who received each score, as shown in Figure 4.2a. If bars are drawn instead of Xs to represent the score frequencies, the result is a *bar graph*, as shown in Figure 4.2b. Likewise, when dots are placed where the top X would be at each score value and are then connected by lines, the result is a *frequency polygon*, as shown in Figure 4.2c. All three of these ways of displaying test results are important because they can help teachers to understand what happened when their students took a test. Another excellent reason for teachers to understand how such graphs work is that such techniques are sometimes used to misrepresent or distort information very graphically (see Huff & Geis 1954). Thus, understanding how graphs work can help teachers to defend their program successfully against harmful external misrepresentations about enrollments, budgets, teaching loads, and so forth.

Descriptions of language tests most often omit these very useful forms of graphs. Hence, test developers and test score users are missing out on one kind of test description that could help them to understand what the

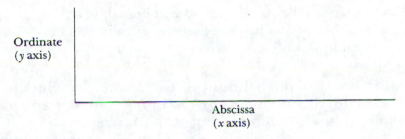

Figure 4.1:   Abscissa and Ordinate

a. Histogram

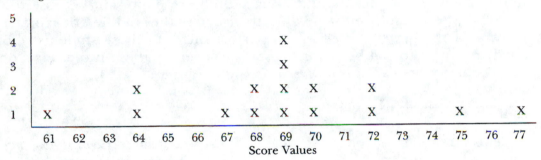

b. Bar Graph

c. Frequency Polygon

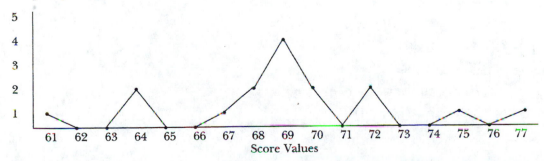

Figure 4.2: Graphic Representation of Frequency Distributions

scores on the test mean. I strongly advise teachers to graph their test results in one way or another and consider what the graphs may be showing them. Fortunately, graphing numbers has become relatively easy in today's personal-computer-oriented world.

At a minimum, teachers should examine the descriptive statistics whenever they administer a test. **Descriptive statistics** are numerical representations of how a group of students performed on a test. Generally, test developers are responsible for providing descriptive statistics (see American Psychological Association 1985) so that all test result users can create a mental picture of how the students performed on the test. Two aspects of group behavior are considered in descriptive statistics: the middle of the group and the individuals. Both are important because the user of the test results must be able to visualize the middle (or typical) behavior of the group as well as the performances of those students who varied from the typical behavior. In statistical terms, these two aspects of group behavior are called *central tendency* and *dispersion*.

CENTRAL TENDENCY

Central tendency is the first aspect of a test to consider. **Central tendency** describes the most typical behavior of a group. Four statistics are used for estimating central tendency: the mean, the mode, the median, and the midpoint.

Mean

The **mean** is probably the single most important indicator of central tendency. The mean is virtually the same as the arithmetic average that most teachers calculate in grading classroom tests. The mean is symbolized in writing by $\overline{X}$ said "ex bar"). Another way to define a statistical concept is to give its formula, so let me also define the mean as:

$$\overline{X} = \frac{\Sigma X}{N}$$

Where $\overline{X}$ = mean

X = scores

N = number of scores

Σ = sum (or add)

In order to help clarify the reading of such formulas, I will briefly explain this one in a step-by-step manner. The formula simply says: To get the mean ($\overline{X}$), *sum* (or add up) (Σ) the *scores* (X), and divide by the *number of scores* (N). These steps are shown in Table 4.5. To find the mean in the example: (a) sum, or add up the scores, (b) find the number of scores, and (c) divide the sum of the scores by the number of scores. So the mean in the example in Table 4.5 would be 69. As mentioned above, this set of calculations probably looks very familiar since most teachers use the arithmetic average in looking at the results of a classroom test. What they are checking in the process is almost exactly the same as the mean and therefore is an indicator of the central tendency, or typical performance, of their class on the test.

As with the formula for the mean, all other formulas in this book are always explained recipe-book style with plenty of examples. In the case of this formula, the steps seem very easy because the formula and the concept of the mean are just another way of expressing something that teachers already know how to do. However, in general, formulas provide more mathematical precision for defining and discussing statistical concepts. So

Table 4.5: Calculating the Mean

Students	Scores (X)	Calculations
Robert	77	a. ΣX = sum of scores = 77 + 75 + 72 +
Millie	75	72 + 70 + 70 + 69 + 69 + 69 + 69 +
Dean	72	68 + 68 + 67 + 64 + 64 + 61 = 1104
Shenan	72	b. N = number of scores = 16
Cuny	70	c. $\overline{X} = \dfrac{\Sigma X}{N} = \dfrac{1104}{16} = 69$
Bill	70	
Corky	69	
Randy	69	
Monique	69	
Wendy	69	
Henk	68	
Elisabeth	68	
Jeanne	67	
Iliana	64	
Archie	64	
Lindsey	61	

language testers use such formulas much as linguists and language teachers use terms like "syntax" and "phonology" when everyone else calls these concepts grammar and pronunciation. Such formulas are just part of learning to "speak" language testing.

Mode

Another indicator of central tendency is the mode. The *mode* is that score which occurs most frequently. In Table 4.5, what would the mode be? It would be 69, the only score received by four students. A memory device that I use to keep the mode straight in my mind is that "mode" can mean fashionable (as in *à la mode*). Thus, the mode would be that score which is most fashionable, or the one received by the most students. No statistical formula is necessary for this straightforward idea. However, note that a set of scores can have two or more modes. Such distributions of scores are referred to as being *bimodal*, *trimodal*, and so on.

Median

The *median* is that point below which 50% of the scores fall and above which 50% fall. Thus, in the set of scores 100, 95, 83, 71, 61, 57, 30, the median is 71, because 71 has three scores above it (100, 95, and 83) and three scores below it (61, 57, and 30). What is the median for the following set of scores: 11, 23, 40, 50, 57, 63, 86? Fifty, right?

In real data, cases arise that are not so clear. For example, what is the median for these scores: 9, 12, 15, 16, 17, 27? In such a situation, when there is an even number of scores, the median is taken to be midway between the two middle scores. In this example, the two middle scores are 15 and 16, so the median is 15.5. Does that make sense? If so, what is the median for these scores: 11, 28, 33, 50, 60, 62, 70, 98? Your answer should be 55 because that is the point halfway between the two middle scores, 50 and 60.

In some cases, there is more than one numerically equal score at the median—for instance, 40, 45, 49, 50, 50, 50, 57, 64, 77. Here, the midpoint is clearly 50 because there is an odd number of like scores at the median separating equal numbers of scores on either side.

Still other situations may arise in determining the median, but the important thing to remember is that the median is the point that divides the scores 50/50, much like the median in a highway divides the road into two equal parts. However, in sets of test scores, the median may have a fraction because students rarely cooperate to the degree that highways do.

Midpoint

The *midpoint* in a set of scores is that point halfway between the highest score and the lowest score on the test. The formula for calculating the midpoint is:

$$\text{Midpoint} = \frac{\text{High} + \text{Low}}{2}$$

For example, if the lowest score on a test was 30 and the highest was 100, the midpoint would be halfway between these two scores. To use the formula: (a) identify the high and low scores (100 and 30 here), (b) add the low score to the high one (100 + 30 = 130), and (c) divide the result by 2 as follows:

$$\text{Midpoint} = \frac{100 + 30}{2} = \frac{130}{2} = 65$$

To review central tendency briefly, four such measures exist: the mean, the mode, the median, and the midpoint. These are all measures of central tendency, and each has its strengths and weaknesses. None is necessarily better than the others, though the mean is most commonly reported. They simply serve different purposes and are appropriate in different situations, as you will see at the end of the chapter.

To further review central tendency, look at Table 4.5. I have explained that the mean, or arithmetic average, in Table 4.5 is 69. The mode, or most frequent score, also turned out to be 69. The median, that score which divided the scores 50/50, was also 69. The midpoint, halfway between the high score of 77 and the low score of 61, was also 69. In this contrived example, all four measures of central tendency turned out to be the same—69. However, as you will see in Table 4.8, these four indices for actual test data are seldom so universally well-centered and in agreement on what constitutes the typical behavior, or central tendency, of a group of scores. For that reason alone, all four should be used. Furthermore, as I explain in Chapter 5, the degree to which these four indices of central tendency are similar is one indication of the degree to which a set of scores is *normally* (as in *norm*-referenced) distributed.

DISPERSION

With a clear understanding of how to examine the central tendency of a set of scores in hand, the next step is to consider *dispersion*, or how the individual performances vary from the central tendency. Three indicators of the dispersion are commonly used for describing distributions of test scores: the range, the standard deviation, and the variance.

Range

Most teachers are already familiar with the concept of *range* from tests that they have given in class. Simply put, the range is the number of points between the highest score on a measure and the lowest score plus one (one is added because the range should include the scores at both ends). Thus, in Table 4.5, where the highest score is 77 and the lowest is 61, the range is 17 points ($77 - 61 + 1 = 17$). The range provides some idea of how individuals vary from the central tendency.

However, the range only reflects the magnitude of the outer edges (high and low) of all the variation in scores and therefore can be strongly affected by any test performance which is not really representative of the group of students as a whole. For instance, if I add another student named Emma, who scored 26, to the bottom of Table 4.5, the range will be much larger than 17. With Emma included, the range is 52 ($77 - 26 + 1 = 52$). However, her performance on the test is so different from the performances of the other students that she does not appear to belong in this group. Such a person may be an *outlier*, a person who, for some reason, does not belong to the group. To check this, I would talk to Emma in an attempt to discover what was going on during the test. Perhaps she will reveal that she had already decided to drop the course at the time of the test so she did not study and had to guess on most of the test. If she is included in calculating the range, a value of 52 is obtained. If she is excluded, a value of 17 is the result. These ranges are quite different. In a sense, the range of 52 (obtained with the outlier included) is wrong in that it does not really represent the group performance. So I might be tempted to exclude her and report the range as 17. However, I can never be 100% sure that an outlier is not a natural part of the group, so I am more likely to be open and honest about the situation and report the range with and without the outlier. I would also want to explain why I think that the outlier is not part of the group.

In short, the range is a weak measure of dispersion because factors like Emma's personal decision can strongly affect it even though they are extraneous to the students' performances on the test. Regardless of this problem, the range is usually reported as one indicator of dispersion and should be interpreted by test score users as just what it is: the number of points between the highest and lowest scores on a test, including both of them.

Standard Deviation

The standard deviation is an averaging process; as such, it is not affected as much by outliers as the range. Consequently, the standard deviation is generally considered a stronger estimate of the dispersion of scores. I define the ***standard deviation*** as a sort of average of the differences of all scores from the mean (Brown 1988a). This is not a rigorous statistical definition but rather one that will serve well for conveying the meaning of this statistic. The formula used to calculate the statistic says very much the same thing but in mathematical shorthand. Remember that $\overline{X}$ is the symbol for the mean, that X represents the scores, that Σ indicates that summation (adding something up) is necessary, and that N stands for the number of scores. The formula for the standard deviation (S, s, or S.D.) is:

$$S = \sqrt{\frac{\Sigma(X - \overline{X})^2}{N}}$$

Starting from the inside and working outward, subtract the mean from each score $(X - \overline{X})$, square each of these values $(X - \overline{X})^2$, and add them up $\Sigma(X - \overline{X})^2$. This sum is then divided by the number of scores $\Sigma(X - \overline{X})^2 / N$ and the square root of the result of that operation

$$\sqrt{\frac{\Sigma(X - \overline{X})^2}{N}}$$

is the standard deviation. Let's take a look at Table 4.6 to make this clear.

Remember that the mean in Table 4.5 was 69. Using the same scores and mean, Table 4.6 illustrates the steps required to calculate the standard deviation: (a) line up each score with the mean; (b) subtract the mean from each score; (c) each of the "differences" from the mean is squared; (d) the squared values are added up; and (e) the appropriate values can be inserted into the formula. In the example, the result after taking the square root is 3.87. I will now go back to the original definition to make sure all this is crystal clear.

In my definition, the standard deviation is "a sort of average" (ignoring the squaring and square root, notice that something is added up and divided by N—similar to what happens in calculating an average) "of the differences of all scores from the mean" (so it turns out that the difference of each student's score from the mean is what is being averaged). Thus, the standard deviation is a sort of average of the differences of all scores from the mean. These differences from the mean are often called ***deviations*** from the mean—hence the label "standard deviation."

Table 4.6: Standard Deviation

Students	Score a. (X)	−	Mean $(\bar{X})$		Difference b. $(X-\bar{X})$	Difference Squared c. $(X-\bar{X})^2$
Robert	77	−	69	=	8	64
Millie	75	−	69	=	6	36
Dean	72	−	69	=	3	9
Shenan	72	−	69	=	3	9
Cuny	70	−	69	=	1	1
Bill	70	−	69	=	1	1
Corky	69	−	69	=	0	0
Randy	69	−	69	=	0	0
Monique	69	−	69	=	0	0
Wendy	69	−	69	=	0	0
Henk	68	−	69	=	−1	1
Elisabeth	68	−	69	=	−1	1
Jeanne	67	−	69	=	−2	4
Iliana	64	−	69	=	−5	25
Archie	64	−	69	=	−5	25
Lindsey	61	−	69	=	−8	64

$$\text{d.} \quad \Sigma (X-\bar{X})^2 = 240$$

$$\text{e.} \quad S = \sqrt{\frac{\Sigma(X-\bar{X})^2}{N}} = \sqrt{\frac{240}{16}}$$

$$= \sqrt{15} = 3.87$$

I call the standard deviation a "sort of" average because it involves squaring certain values and taking a square root at the end. In the example in Table 4.6, the deviations are reported in column b. under $(X-\bar{X})$. Notice that adding up the deviations including both the positive and negative values will yield zero. Such a result will usually be obtained because typically about half the deviations will be positive (above the mean) and half will be negative (below the mean). Thus, they will usually add to zero or a value very close to zero. To get around this problem, each value is squared, as shown in column c. under $(X-\bar{X})^2$. Then the resulting numbers can be added with a result other than zero. After the sum of these numbers is divided by N in the averaging process, the result is brought back down to a score value by taking its square root. In other words, the square root is taken to counteract the squaring process that went on earlier.

The standard deviation is a very versatile and useful statistic, as I explain in much more detail in the next chapter, but for now, keep in mind that the standard deviation is a good indicator of the dispersion of a set of test scores around the mean. The standard deviation is usually better than the range because it is the result of an averaging process. By averaging, the effects are lessened of any extreme scores not attributable to performance on the test (that is, outliers like Emma with her personal problem).

Sometimes, a slightly different formula is used for the standard deviation:

$$S = \sqrt{\frac{\Sigma(X - \overline{X})^2}{N - 1}}$$

This version (called the "$N - 1$" formula) is only appropriate if the number of students taking the test is less than 30. Note that the sample size in Table 4.6 is 16. Hence, I should have used the $N - 1$ formula. I did not do so because I wanted to save space and to demonstrate the more commonly used formula—a prime example of do-as-I-say-not-as-I-do.

Variance

The variance is another descriptive statistic for dispersion. As indicated by its symbol, S^2, the test variance is equal to the squared value of the standard deviation. Thus, the formula for the test variance looks very much like the one for the standard deviation except that both sides of the equation are squared. Squaring the left side of the standard deviation equation is easy. Just change S to the power of 2—that is, S^2. To square the right side of the standard deviation equation, all that is necessary is to take away the square root sign. What is left is the formula for the test variance.

$$S^2 = \frac{\Sigma(X - \overline{X})^2}{N}$$

Hence, *test variance* can easily be defined, with reference to this formula, as the average of the squared differences of students' scores from the mean. Test variance can also be defined as the square of the standard deviation, or as an intermediary step in the calculation of the standard deviation. For much more discussion of this concept, see Chapters 6, 7, and 8.

REPORTING DESCRIPTIVE STATISTICS

What Should Be Included?

To review briefly then, test developers often write up a report of the results of administering their test. In such reports, they typically describe at least two aspects of the results on a test: central tendency and dispersion. *Central tendency* indicates the middle, or typical, score for the students who took the test. Central tendency indicators come in four forms: the *mean* (arithmetic average), *mode* (most often received score), the *median* (score that splits the group 50/50), and the *midpoint* (the score halfway between the highest and lowest scores)

In addition, test developers usually provide indicators of the *dispersion* of scores, or the way individuals varied around the typical behavior of the group. Dispersion indicators come in three forms: the *range* (the difference between the highest and lowest scores, including both), the *standard deviation* (a sort of average of how far individuals varied from the mean), and the *test variance* (a sort of average of the squared differences of students' scores from the mean).

Two other descriptive statistics are commonly reported. Mercifully, these statistics do not require any calculations. The **number of students** who took the test (N) is one such statistic. For instance, if 130 students took the test, the test developer should report that $N = 130$. Likewise, he or she should report the **number of items** (k) that were on the test. Thus, on a test with fifty items, the test developer should report that $k = 50$.

Under circumstances where one focus of the report is on the individual test items or on selecting items for revising and improving the test, the means for the following item statistics might be reported as well: the item facility index, the item discrimination index, the difference index, and the *B*-index. These mean item statistics are calculated just like the mean for a set of scores, but the individual item statistics are used instead of students' scores.

So far in this chapter, I have covered numerous statistics that can aid in analyzing and reporting test results. Deciding which indicators to calculate and report in a particular testing situation depends on whether the test is an NRT or CRT, on the statistical sophistication of the audience (the test users), and on how clear the results need to be. But in most cases, test developers should consider all these graphic and statistical ways of describing test data so that they can provide the clearest possible description of how the students performed on the test. The best rule of thumb to follow is, when in doubt, report too much information rather than too little.

How Should Descriptive Test Statistics be Displayed?

The next step is to consider how to present the statistics once they are calculated. Test developers may find themselves presenting test results to colleagues, to funding agencies, or to a journal in the form of research. Most often, the purpose is to summarize the information so that everyone involved can better understand how well the tests worked or how well the students performed on it. In most cases, descriptive test statistics are displayed in the form of a table.

Table 4.7: Fall 1986 (First Administration) ELIPT Results

	Subtests			
Statistics	Listening	Reading	Vocabulary	Writing
N	153.00	153.00	154.00	153.00
Total items (k)	55.00	60.00	100.00	100.00
Mean ($\overline{X}$)	34.76	40.64	69.34	75.08
Mode	32.00	43.00	86.00	77.00
Median	34.45	41.00	71.67	75.50
Midpoint	34.50	39.00	59.50	69.00
Low–High	17–52	21–57	20–99	44–94
Range	36.00	37.00	80.00	51.00
S	7.29	7.48	16.08	8.94

Table 4.7 shows one way to display such statistics. The table shows very real test results from a now retired version of the English Language Institute Placement Test (ELIPT) at the University of Hawaii at Manoa (UHM). Most incoming foreign students admitted to the university took this battery of tests. To be admitted, they first had to take the *Test of English as a Foreign Language* (TOEFL) (Educational Testing Service 1994) and score at least 500. If they score higher than 600 on the TOEFL, they do not have to take our placement examination. The ELIPT battery is administered three to five times each semester to determine what levels of study the students must take in the various ESL reading, writing, and listening courses that we offer. Depending on their scores, students may also be exempt in one or more of the skill areas.

The results shown in Table 4.7 are for the largest two of five Fall semester administrations in 1986. Notice how very neatly and clearly this table presents a great deal of information that can be easily examined and interpreted by the test user. This clarity results partly from the fact that the table is not cluttered by vertical lines. The columns of numbers are enough to orient the reader's eye both horizontally and vertically. The horizontal lines that do appear serve only to define the boundaries of the table itself and to separate the column labels from the statistical results. This table follows American Psychological Association (1994) format recommendations, as do many of the language journals because this format is uncluttered and easy to read. Notice also how each number (except those for the low–high) has been carried out to two decimal places, even when not necessary (for instance, those for N and total possible), for the sake of presenting a neat and symmetrical table.

Table 4.8: Fall 1986 ELIPT Results

Subtest	N	k	$\bar{X}$	Mode	Median	Midpoint	Low–High	Range	S
			Central Tendency				**Dispersion**		
Listening	153	55	34.76	32	34.45	34.50	17–52	36	7.29
Reading	153	60	40.64	43	41.00	39.00	21–57	37	7.48
Vocabulary	154	100	69.34	86	71.67	59.50	20–99	80	16.08
Writing	153	100	75.08	77	75.50	69.00	44–94	51	8.94

Table 4.8 displays the same information with the column labels changed to row labels and vice versa. Many other possible variations exist, and the form that test developers choose to use will depend on their purposes in displaying the statistics. In some cases, they may wish to present data in a histogram, bar graph, or frequency polygon. For instance, histograms for each of the ELIPT subtests helped us to examine the degree to which each subtest was producing a normal, or bell, curve. The histogram for the ELIPT listening subtest is shown in Figure 4.3, just as it came off of the computer. Notice that the orientation of the graph is different from the histograms elsewhere in this chapter. The sideways orientation resulted from the fact that the scores were plotted on the ordinate (or vertical y axis) and the frequencies along the abscissa (or horizontal x axis). This orientation is a product of the way the computer program "thinks" and prints rather than a question of convenience for the humans who must interpret the graph. Nevertheless, nobody should have any problem visualizing the distribution of scores the way they are presented, though some may have to turn the book sideways to do so.

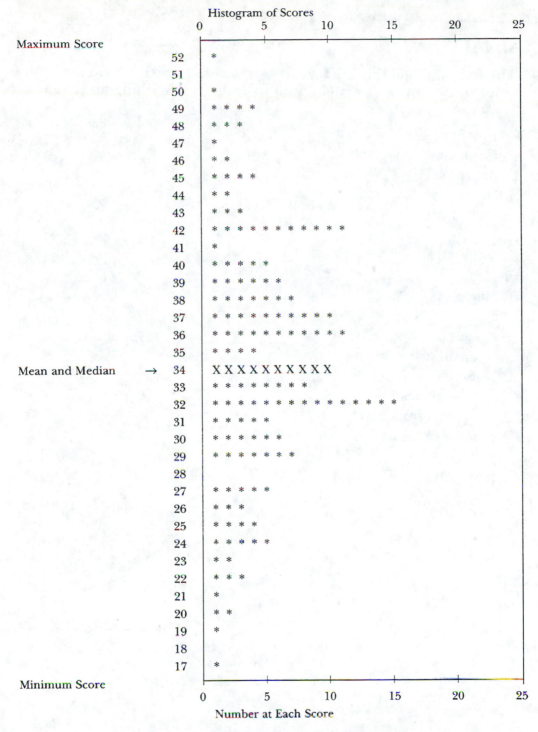

Figure 4.3: Histogram ELIPT Listening Subtest

SUMMARY

The following checklist may help you to recall which of the descriptive graphics and statistics you might want to cover in describing and reporting your test results.

- ☐ Graphical
  - ☐ Histogram
  - ☐ Bar graph
  - ☐ Frequency polygon
- ☐ Central tendency
  - ☐ Mean
  - ☐ Mode
  - ☐ Median
  - ☐ Midpoint
- ☐ Dispersion
  - ☐ Range
  - ☐ Standard deviation
  - ☐ Test variance
- ☐ Other possibilities
  - ☐ Number of students (N)
  - ☐ Number of items(k)
  - ☐ Mean IF
  - ☐ Mean ID

TERMS AND SYMBOLS

abscissa (x axis)
bar graph
bimodal
categorical scale
central tendency
cumulative frequency
cumulative percentage
data
descriptive statistics
deviations
dichotomous scale
dispersion
frequency
frequency distribution
frequency polygon
histogram
interval scale
mean ($\overline{X}$)
median
midpoint
mode
nominal scale
number of items (k)
number of students (N)
ordinal scale
ordinate (y axis)
outlier
range
ratio scale
scores (X)
standard deviation (S or SD)
sum (Σ)
test variance (S^2)
trimodal

REVIEW QUESTIONS

1. What is a nominal scale? An ordinal scale? An interval scale? A ratio scale?

2. How can you convert one scale to another? Which ones can be converted into which other ones?

3. How would you define central tendency? What are four ways to estimate it? Which is most often reported? Why?

4. What is dispersion? Which of the three indices for dispersion are most often reported?

5. Why should you describe your students' behavior on a measure in terms of both central tendency and dispersion?

6. What is a frequency distribution? Why might you want to use a frequency distribution to describe the behavior of your students on a test if you already have the descriptive statistics?

7. Which of these axes is the ordinate, and which the abscissa? Go ahead and label them.

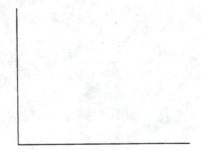

8. Which of these three graphs is a bar graph? A histogram? A frequency polygon?

a.

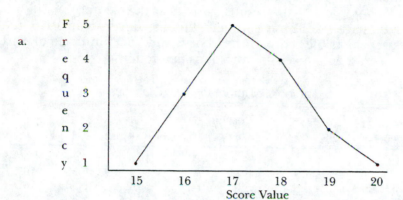

b.

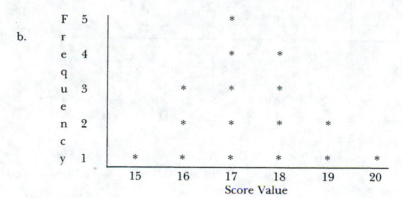

c.

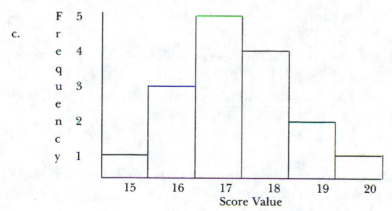

APPLICATION EXERCISES

A. The results shown in Table 4.9 are adapted from Hinofotis (1980). This table shows a portion of the results for tests at the Center for English as a Second Language (CESL) at Southern Illinois University in 1976. (Notice that she uses "possible score" instead of *k*, and "SD" in place of *S*.) Look the table over; then answer the questions that follow.

Table 4.9: Summary Test Statistics

Measure	Possible Score	Mean	SD	N
Cloze	50	15.3	7.30	107
Total CESL Placement	300 ÷ 3 = 100	50.8	16.23	107
CESL Listening	100	50.4	18.50	107
CESL Structure	100	50.4	20.80	107
CESL Reading	100	51.3	16.01	107
Total TOEFL	ca. 700	422.1	56.06	52

A1. a. Do you remember (from Chapter 2) what a cloze test is?   b. How many subtests are there on the CESL?   c. Do you know what the TOEFL is?

A2. a. What is the mean for the CESL Reading subtest?   b. How many total points does it have?   c. What is the standard deviation?   d. And, how many students took it?

A3. a. Why do you suppose the possible score for Total CESL Placement indicates 300 ÷ 3 = 100?   b. And why does Total TOEFL show "ca. 700"?

A4. a. Which test has the smallest total possible?   b. Which appears to have the largest?   c. What is the number of items in the Cloze test?

A5. a. Which test had the smallest number of students taking it?   b. And why do you suppose this is the case?

A6. a. Which test appears to have the widest dispersion of scores?   b. How do you know that?

A7. What additional information would you have liked to see in this table to help you interpret the results of these tests?

B. The scores shown in Table 4.10 are based on a subsample of thirty Sri Lankan high-school students who took four different 30-item variations of the cloze type of test (see Premaratne 1987 for more details). The four variations are labeled A – D for convenience. Look at the data, and answer the following questions.

Table 4.10: Sri Lankan High-School Cloze Test Data

Student ID Number	Test A	Test B	Test C	Test D
1	27	19	28	28
2	27	20	27	29
3	20	16	18	23
4	21	17	24	25
5	21	15	26	19
6	18	13	25	26
7	11	6	24	23
8	16	11	24	21
9	17	12	24	23
10	14	8	22	17
11	12	8	19	18
12	24	18	28	29
13	10	8	10	23
14	14	8	26	21
15	13	7	26	22
16	19	13	24	19
17	18	15	25	18
18	18	14	23	24
19	17	14	20	25
20	26	20	24	28
21	15	11	17	24
22	16	11	22	21
23	12	9	20	18
24	16	11	21	21
25	14	12	22	22
26	13	11	17	21
27	18	13	20	24
28	8	8	14	19
29	26	21	25	27
30	18	13	21	23

B1. Begin by graphing the results of each test in the spaces provided below. Use a histogram, bar graph, or frequency polygon, as you see fit, or mix and match.

Test A:

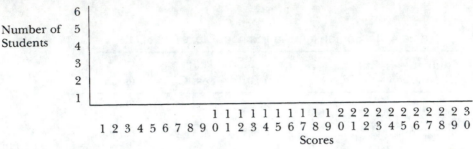

Test B:

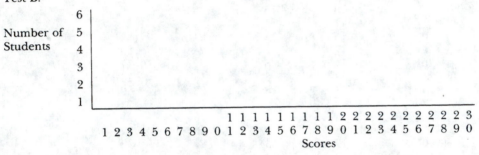

Test C:

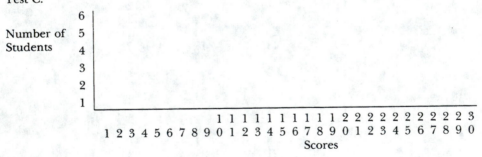

Test D:

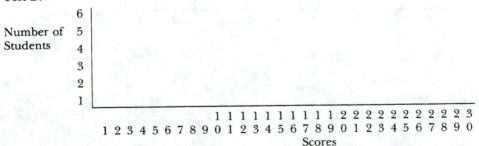

B2. Look back to the brief prose description under part B. How many students took each test? How many items were on each test? Put your answers in the table below in the rows labeled N and k, respectively. Fill in the rest of the table by calculating the four indicators of central tendency and the four for dispersion.

Sri Lankan High-School Cloze Test Results

Statistic	Test A	Test B	Test C	Test D
N				
k				
Mean				
Mode				
Median				
Midpoint				
S				
Variance				
Low–High				
Range				

CHAPTER 5

INTERPRETING TEST SCORES

The purpose of developing language tests, administering them, and sorting through the resulting scores is to make decisions about your students. The sorting process is sometimes called *test score interpretation*. This chapter is about interpreting the performances of students on both norm-referenced and criterion-referenced tests. The descriptive statistics discussed in the previous chapter help teachers to visualize the students' performances in terms of central tendency and dispersion. As explained in this chapter, descriptive statistics can also help language teachers to understand more complex patterns in the test behavior of their students. As a foundation, the discussion begins with three concepts: probability distributions, the normal distribution, and standardized scores. Knowing about these three concepts helps teachers to understand what has happened on a test administration and enables them to report students' scores in the context of the entire score distribution. As a result, each score has more meaning to the students themselves, as well as to the administrators and teachers involved.

PROBABILITY DISTRIBUTIONS

Early in life, most people discover that the *probability* of getting heads on any given flip of a coin is 50/50. This probability can also be expressed as a "1 in 2 chance" or 50%. Regardless of how it is phrased, the concept is a familiar one. In more formal terms, such a probability is determined by dividing the number of expected outcomes (one—heads in this case) by the number of possible outcomes (two—both heads and tails are possibilities). In the case of the coin flip, one expected outcome is divided by the number of possibilities to yield 1/2, or .50, which indicates a 50% probability of getting heads on any particular flip of a coin.

Since probability is clearly a function of expected outcomes and possible outcomes, I would like to explain these concepts in a bit more detail. *Expected outcomes* represent those events for which a person is trying to determine the probability (heads in the example above). The *possible outcomes* represent the number of potentially different events that might occur as the events unfold (two in the example). The probability of a given event, or set of events, is the ratio of the expected outcomes to the possible outcomes. This ratio ranges from 0 to 1.0 and is commonly discussed in percentage terms. Thus, a ratio of .50, as discussed above, is also referred to as a 50% chance of getting heads.

Another way of keeping track of probabilities is to plot them out as they occur, perhaps in the form of a histogram, like the ones in the previous chapter. Typically, a histogram is designed so that the number of actual outcomes is on the ordinate and possible outcomes is on the abscissa. Figure 5.1a shows how the histogram would look for coin flips if they were to occur as follows: tails, heads, heads, tails, tails, heads, tails, tails.

The result of plotting the coin flips as they occurred is a graph of the *distribution,* or arrangement, of the outcomes. This distribution helps us to picture the events that occurred in a more vivid manner than simply knowing the numbers (three heads and five tails). Another way to plot the events involved in coin flipping is to plot the probable, or likely, distributions for many more than the two possible events described above. Consider, for instance, the possibilities for outcomes of heads only but for two coins instead of one. A typical distribution for heads on two coins given four flips is shown in Figure 5.1b. Notice that the distribution in Figure 5.1b shows heads only and that the histogram indicates all possible outcomes for heads (that is, 0, 1, or 2 heads). Notice also that the following events are plotted: zero heads one time, one head two times, and two heads one time. Figure 5.1c shows the distribution for heads on three coins given eight flips. Notice that the distribution of events grows more complex as the number of coins is increased. Consider what would probably happen if I were to plot the occurrences of heads for 100 coins in thousands of flips and connect the tops of each column. The resulting frequency polygon would look like the one shown in Figure 5.1d. This figure will look familiar to anyone who has worked with the concept of the normal distribution, or bell curve. Such normal distributions always occur in distributions like those I just discussed as long as enough coin flips are involved. Notice that these distributions occur purely because of the probabilities of those coins landing on the various possible numbers of heads.

NORMAL DISTRIBUTION

The normal distribution does occur. The graphs of the coin flip distributions demonstrate that. Moreover, as the number of possible events gets larger, plots of those events increasingly take the shape of the bell curve. Additional evidence comes from the biological sciences, where repeated observations generally show that living organisms grow, multiply, and behave in relatively predictable patterns. Many of these patterns take the shape of the *normal distribution.* For example, consider the 28 trees that grow in Mauka Park near where I live. If I were to measure them, I could plot their heights roughly as shown in Figure 5.2a. Each tree is represented by an "x" on the 5-foot height closest to the actual height of the tree. Notice

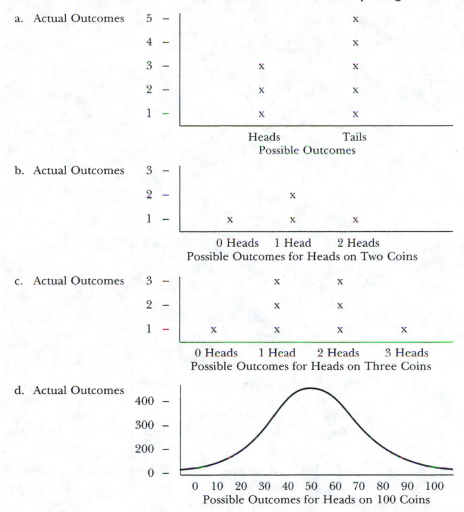

Figure 5.1: Histograms of Coin Flips

that the result is a histogram of the distribution of heights among the trees in Mauka Park. Such visual representation could be accomplished equally well by using a frequency polygon (as shown in Figure 5.2b). Notice how the shape of the curve in the polygon looks suspiciously, but not exactly, like the normal distribution.

The numbers along the abscissa could have been just as easily the measurements of another type of organism—that is, scores measuring the language performance of students, perhaps on a 100-point test, as shown in Figure 5.3. Notice that their scores look reasonably normal, a distribution that is quite common among language students. Similar distributions

a. Histogram

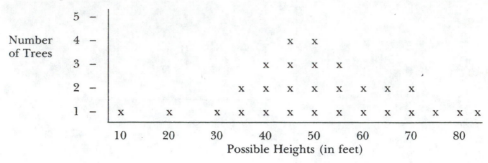

Possible Heights (in feet)

b. Frequency Polygon

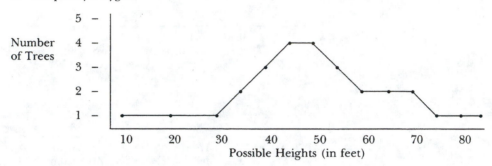

Possible Heights (in feet)

Figure 5.2: Distribution of the Heights of Trees

would likely occur in graphs of their ages, their heights, and their IQ scores as well.

So the normal distribution is often observed in the behavior of language students. In fact, I have done so repeatedly over the years. However, as with the coin-flip examples, as the number of outcomes increases, the distributions will tend to look more and more normal. Hence, teachers should remember that in a small number of outcomes, the distribution may be somewhat lopsided, as in Figures 5.2 and 5.3. As the number of outcomes increases, teachers can reasonably expect the distribution to become increasingly normal. However, they should never take this for granted. Visual inspection of a distribution will provide valuable information about the normality of the distribution of events involved; that is, inspection can reveal just how wide, lopsided, or normal the distribution is. Remember also that a class of, say, fifteen students is typically too small a group to expect a perfectly normal distribution of scores on even the best norm-referenced test. But what is a large enough group? Well, 1 million students would certainly be enough. But in more realistic terms, a good rule of thumb to remember is that events tend to approach normal distribution (if indeed it

a. Histogram

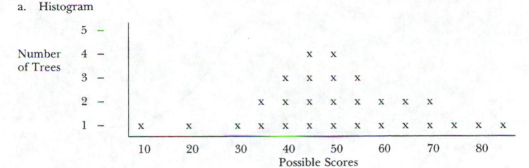

b. Frequency Polygon

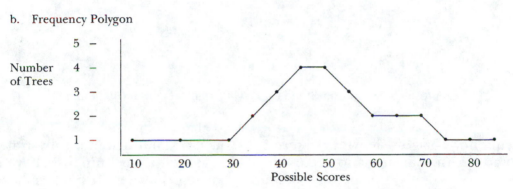

Figure 5.3: Student Scores on Hypothetical Language Test

exists) when the number of observations is about thirty. This rule of thumb seems to work out fairly well in reality. However, in most norm-referenced test development situations, the developers should try to get the largest sample of students possible in order to maximize the chances of getting a normal distribution. After all, creating a normal distribution of scores is a major goal of norm-referenced tests.

In the previous chapters, I explained that criterion-referenced decision making may be almost completely independent of the normal distribution. Nonetheless, plotting the CRT scores of a group of students can never hurt. While CRT distributions are often quite different from NRT distributions, inspecting them can provide as much information about the CRT involved as the normal distribution does about NRTs.

So, to the surprise of many teachers, the normal distribution of scores, or something close to it, really does occur if the purpose of the test is norm-referenced and the number of students is sufficiently large. Hence, teachers should never dismiss out of hand the idea of the normal distribution. With a group of, say, 160 students taking the Hypothetical Language Test, I could reasonably expect a normal distribution that would look something like the

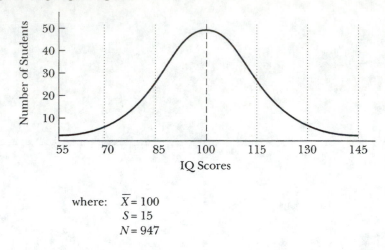

where: $\overline{X} = 100$
$S = 15$
$N = 947$

Figure 5.4: Mean and Standard Deviation in a Normal Distribution

frequency polygon shown in Figure 5.4. This normal distribution illustrates a pattern that occurs and recurs in nature as well as in human behavior. More importantly, this pattern can aid in sorting out the test performance of language students.

CHARACTERISTICS OF NORMAL DISTRIBUTIONS

The two most important characteristics of a normal distribution were covered in the previous chapter: central tendency and dispersion. A third useful characteristic is the notion of percents in the distribution. One way this concept can be useful is in exploring the percents of students who fall within different score ranges on a test. Mostly, I explore the notion of percents in terms of the normal distribution, but later in the chapter I also discuss potential exceptions to the theoretical model of normal distribution.

Central Tendency

Recall that *central tendency* indicates the typical behavior of a group and that four different estimates can be used: the mean, mode, median, and midpoint. All four of these estimates should be somewhere near the center or middle if a distribution is normal. In fact, in a perfectly normal distribution, all four indicators of central tendency would fall on exactly the same score value, as shown in Figure 5.4, right in the middle of the distribution. Note in Figure 5.4 that the mean, mode, median, and midpoint are all equal to the same value, 41.

Dispersion

As with central tendency, *dispersion* is predictable in a normal distribution. Remember that dispersion describes how the individual scores disperse, or vary, around the central tendency. This concept is commonly estimated statistically by using the range and standard deviation. In a theoretical normal distribution, testers expect the lowest score on the test (11 in Figure 5.4) and highest score (71 in the example) to be exactly the same distance from the center, or mean. This is apparently true in the example. Both are 30 points above or below the mean. Thus, in this case, the *range* is symmetrical.

The other indicator of dispersion is, of course, the standard deviation. Conveniently, the standard deviation in Figure 5.4 is a nice round number, 10. Typically, the standard deviation in a normal distribution will fall in the pattern shown in Figure 5.4. One standard deviation above the mean ($+1S$) will fall on the score that is equal to $\overline{X} + 1S$ or, in this case, $41 + 10 = 51$. Similarly, two standard deviations below the mean will fall on the score that is equal to $\overline{X} - 2S$, or $41 - 20 = 21$. In short, the *standard deviation* is a regular distance measured in score points that marks off certain portions of the distribution, each of which is equal in length along the abscissa.

Consider a hypothetical situation in which teachers administered an IQ (Intelligence Quotient) test to 947 elementary-school students. The mean, mode, median, and midpoint all turned out to be 100, and the standard deviation was 15, with a range of 91 points (low score = 55, and high = 145). Can you imagine what such a distribution of scores might look like under these conditions? Try to make a rough sketch of the distribution. Start with a vertical line for the mean, and assume that mean = mode = median = midpoint. Now put in a line for each of three standard deviations above the mean and three below, as well. Then draw a rough normal curve to fit the standard deviation markers. Finally, compare the drawing to the distribution shown in part A of the Application Exercises section at the end of the chapter. Both distributions should look about the same.

Percents

Once central tendency and dispersion are understood as they apply to the normal distribution, some inferences can be made about the *percents* of students who are likely to fall within certain score ranges in the distribution. First, recall that the mean, mode, median, and midpoint should all be the same in a normal distribution. Also recall that the median is the score below which 50% of the cases should fall, and above which 50% should be. Given these facts, teachers can predict with fair assurance that 50% of their

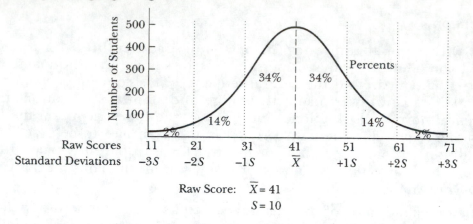

Raw Score: $\overline{X} = 41$
$S = 10$

Figure 5.5: Approximate Percentages under the Normal Distribution*
*The more precise percents (shown in Figure 5.6) are 34.13%, 13.59%, and 2.14%.

students' scores will be above the median (or mean, or mode, or midpoint) in a normal distribution. In like manner, researchers have repeatedly shown that approximately 34% of the scores will fall within one standard deviation above the mean, as shown in Figure 5.5. That means that about 34% of the students scored between 41 and 51 points on this particular test. Since the distribution under discussion is normal and therefore bell-shaped, the curve is symmetrical. Thus, 34% of the students are also likely to score between 31 and 41 points on the test, or within one standard deviation below the mean.

Thus, in a normal distribution, 68% of the students (34% + 34% = 68%) are likely to fall within one standard deviation on either side of the mean (plus or minus). But that leaves 32% of the students (100% − 68% = 32%) not yet explained in the distribution. Notice in Figure 5.5 that roughly 14% of the students scored between the first and second standard deviations (+1S to +2S) above the mean (or between 51 and 61 score points in this particular distribution). Likewise, 14% will usually score between one standard deviation below the mean (−1S) and two standard deviations below the mean (−2S) (or between 21 and 31 score points in this case).

At this point, 96% of the students in the distribution are accounted for (34% + 34% + 14% + 14% = 96%). The remaining 4% of the students are evenly divided above and below the mean: a little less than 2% in the area between the second and third standard deviations above the mean (+2S to +3S) and about the same 2% in the area between the second and third standard deviations below the mean (−2S to −3S). This pattern of percents for students' scores within the various areas under the curve of the normal distribution is fairly regular and predictable, and some interesting things that can be learned from such patterns, as I explain in the next section.

LEARNING FROM DISTRIBUTIONS

I should stress that so far I have been discussing the ***theoretical normal distribution***—that is, the normal distribution in its purest idealized form, or the distribution that testers would like to find in their NRT results. I am not implying that the same patterns do not occur in reality or that they do not exist. I am not skeptical about the existence of such distributions nor about their characteristics. I know that they exist in mathematical probability distributions (as shown in the distributions for coin flips), and I have often seen very close approximations occur in the scores of my own tests. These distributions have also been observed by countless other testers and researchers in our discipline and in other disciplines. Such distributions do occur with the same regularity as the distribution of 50% heads and 50% tails for coin flips IF THE NUMBER OF SCORES IS LARGE ENOUGH.

Once teachers have accepted the notion of normal distribution, they can benefit from a number of inferences that can be made from this predictable pattern of scores. In addition to knowing the percents of students who will score within certain score ranges on a measure, they can learn what percentiles mean in terms of exactly where an individual's score falls in the normal distribution. Perhaps more important, they can learn what happens when departures from the normal distribution occur (that is, when distributions are *not* normal) and what language testers do when things go wrong and deviate from the normality.

Using Percents

Obviously, the concept of *percents* needs very little explanation. If I ask teachers what percent of their paychecks goes to buying food each week, they can figure it out easily. They would simply divide the amount of money they spend on food each week by the total amount they earn per week. Similarly, referring back to Figure 5.5, the following questions should be easy to answer:

1. What percent of students have scores above the mean?

2. What percent have scores falling between 31 and 41 points on this test? Or between the mean and one standard deviation below the mean?

3. About what percent fall within one standard deviation of the mean, plus and minus—that is, between 31 and 51 on this test?

4. Approximately what percent have scores below 31, or lower than the first standard deviation below the mean?

To answer *question 1*, remember that 50% of the students should fall below the mean and 50% above it. A more awkward way to get the same answer would be to add up all the percents shown in Figure 5.5 that fall below the mean (that is, 2% + 14% + 34% = 50%). For *question 2*, examine the percent shown in the space between the scores of 31 and 41. This should be 34%, right? For *question 3*, add the two percents given in the spaces between 31 and 51 (that is, 34% + 34% = 68%). To answer *question 4*, find the percent of the students who scored 31 or below (that is, 2% + 14% = 16%).

Another category of inferences, percentiles, stems from the foregoing notion of percents under the normal distribution. However, as I explain in the following section, percentiles relate more directly to the performance of each individual student.

Percentiles

Percentiles are not any trickier than percents. In effect, question 4 in the previous section was about percentiles because it could be rephrased as follows: what percentile would a score of 31 represent? Such a score would represent the 16th percentile. Thus, a *percentile* can be defined as the total percent of students who scored equal to or below a given point in the normal distribution.

Given this definition, what percentile would a score of 21 represent in Figure 5.5? Or 31? Or 51? Or 61? They would be about the 2nd, 16th, 84th, and 98th percentile, respectively. To make this idea somewhat more personal, any teacher should be able to think back to the percentile score he or she received on any standardized test (for instance, ACT, SAT, or GRE)? I recall once scoring in the 84th percentile on the GRE quantitative subtest. This means that my score was equal to or higher than 84% of the other students who took the test (but also lower than 16%).

The concepts of percent, percentage, and percentile are being used fairly carefully in this book. Since they were used in Chapter 1 to delineate very real differences between NRTs and CRTs, they will continue to enter the discussion. For the moment, remember that percentages are associated with CRTs and that the percentiles just discussed are very much a part of NRT decisions, as are the standardized scores that come next.

Standardized Scores

One result of the different ideas discussed above has been the evolution of different scoring systems. The best place to begin in discussing these different scoring systems is with the notions of raw scores and weighted scores. *Raw scores* are the actual number of items answered correctly on a test (assuming that each item gets one point). Most teachers are familiar with this type of score. *Weighted scores*, on the other hand, are those scores which are based on different weights for different questions in a test. For instance, a teacher might give one point for the first twenty questions on a test, then three points each for the next ten questions, and five points each for the last five questions. This type of scoring is fairly common in language courses. Standardized scores are yet a third way to record, interpret, and report test results. Unfortunately, standardized scores are often somewhat mysterious to language teachers, so I attempt now to make this concept more concrete.

Remember that percentiles, or *percentile scores*, indicate how a given student's score relates to the test scores of the entire group of students. Thus, a student with a percentile score of 84 had a score equal to or higher than 84% of the other students in the distribution and a score equal to or lower than 16%. *Standard scores* represent a student's score in relation to how far the score varies from the test mean in terms of standard deviation units. The three most commonly reported types of standard scores are z, T, and CEEB scores.

z scores. The *z score* is a direct indication of the distance that a given raw score is from the mean in standard deviation units. The z score for each student can be calculated on any test by using the following formula:

$$z = \frac{X - \overline{X}}{S}$$

In other words, to calculate a student's z score, first subtract the mean from the student's score; then divide the result by the standard deviation for the test. If a student scored 61 in the distribution shown in Figure 5.5, where $\overline{X}$ = 51 and $S = 10$, the z score for that student would be as follows:

$$z = \frac{61 - 51}{10} = \frac{10}{10} = 1 = +1.0$$

This student's z score would be +1.0, or one standard deviation unit above the mean. If another student scored 31 raw score points on the same test, that student's z score would be:

$$z = \frac{31 - 51}{10} = \frac{-20}{10} = -2 = -2.0$$

The student with a z score of −2.0 is two standard deviations below the mean.

A quick look at Figure 5.6 reveals that z scores, which are labeled three rows below the bottom of the distribution, are in exactly the same positions as those points marked off for the standard deviations just above them. Observe that the mean for the z scores is zero and that logically the standard deviation for any set of z scores will be 1.0. Again with reference to Figure 5.6, notice that the raw scores have a mean of 41 and a standard deviation of 10. In view of that information, answer the following questions:

1. How many standard deviations above the mean would a raw score of 51 be?

2. What would be the z score for a student whose raw score was 11?

3. What would the z score be for a raw score of 71?

4. Now the tricky one. How many z scores above or below the mean would a raw score of 41 be?

To answer *question 1*, just remember that a raw score of 51 is one standard deviation above the mean (equivalent to a z score of +1.0). For *question 2*, subtract the mean of 41 from the score of 11 (11 − 41 = −30) and divide the result by the standard deviation (−30 ÷ 10 = −3.0). Thus, z = −3.0. To answer *question 3*, look at Figure 5.6 and decide how many standard deviations a score of 71 is above the mean. Three, right? If it is three standard deviations above the mean, the equivalent z score must be +3.0. To answer *question 4*, just remember that in this example the mean is 41, so a raw score of 41 is neither above nor below the mean of 41 (it *is* the mean), and the mean for a set of z scores is always 0.0.

In short, a z score indicates the number of standard deviations that a student's score falls away from the mean. This value will always be plus (+) if the student scored above the mean and minus (−) if the score was below the mean. Note that z scores seldom turn out to be perfectly round numbers like those found in the examples above. These were used so that the demonstration would be clear. In fact, uneven z scores, like +1.67, 0.71, or −3.13, are much more likely to occur in real test data. Nevertheless, the steps involved in calculating z will be exactly the same.

Also note that one aspect of Figure 5.6 is quite different from Figure 5.4: The percents that are shown for the areas under normal distribution are carried out to two places instead of being rounded off to the nearest whole percent. The fact that these values are expressed more exactly should make no difference in the way readers think about the percents—they are simply more precise ways of expressing the same information.

T scores. When reporting z scores to students, several problems may arise. The first is that z scores can turn out to be both positive or negative. The second is that z scores are relatively small, usually ranging from about −3.00 through 0.00 to +3.00. Third, z scores usually turn out to include several decimal places. Most students (and their parents) just will not understand if they get a score of −1 on a test, or 0.00, or +3.43. Such scores are difficult to understand without a long and involved explanation like the one I have presented. One technique that language testers have used to

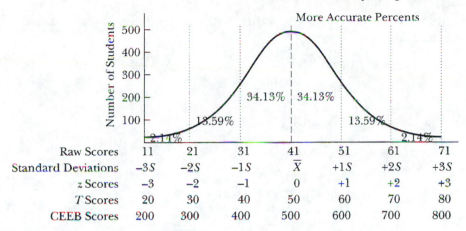

Figure 5.6: Comparison of Standard Score Distributions

circumvent these problems is to transform the z scores into ***T scores***. The T score transformation is done by rather arbitrarily multiplying the z score by 10 and adding 50. The formula for this simple transformation is:

$$T = 10z + 50$$

The following are some examples of applying this T score transformation:

For $z = -2$:
$$\begin{aligned} T &= 10(-2) + 50 \\ &= -20 + 50 \\ &= 30 \end{aligned}$$

For $z = 0$:
$$\begin{aligned} T &= 10(0) + 50 \\ &= 0 + 50 \\ &= 50 \end{aligned}$$

For $z = +1$:
$$\begin{aligned} T &= 10(+1) + 50 \\ &= 10 + 50 \\ &= 60 \end{aligned}$$

T scores at least give the illusion of looking more like "real" scores than z scores and will probably be more readily accepted by students and their parents. Note that row four of Figure 5.6 shows a mean for T scores of 50 and a standard deviation of 10 for the distribution of T scores. In the same sense that the mean and standard deviation for a set of z scores should always be 0 and 1, respectively, the mean and standard deviation for a set of T scores will always be 50 and 10.

CEEB scores. College Entrance Examination Board (CEEB) scores are another variation of the z score that is often reported in the U.S.A. To convert z scores to ***CEEB scores***, multiply the z score by 100 and add 500, as follows:

$$CEEB = 100z + 500$$

The results for transforming the same z scores as those shown above for T scores are as follows:

For $z = -2$:
$$CEEB = 100(-2) + 500$$
$$= \quad -200 + 500$$
$$= 300$$

For $z = 0$:
$$CEEB = 100(0) \quad + 500$$
$$= \quad 0 \quad + 500$$
$$= 500$$

For $z = +1$:
$$CEEB = 100(+1) + 500$$
$$= \quad 100 \quad + 500$$
$$= 600$$

Clearly, CEEB scores are very similar to T scores. In fact, they are exactly the same except that CEEB scores always have one extra zero. So to convert from a T score to CEEB, just add a zero. In other words, if a student's T score is 30, his or her CEEB score will be 300. The mean for a distribution of CEEB scores will always be 500, with a standard deviation of 100. The fifth row of Figure 5.6 confirms these facts.

Standardized and percentile scores. Even though standardized scores are generally clear to test developers, percentile scores are more widely and easily understood by students, teachers, and the general public. Thus, percentile score reports will be clearer to many people than standardized scores. Table 5.1 is a conversion table for z, T, and CEEB scores to percentiles, or vice versa. Note that these conversions assume that the raw scores are normally distributed, and the conversions are only accurate to the degree that this assumption of normality is met.

To use Table 5.1, begin by finding the correct standard score column; then find the actual standard score that is to be converted into a percentile, and look across the row for the percentile equivalent. For example, to convert a z score of 1.7 to a percentile score, look down the left column (labeled z) for the z score of 1.7; then search three columns to the right (in the column for percentiles), and find the percentile equivalent, which is 95.5. All other conversions will work about the same way.

The Importance of Standardized Scores

All language teachers should understand standardized scores for a number of reasons. First, knowing about standardized scores can help teachers to understand standardized test score reports, which are often reported as T or CEEB scores and sometimes as percentiles. One example of this is the TOEFL test. Educational Testing Service reports the subtest scores for listening comprehension, writing and analysis, and reading

Table 5.1: Converting Standardized Scores to Percentiles

z	T	CEEB	Percentile	z	T	CEEB	Percentile
3.0	80	800	99.9	−0.1	49	490	46.0
2.9	79	790	99.8	−0.2	48	480	42.1
2.8	78	780	99.7	−0.3	47	470	38.2
2.7	77	770	99.6	−0.4	46	460	34.5
2.6	76	760	99.5	−0.5	45	450	30.9
2.5	75	750	99.4	−0.6	44	440	27.4
2.4	74	740	99.2	−0.7	43	430	24.2
2.3	73	730	98.9	−0.8	42	420	21.2
2.2	72	720	98.6	−0.9	41	410	18.4
2.1	71	710	98.2	−1.0	40	400	15.9
2.0	70	700	97.7	−1.1	39	390	13.6
1.9	69	690	97.1	−1.2	38	380	11.5
1.8	68	680	96.4	−1.3	37	370	9.7
1.7	67	670	95.5	−1.4	36	360	8.2
1.6	66	660	94.5	−1.5	35	350	6.7
1.5	65	650	93.3	−1.6	34	340	5.5
1.4	64	640	91.9	−1.7	33	330	4.5
1.3	63	630	90.3	−1.8	32	320	3.6
1.2	62	620	88.5	−1.9	31	310	2.9
1.1	61	610	86.4	−2.0	30	300	2.3
1.0	60	600	84.1	−2.1	29	290	1.8
0.9	59	590	81.6	−2.2	28	280	1.4
0.8	58	580	78.8	−2.3	27	270	1.1
0.7	57	570	75.8	−2.4	26	260	0.8
0.6	56	560	72.6	−2.5	25	250	0.6
0.5	55	550	69.1	−2.6	24	240	0.5
0.4	54	540	65.5	−2.7	23	230	0.4
0.3	53	530	61.8	−2.8	22	220	0.3
0.2	52	520	57.9	−2.9	21	210	0.2
0.1	51	510	54.0	−3.0	20	200	0.1
0.0	50	500	50.0				

comprehension as *T* scores. Thus, an "average" student might score 51, 50, and 49 on these three subtests. On the other hand, the total TOEFL score is reported as a CEEB score. Hence, my example "average" student might have a total TOEFL score of 500.

Second, knowing about standardized scores can help language teachers to examine the relationships between performances of different groups on two or more tests of different lengths. Such comparisons are difficult to make unless the scores are converted to a common scale. If the scores of interest are first converted to standardized scores and then compared, the problem of different lengths is effectively circumvented, as shown in Figure 5.7. Notice in Figure 5.7 that a comparison is being made between the relative performances of graduate and undergraduate foreign students on six different ESL tests (which were all of different lengths). To make these comparisons, the researcher (Farhady 1982) first converted the raw scores into standardized *T* scores. He could equally well have used CEEB scores or even *z* scores.

Third, knowing about standardized scores can help teachers to examine the relative position of any individual student on different tests or on different administrations of the same test. Thus, a student can be monitored over time, using different forms of the same overall proficiency test to see if his or her position has changed relative to other students in the distributions.

In short, percentiles and standardized scores, including *z* scores, *T* scores, and CEEB scores, are becoming increasingly common throughout the world. As such, knowing about standardized scores is essential to making responsible norm-referenced decisions and to reporting the results of norm-referenced tests.

Skewed Distributions

At this point, the primary characteristics of normal distributions and the types of inferences that can be drawn from them should be clear. However, for a variety of reasons, the distributions of language students' scores may not always be normal. Several things can go wrong, but the most common problem is that a distribution will be skewed. Skewing usually occurs because the test was either too easy or too difficult for the group of students who took it. However, as I explain later, a skewed distribution is not always bad.

Skewedness. A *skewed* distribution is easiest to spot by visual inspection of a histogram, bar graph, or frequency polygon of scores. A skewed distribution is one that does not have the prototypical, symmetrical bell shape. In Popham's rather nontechnical terms, a skewed distribution is one where the scores are "scrunched up" (Popham 1981). The scores may be scrunched up toward the higher end of the scale, as shown in Figure 5.8a, in which case the distribution is said to be negatively skewed. Or the scores may be scrunched up toward the lower end of the scale, as in Figure 5.8b. In this latter case, the distribution would be considered positively skewed. I have always found the assignment of the negative and positive distinctions in discussions of skewedness to be counter-intuitive. To keep them straight, I always try to remember that skewed distributions characteristically have a "tail" pointing in one of the two possible directions. When the tail is pointing in the direction of the lower scores (−), the distribution is said to be *negatively skewed*. When the tail points toward the higher scores (+), the distribution is *positively skewed*.

A number of implications may arise from such non-normal distributions. First, many of the statistics used to analyze tests assume a normal distribution. In most cases, such statistics are based on comparisons of the central tendency and dispersion of scores. When a distribution of test

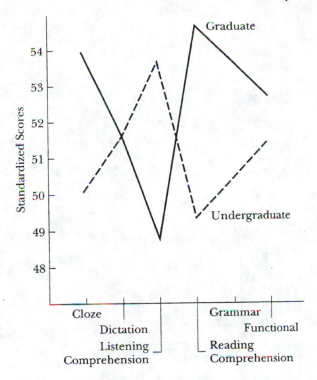

Figure 5.7: Difference Due to University Status in Student Performance on Study Measures. (Adapted from Farhady 1982, p. 49.)

scores is non-normal, perhaps negatively skewed, most of the students have scored well. Thus, they are "scrunched up" toward the top of the scale, and the usual indicators of dispersion (range, standard deviation, and variance) are depressed by what is sometimes called a ***ceiling effect***. If all the students have scored so high on a measure that the dispersion is depressed, the related statistics may be impossible to interpret. Under such conditions, particularly in examining NRT results, the assumption of normality that underlies most of the common testing statistics cannot be said to have been met. Thus, applying such statistics may become an exercise in futility. The results of such analyses are difficult, if not impossible, to interpret responsibly. As a result, all language testers must learn to spot skewed distributions in their norm-referenced test results so that they can make proper interpretations based on the statistics being used.

In other words, when language testers look at the descriptive statistics for a test, a picture of the distribution should come to mind. Consider a test administered to 112 students, which has a range of 56 raw score points (45 to 100), a mean of 71, and a standard deviation of 9. What would the distribution look like? Can you draw it? Consider another administration of

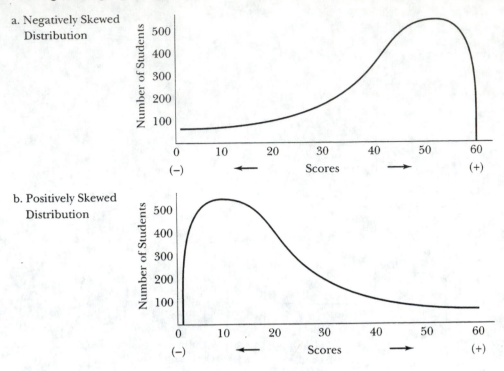

Figure 5.8: Skewed Distributions

the same test where the range is 70 points (31 to 100), but the mean is 92, and the standard deviation is 8.25? What would this distribution look like? The distribution would be skewed, right? Notice that the top score is 100 and the mean is 92, so only one standard deviation of 8.25 can fit between the mean of 92 and the top score of 100. So the distribution is skewed, but which way (positive or negative) is it skewed? Remember, when in doubt, just sketch out the distribution and examine the "tail." Which way is the tail pointing—toward the low scores (negative skew) or toward the high scores (positive skew)?

Another relatively easy way to detect a skewed distribution is to examine the indicators of central tendency. As pointed out in the previous chapter, the four indicators of central tendency (mean, mode, median, and midpoint) should be the same, or very similar, if the distribution is normal. Conversely, if they are very different, the distribution is probably skewed. In fact, the more skewed a distribution is, the more these indicators are likely to diverge. Note also that they will diverge in different directions for positive and negative skewing. As pointed out in Figure 5.9, a negatively skewed distribution will likely have indicators that vary from low to high as follows: midpoint, mean, median, and mode. A positively skewed distribution will usually have indicators that vary in the opposite order from low to high: mode, median, mean, and midpoint. Thus, when differences in central tendency estimates occur, especially large differences, remember to inspect a histogram of the scores to check for skewing.

A skewed distribution on an NRT usually means that the test is not functioning well with the particular group of students. However, on a CRT, a skewed distribution may be the very pattern that teachers would most like to find in the scores of their students. For instance, on a pretest, before the students have studied the material in a course, the teacher would want most of the students to score rather poorly on the course CRT, with perhaps a few students doing better than the rest. Such a positively skewed distribution at the beginning of a course would indicate that most of the students do not know the material and therefore need to take the course. At the end of the term, the teacher would hope that most of the students had learned the material and therefore that they would score very well on the CRT. Hence, a negatively skewed distribution would indicate that most of the students had learned the material well and that the teaching and learning had gone well. As with many other aspects of language testing,

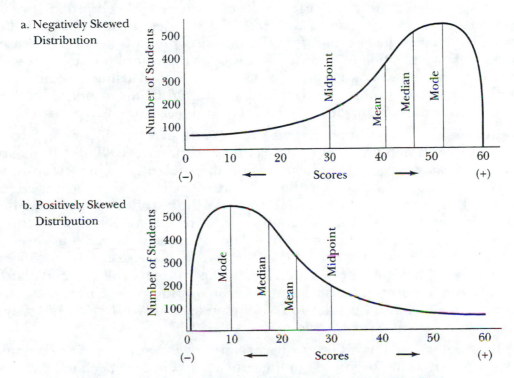

Figure 5.9: Indicators of Central Tendency in Skewed Distributions

interpretation of the distributions of scores is related to the purpose of administering the test.

Peaked distributions. Even if a distribution is not skewed, the height of the distribution relative to its width is important. *Kurtosis* is one way of looking at the degree to which the curve in the middle of a distribution is steep, or the degree to which the distribution is peaked. If the height of the peak, relative to the width, is too different from what would be expected in a normal distribution—that is, either too peaked or too flat—problems may arise in applying testing statistics. Hence, testers should always check for this condition. Simple inspection of a histogram reveals the degree to which the distribution appears to have a normal shape or appears to depart from that shape.

Both abnormally skewed and peaked distributions may be signs of trouble in a norm-referenced test, so language testers should always verify, at least by visual inspection of a graph of the scores, that the distribution is normal.

NRT AND CRT DISTRIBUTIONS

The foregoing discussion of the normal distribution and standardized scores applies to interpreting the results of norm-referenced proficiency or placement tests. Recall from Chapter 1 that the decisions based on NRTs are called *relative decisions* and that the interpretation of the scores focuses on the relative position of each student vis-à-vis the rest of the students with regard to some general ability. Thus, the normal distribution and each student's position in that distribution, as reflected by his or her percentile or standardized score, make sense as viable tools for score interpretation.

Recall also that interpreting the results of criterion-referenced diagnostic and achievement tests is entirely different. CRT decisions are labeled *absolute* because they focus not on the student's position relative to other students but rather on the percent of material that each student knows, largely without reference to the other students. Thus, at the beginning of a course, the distribution of scores on a CRT is likely to be positively skewed if the students actually need to learn the material covered in the course. However, at the end of the course, if the test actually reflects the course objectives, the teacher hopes the students will all score fairly high. In other words, the distribution of scores at the end of instruction will be negatively skewed on a good CRT if reasonably efficient language teaching and learning are taking place.

Item selection for CRTs involves retaining those items that students answer poorly at the beginning of the course (that is, they need to learn the material) and answer well at the end of instruction (that is, they learned it).

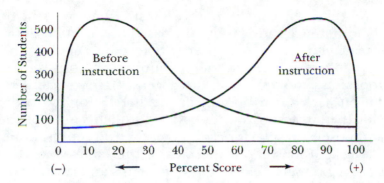

Figure 5.10: Ideal CRT Distributions

This pattern shows up in the IFs on the pretest and posttest as well as in the difference index (DI). The result of revising the CRTs on the basis of these item statistics is usually a magnification of any existing differences between the pretest and posttest distributions. So certain conditions exist under which a skewed distribution is not only desirable but also something that testers may aim for in revising their CRTs. Ideal distributions for a CRT are shown in Figure 5.10.

The trick is not just to create the negatively skewed distribution at the end of instruction. After all, such a distribution can be created by simply making the test much too easy for the students. The trick is to create *through instruction* a negatively skewed distribution on a well-designed test that previously indicated a positively skewed distribution before the instruction took place. In other words, students who needed the instruction (as shown by the positively skewed pretest distribution) learned from that instruction (as shown by the negatively skewed posttest results).

One problem that arises in trying to set up this type of test analysis is the potential problem of *practice effect.* The practice effect occurs when the scores on a second administration are higher, not because of instruction but rather because the students have already experienced, or "practiced," the same test on a previous occasion. One way around this is called *counterbalancing.* To do counterbalancing, testers need to develop two parallel forms (for instance, forms A and B) of the CRT so that they are very similar, objective-by-objective. During the pretest, half of the students (randomly selected) take Form A and half take Form B. After instruction, the first half then takes Form B and the second half takes Form A. Put the students' names on the tests ahead of time for the second administration so that the right students take the right form. The point is that this strategy helps to ensure that no student takes exactly the same test twice. Hence, the practice effect is minimized.

At the same time, the appropriate CRT statistics can still be applied. Recall that the difference index is usually based on an intervention strategy in which the teacher administers a pretest before instruction, intervenes by teaching whatever is relevant, and then administers a posttest. Even though no student took the same test twice, the difference index can be calculated for each item on each form by subtracting the IF for the pretest results from the IF for the posttest. Even though the students are not the same on the pretest and posttest results for each item, they do represent non-masters at the beginning and masters at the end of the course, so DIs based on these results are legitimate. Selecting "good" items and revising on the basis of these statistics remains logical as do any other comparisons of the distributions of scores that the teacher may wish to make. In other words, the teacher can make inferences from the performances on these two forms in a pretest and posttest—but without worrying too much about a potential practice effect.

SUMMARY

I have explored a number of ideas in this chapter that relate to test score interpretation for both NRTs and CRTs. These ideas are central to all language testing endeavors. I have examined how some statistics and patterns in those statistics can help teachers to understand complex distributions of language test scores. I ended by considering some of the ways that such information can be used to help teachers sort through the scores that result from a test administration and report the patterns found to the students (as well as to colleagues if that is desirable). The patterns described in this chapter do exist and do occur among language students. Thus, concepts like probability distributions, normal distributions, raw scores, percentile scores, standard scores, and skewedness help teachers to do their job but only if they actually take the time to look at the scores generated by the students. Go ahead and plot out their scores, and try to analyze what is going on.

TERMS AND SYMBOLS

CEEB scores
ceiling effect
central tendency
counterbalancing
dispersion
distribution
expected outcomes
kurtosis
negatively skewed
normal distribution
percentile
percentile scores
percents
positively skewed
possible outcomes
practice effect
probability
range
raw scores
skewed
standard deviation
standard scores
T scores
theoretical normal distribution
weighted scores
z scores

REVIEW QUESTIONS

1. What is the probability of drawing a queen of spades from a deck of 52 cards? How many expected outcomes are involved? How many possible outcomes? What is the ratio of expected to possible outcomes? What is the probability of drawing the queen of hearts? Of drawing any queen?

2. Draw an ideal normal distribution. Start by drawing two lines—an ordinate and an abscissa. Then mark off a reasonable set of scores along the abscissa and some sort of frequency scale along the ordinate. Make sure that you represent the mean, mode, median, and midpoint with a vertical line down the middle of the distribution. Also include six lines to represent each of three standard deviations above and below the mean. Remember to include the following standard deviation labels: $-3S$, $-2S$, $-1S$, 0, $+1S$, $+2S$, $+3S$. Then actually draw a normal curve to fit the data.

3. Now go back and put in the approximate percents of students that you would expect to find within each score range on the distribution (between the lines that mark off the standard deviations).

4. Can you also label the main z scores that would correspond to the standard deviation lines? And the equivalent T scores? And CEEB scores, too?

5. About what percent of students would you expect to score within plus and minus one standard deviation of the mean?

6. About what percentage of students would you expect to score below a z score of -1? Below a T score of 60? Below a CEEB score of 500?

7. What would the percentile score be for a z score of $+1$? A T score of 40? A CEEB score of 650?

8. What would a positively skewed distribution look like? What about a negatively skewed distribution? For what category of tests would skewed distributions be a sign that there is something wrong? For what category of tests would a skewed distribution be a good sign? How is this possible, and how does it work?

9. Why is counterbalancing a good idea in a CRT development project? How does it work? And what is the practice effect?

10. Do you now believe that normal distribution occurs? Under what conditions? Do you now know what the normal distribution indicates and what you should do for various kinds of tests if the normal distribution does not occur for some reason?

APPLICATION EXERCISES

A. Look at the frequency polygon, and answer the questions that follow.

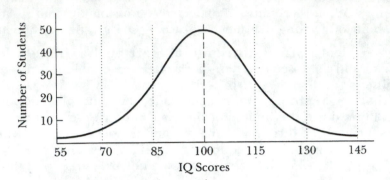

where: $\bar{X} = 100$
$S = 15$
$N = 947$

A1. What percentile score would an IQ score of 85 represent?

A2. About what percentage of students scored between 70 and 115?

A3. If Iliana had a score of 177 on this test, about how many standard deviations would she be above the mean? Does this mean that she is really intelligent?

A4. What would Iliana's z score be? *T* score? CEEB score?

B. In the table below, the raw score mean is 50, and the raw score standard deviation is 7. Fill in all the missing spaces by using the available information and what you now know about distributions and standardized scores.

Student	Raw score	z score	*T* score	CEEB score
A	64		70	
B	50			
C		−1		
D		−1.5		350
etc.				

C. Study the table below, and answer the questions that follow.

Test	Raw scores			Standardized scores	
	k^*	$\overline{X}$	S	$\overline{X}$	S
A	110	60	25	500	100
B	75	60	15	50	10
C	50	11	4	0	1

* Remember, k = number of items on the test

C1. Which test (A, B, or C) shows standardized scores that are probably:

    a. *z* scores?   _____

    b. *T* scores?   _____

    c. CEEB scores?   _____

C2. In raw scores, which test has:

    a. the largest standard deviation?   _____

    b. the lowest mean?   _____

    c. the largest number of items?   _____

    d. a negatively skewed distribution?   _____

C3. In test C, a raw score of:

    a. 11 equals what *z* score?   _____

    b. 7 equals what *T* score?   _____

    c. 19 equals what CEEB score?   _____

D. In Table 4.3 of the previous chapter, there were some scores given for Robert, Millie, and others. To practice calculating standardized scores, lay out a new table that gives not only their raw scores but also the *z*, *T*, and CEEB score for each student. (*Hint:* This process is very easy and can be done without too many calculations because much of the information that you need is already available in Table 4.6, p. 108—for the purpose of this exercise, round the standard deviation to 4.00.)

E. Collect some data from your students, plot them out, and decide for yourself whether they are normally distributed. Remember to collect a fairly large number of scores, or ages, or heights, or whatever you decide to measure.

CHAPTER 6

CORRELATION

In the last two chapters, I discussed the importance of descriptive statistics and various interpretations of those statistics—whether for adopting, developing, or adapting norm-referenced or criterion-referenced tests. However, a test can have wonderful descriptive statistics, produce scores that are beautifully distributed, and still have problems. Before examining these potential problems, which have to do with the reliability and validity of tests, I must cover a set of useful test analysis tools called *correlational analyses*. This family of statistical analyses helps teachers to understand the degree of relationship between two sets of numbers and whether that relationship is significant (in a statistical sense), as well as meaningful (in a logical sense). With these concepts in hand, teachers are then in a position to consider two fundamental test characteristics, test reliability and validity, which are presented in Chapters 7 and 8.

PRELIMINARY DEFINITIONS

One of the most valuable sets of analytical techniques covered in this book is the correlational family of statistics. The purpose of **correlational analyses** in language testing is to examine how the scores on two tests compare with regard to dispersing, or spreading out, the students. Essentially, **correlation** is the "go-togetherness" of two sets of scores. Figure 6.1a shows two sets of scores lined up in columns. Notice that the two sets are in exactly the same order—that is, the student who scored highest on Test X did so on Test Y; the same is true for the second highest, third highest, fourth highest, and so forth.

The degree to which two sets of scores *covary*, or vary together, is estimated statistically by calculating a **correlation coefficient**. Such a coefficient can reach a magnitude as high as +1.0 if the relationship between the scores on two tests is perfectly direct, or positive (see Figure 6.1a). Alternatively, a correlation coefficient can be negative with a value as strong as −1.0 if the relationship is perfectly opposite, or negative (see Figure 6.1b). A zero can also result if no relationship exists between the two sets of numbers.

To begin doing correlational analysis, testers line up the scores side-by-side as shown in Figure 6.1. Setting up a table of scores is easy. Consider the scores tabled in Figure 6.1a. Three columns are labeled, in this case one for

a. $r = +1.0$

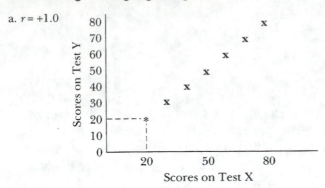

Scores		
Students	Test X	Test Y
Dean	21	20
Randy	31	30
Iliana	41	40
Jeanne	51	50
Elisabeth	61	60
Shenan	71	70
Monique	81	80

b. $r = -1.0$

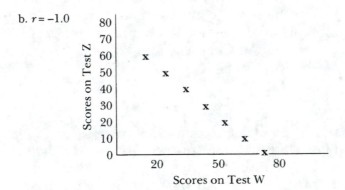

Scores		
Students	Test W	Test Z
Dean	12	61
Elisabeth	22	51
Shenan	32	41
Iliana	42	31
Randy	52	21
Jeanne	62	11
Monique	72	01

Figure 6.1: Perfect Correlations

the students' names, a second for their scores on Test X, and a third for their scores on Test Y. This table also organizes the data in such a way that each row in the table represents one student's record for these tests.

A scatterplot of the information may also prove useful in examining correlations. A *scatterplot* is a form of visual representation, similar to the histogram, bar graph, and frequency polygon described in Chapter 4, that allows for representing two sets of scores at the same time and examining their relationship. Usually, the increments in the range of possible scores for one test will be marked off along the *x* axis (or abscissa) and those for the other test along the *y* axis (or ordinate). A mark is then plotted for each student at the point where the coordinates for that student's two scores meet. For instance, in the scatterplot shown in Figure 6.1a, Dean scored 21 on Test X and 20 on Test Y. If you were to draw a line straight up from 21 on the horizontal axis and another line straight across from a score of 20 on Test Y, they would intersect at the point represented by an **x** in the figure. If you repeat the process for each of the other students, the results will look like the **x** marks plotted in the same figure. Notice that the scatterplot presents exactly the same information as the corresponding table but that the scatterplot displays the data in an entirely different way.

A correlation coefficient that represents a perfect relationship like that shown in Figure 6.1a is positive and takes on the maximum value of +1.0. Such a correlation occurs only if the two sets of scores line up the students in exactly the same order—that is, only if the scores are 100% similar. Such a correlation coefficient indicates a very strong positive correlation, and the plot for a perfect correlation always forms a straight line like that shown in Figure 6.1a. This line is the reason such relationships are called *linear* (more about this below).

A correlation coefficient can also be negative in value and as high in magnitude as −1.0. For such a high negative correlation to occur, the relationship between the two sets of scores must be exactly the opposite, or negative, as shown in Figure 6.1b. In other words, as the scores on one test go up, the scores on the other go down; put another way, students who scored high on one test scored low on the other, and vice versa. The negative sign in front of the coefficient shows that the relationship between the two tests is in the opposite direction. Although negative, the relationship shown in Figure 6.1b is nevertheless very strong because students who have high scores on Test W scored low on Test Z, and vice versa.

When there is absolutely no relationship at all between two sets of numbers, the coefficient is 0 or something very close to 0. Coefficients either positive or negative up to about +.40, or down to about −.40, indicate fairly weak relationships. Relatively strong correlations are those that range from +.80 to +1.0, or −.80 to −1.00. Just remember that the further a coefficient is from 0 toward +1.0 or −1.0, the stronger the relationship is between whatever sets of numbers are involved and that the sign indicates the direction of the relationship.

Table 6.1 presents a slightly more realistic situation because real scores seldom line up perfectly. The correlation coefficient I am focusing on now is called the **Pearson product-moment correlation coefficient,** which is the statistic of choice for comparing two sets of interval or ratio scale data like the scores shown in the table. In this case, the correlation coefficient turns out to be .78. A coefficient of this magnitude indicates that there is a fairly strong positive correlation between these two groups of data. In other words, the two tests are spreading the students out in much the same way. Note also, though, that the students are not in exactly the same order on the two tests and that the distances between students are not exactly the same on each scale. In fact, the descriptive statistics given at the bottom of

Table 6.1: Correlation of Two Sets of Test Scores
(Based on Scores from Tables 4.2 and 4.3)

Students	Test Y Scores (Table 4.2)	Test X Scores (Table 4.3)
Robert	97	77
Millie	85	75
Iliana	82	64
Dean	71	72
Cuny	70	70
Bill	70	70
Corky	69	69
Randy	68	69
Monique	67	69
Wendy	67	69
Henk	67	68
Shenan	66	72
Jeanne	62	67
Elisabeth	59	68
Archie	40	64
Lindsey	31	61

Summary of Descriptive Statistics:

N	16	16
Mean	66.94	69.00
S	15.01	3.87
Range	67	17

Table 6.1 indicate that the two tests are different in central tendency (as indicated by the means) and even more so in dispersion (as indicated by the standard deviations and ranges). Nevertheless, the correlation coefficient provides evidence that the two sets of scores "go together" to a fairly high degree.

CALCULATION OF THE PEARSON PRODUCT-MOMENT CORRELATION COEFFICIENT

Calculating the Pearson product-moment correlation coefficient, if taken step-by-step, is not any more demanding than calculating the standard deviation was. For reasons that may not be immediately obvious, the Pearson product-moment correlation coefficient is usually symbolized by r, or r_{xy}.

As mentioned above, the process of looking at the degree of relationship between two sets of numbers begins with lining up the scores for two tests administered to the same group of students, or collecting any two sets of interval scale information (like age, years of language study, and so forth). Ultimately, pairs of interval scale numbers for each student should be lined up in two columns like those shown in Table 6.1. In cases where there are *missing data*—that is, when there is only one score for a given student—leave that student out of the analysis. Once the data are lined up properly in two columns with no missing data, everything is ready for calculating a Pearson product-moment correlation coefficient.

The formula for the Pearson product-moment correlation coefficient is explained in terms of two sets of test scores because this is a language testing book, but remember that the numbers could equally well be any other interval scale data. The best formula for calculating and for understanding the Pearson product-moment correlation coefficient is the following:

$$r_{xy} = \frac{\Sigma(Y - \bar{Y})(X - \bar{X})}{N\,S_y\,S_x}$$

where
r_{xy} = Pearson product-moment correlation coefficient

Y = each student's score on Test Y

$\bar{Y}$ = mean on Test Y

S_y = standard deviation on Test Y

X = each student's score on Test X

$\bar{X}$ = mean on Test X

S_x = standard deviation on Test X

N = the number of students who took the two tests

Notice that the formula has many elements but that none of them are completely unfamiliar. First look at $(X - \bar{X})$, or the deviation of each student from the mean on Test X, and then N and the S_x. Several symbols, Y, $\bar{Y}$, and S_y, at first appear to be new, but they just represent the students' scores on the second test, the mean of those scores on that test, and the standard deviation, respectively. Thus, $(Y - \bar{Y})$ is the deviation of each student from the mean on test Y. Given this information, calculation of a correlation coefficient is not difficult at all.

Table 6.2 shows the calculations for the data set shown in Table 6.1.

1. The data were copied, and the mean and standard deviation were calculated for each set. These descriptive statistics are shown at the bottom of columns 2 and 5 of Table 6.2 for Test Y and Test X, respectively.

2. The means for Test Y and for Test X were placed repeatedly in columns 3 and 6 so that they could easily be subtracted from each score on each test. The results of these repeated subtractions were placed in columns 4 and 7 for Test Y and Test X, respectively. For example, Robert's score of 97 on Test Y (column 2) minus the mean of 66.94 on Test Y (column 3) is 30.06

Table 6.2: Calculating a Correlation Coefficient (for Table 6.1 Data)

Column 1 Students	2 Y	$-$	3 $\bar{Y}$	$=$	4 $(Y-\bar{Y})$	5 X	$-$	6 $\bar{X}$	$=$	7 $(X-\bar{X})$	8 $(Y-\bar{Y})(X-\bar{X})$
Robert	97	$-$	66.94	$=$	30.06	77	$-$	69.00	$=$	8.00	240.48
Millie	85	$-$	66.94	$=$	18.06	75	$-$	69.00	$=$	6.00	108.36
Iliana	82	$-$	66.94	$=$	15.06	64	$-$	69.00	$=$	-5.00	-75.30
Dean	71	$-$	66.94	$=$	4.06	72	$-$	69.00	$=$	3.00	12.18
Cuny	70	$-$	66.94	$=$	3.06	70	$-$	69.00	$=$	1.00	3.06
Bill	70	$-$	66.94	$=$	3.06	70	$-$	69.00	$=$	1.00	3.06
Corky	69	$-$	66.94	$=$	2.06	69	$-$	69.00	$=$	0.00	0.00
Randy	68	$-$	66.94	$=$	1.06	69	$-$	69.00	$=$	0.00	0.00
Monique	67	$-$	66.94	$=$	0.06	69	$-$	69.00	$=$	0.00	0.00
Wendy	67	$-$	66.94	$=$	0.06	69	$-$	69.00	$=$	0.00	0.00
Henk	67	$-$	66.94	$=$	0.06	68	$-$	69.00	$=$	-1.00	-0.06
Shenan	66	$-$	66.94	$=$	-0.94	72	$-$	69.00	$=$	3.00	-2.82
Jeanne	62	$-$	66.94	$=$	-4.94	67	$-$	69.00	$=$	-2.00	9.88
Elisabeth	59	$-$	66.94	$=$	-7.94	68	$-$	69.00	$=$	-1.00	7.94
Archie	40	$-$	66.94	$=$	-26.94	64	$-$	69.00	$=$	-5.00	134.70
Lindsey	31	$-$	66.94	$=$	-35.94	61	$-$	69.00	$=$	-8.00	287.52

N	16		16	$\Sigma(Y-\bar{Y})(X-\bar{X}) = 729.00$
Mean	66.94		69.00	
S	15.01		3.87	
Range	67		17	

$$r_{xy} = \frac{\Sigma(Y-\bar{Y})(X-\bar{X})}{N\,S_y\,S_x}$$

$$= \frac{729.00}{16(15.01)(3.87)}$$

$$= \frac{729.00}{929.42} = .7843601$$

$$\approx .78$$

(column 4), or his deviation from the mean on Test Y; his score of 77 on Test X (column 5) minus the mean of 69.00 on Test X (column 6) is 8.00 (column 7), or his deviation from the mean on Test X. This process was repeated for each student.

3. The results of the subtractions for both tests (see columns 4 and 7) were then multiplied for each student, and the results were placed in column 8. For instance, Robert's deviation from the mean of 30.06 on Test Y (column 4) was multiplied by his deviation from the mean of 8.00 on Test X (column 7). The result, or the **cross-product** of Robert's deviations, was 240.48 (column 8). This process was repeated for each student.

4. The cross-products for all the students (column 8) were then summed (added up), as shown at the bottom of column 8, which resulted in a value of 729.00.

5. Returning to the formula for the correlation coefficient (below the table and to the right), the sum of the cross-products was substituted into the

formula as the numerator. The values 16, 15.01, and 3.87 were then appropriately substituted (from the information given below the table to the left) for N, S_y, and S_x, respectively, in the denominator of the formula. When the three numbers in the denominator were multiplied, the result was $16 \times 3.87 \times 15.01 = 929.42$. Dividing the numerator by the denominator, the result was $729.00 \div 929.42 = .7843601$, or approximately .78.

So calculating the Pearson product-moment correlation coefficient really is not difficult, though it may be a bit tedious sometimes. Hence, such calculations are usually done on a computer or advanced hand calculator if at all possible. However, with this formula in hand, teachers are in a position to calculate this correlation coefficient by hand even if the electricity goes out. More importantly, working through the formula should have removed any mystery that surrounds this statistic.

However, calculating the correlation coefficient is far from the final step. The tester must also check the assumptions that underlie this statistic to make sure that they have been met and must interpret the results in terms of statistical significance and meaningfulness.

ASSUMPTIONS OF THE PEARSON PRODUCT-MOMENT CORRELATION COEFFICIENT

I have already discussed one requirement of the Pearson r, which is really a design requirement: the two sets of numbers must both be interval or ratio scales rather than ordinal or nominal scales. I am not saying that correlational analysis cannot be applied to nominal and ordinal scales. I am saying that statistics other than the Pearson product-moment correlation coefficient must be used to do so.

In addition to this design requirement, there are three assumptions that underlie the Pearson product-moment correlation coefficient:

1. *Independence:* Each pair of scores is independent from all other pairs.

2. *Normally distributed:* Each of the two sets of numbers is normally distributed.

3. *Linear:* The relationship between the two sets of scores is linear.

These assumptions must be met for the statistic to be properly applied and interpreted.

The assumption of ***independence*** requires that each pair of scores be unrelated to all other pairs of scores. In other words, when the pairs of test scores are in two columns, no student should appear twice in either column (because, for example, he or she took the two tests twice) and thus create two pairs of scores related to each other, and no student should have copied the answers from another student (also creating related pairs). In short, for the Pearson *r* to be properly applied, there must be no systematic association between pairs of scores. Hence, language teachers who wish to use correlational analysis should ensure that this assumption is met during the test administration and analysis stages.

The second assumption is that each of the sets of scores must be ***normally distributed***. Another way to state this is that neither of the two distributions can be skewed. If one or the other is not normal, the magnitude of any resulting correlation coefficients is affected. Typically, if either distribution is skewed, the value of the correlation coefficient is depressed to an unpredictable degree. The normality assumption can usually be checked by examining the descriptive statistics for each test or by visually inspecting histograms, bar graphs, or frequency polygons of the distributions of scores for skewedness (as described in Chapter 5). The importance of checking for skewedness cannot be overemphasized.

The most important of the three assumptions is that the relationship between the two sets of scores should be ***linear***. In other words, fitting a straight line through the points on the scatterplot must make sense. Figure 6.1 shows ideal situations where a perfect correlation is represented by a perfectly straight line. The scatterplot in Figure 6.1a shows the ideal straight line relationship for a perfect positive correlation (+1.00). The scatterplot in Figure 6.1b illustrates the same thing but for a perfect negative correlation (–1.00). In reality, such perfect linear relationships are seldom obtained.

Figure 6.2 offers alternative situations that may arise in real data. The scatterplots in Figure 6.2a–d are all examples of ***curvilinear*** relationships because they form a curve when plotted out. Curvilinear relationships should not be analyzed using a Pearson *r*. Such relationships often occur when one of the sets of numbers is a function of time. Consider, for instance, a situation in which a teacher is interested in the degree of relationship between the number of division problems a student can correctly answer per minute and the number of minutes elapsed. If the number of division problems correctly solved per minute is plotted on a *y* axis and the number of minutes plotted on the *x* axis, a positive relationship shows up for the first ten or twenty minutes (while the student improves in ability to answer division problems), but the number of problems per minute drops off as the student becomes tired and bored with division. The scatterplot would probably consist of a positive correlation line during the first 20 minutes and a negative line once fatigue set in. The positive and negative relationships combined into the same scatterplot would produce a curvilinear relationship that would probably look something like the one shown in Figure 6.2b.

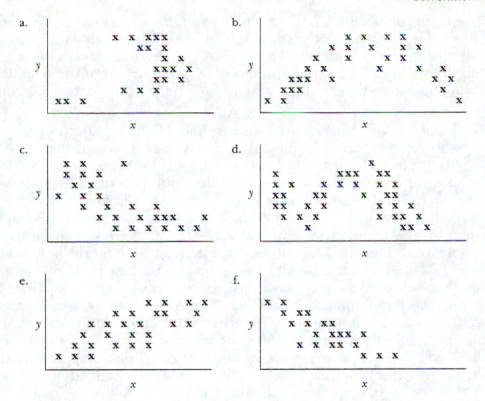

Figure 6.2: Curvilinear (a.–d.) and Linear (e.–f.) Scatterplots

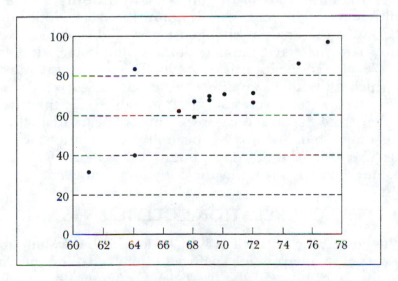

Figure 6.3: Scatterplot for Data in Table 6.2

The scatterplots shown in Figure 6.2e and f are more typical of the form of a linear relationship, with a strong positive correlation (Figure 6.2e) or a strong negative correlation (Figure 6.2f). The best way to check the assumption of linearity is to examine visually a scatterplot of the data. Look for some indication that fitting a straight line through the data would make sense.

Now, once again, consider the data in Table 6.2. A scatterplot of these data is shown in Figure 6.3 (on the previous page). Notice that the data appear to be fairly linear in this scatterplot with one exception: one dot is alone above and to the left of the rest of the plotted points. This data point may be what is referred to as an *outlier* because it is far away from the general clustering of all the other data points. An outlier, if that is what this case is, must be handled with special care. The first trick is to figure out who is involved. Looking carefully at the dot, I can tell that the student had a score of 82 on Test Y and 64 on test X. Looking back at Table 6.1, or 6.2, I notice that Iliana had these scores. Since she was so different from the pattern found for all the other students, I wanted to further investigate why she did so well on one test but so poorly on the other. Interviewing her, I found out that, for personal reasons, she was furious with her father when she arrived at Test X and remained angry throughout the examination. Based on this information, I had to decide if I was logically justified in leaving her out of the analysis. Sometimes doing so is a good idea because, in a sense, an outlier is creating a small curvilinear twist in the data.

In this case, because of her extraordinary anger, I felt justified in eliminating this outlier from the analysis, and doing so made a very dramatic difference in the results, as shown in Table 6.3. Notice that leaving the outlier out of the analysis changed many of the descriptive statistics slightly, and sharply affected the magnitude of the correlation coefficient. Instead of .78, the correlation is now .96. This reanalysis illustrates the degree to which an outlier can affect the results of correlational analysis. Notice in Figure 6.4 (for the results given in Table 6.3), that the outlier is no longer there and that the relationship now appears marvelously linear. Thus, the assumption of linearity has been met. In situations where outliers are an issue, the tester should report both sets of results, with and without the outlier, and should explain why the outlier was removed.

INTERPRETING CORRELATION COEFFICIENTS

Once the correlation coefficient is in hand with the assumptions clearly met, the testers must interpret the coefficient from two different perspectives. First they must check to see if the coefficient is statistically significant; then and only then, they should decide if the coefficient is also meaningful.

Table 6.3: Calculating Pearson *r*
(for Table 6.1 Data, Without Outlier)

Column 1 Name	2 Y	−	3 $\bar{Y}$	=	4 $(Y-\bar{Y})$	5 X	−	6 $\bar{X}$	=	7 $(X-\bar{X})$	8 $(Y-\bar{Y})(X-\bar{X})$
Robert	97	−	65.93	=	31.07	77	−	69.33	=	7.67	238.31
Millie	85	−	65.93	=	19.07	75	−	69.33	=	5.67	108.13
Dean	71	−	65.93	=	5.07	72	−	69.33	=	2.67	13.54
Cuny	70	−	65.93	=	4.07	70	−	69.33	=	0.67	2.73
Bill	70	−	65.93	=	4.07	70	−	69.33	=	0.67	2.73
Corky	69	−	65.93	=	3.07	69	−	69.33	=	−0.33	−1.01
Randy	68	−	65.93	=	2.07	69	−	69.33	=	−0.33	−0.68
Monique	67	−	65.93	=	1.07	69	−	69.33	=	−0.33	−0.35
Wendy	67	−	65.93	=	1.07	69	−	69.33	=	−0.33	−0.35
Henk	67	−	65.93	=	1.07	68	−	69.33	=	−1.33	−1.42
Shenan	66	−	65.93	=	0.07	72	−	69.33	=	2.67	0.19
Jeanne	62	−	65.93	=	−3.93	67	−	69.33	=	−2.33	9.16
Elisabeth	59	−	65.93	=	−6.93	68	−	69.33	=	−1.33	9.22
Archie	40	−	65.93	=	−25.93	64	−	69.33	=	−5.33	138.21
Lindsey	31	−	65.93	=	−34.93	61	−	69.33	=	−8.33	290.97

N	15				15		$\sum(Y-\bar{Y})(X-\bar{X}) = 809.38$		
Mean	65.93				69.33				
S	14.97				3.77				
Range	67				17				

$$r_{xy} = \frac{\sum(Y-\bar{Y})(X-\bar{X})}{N\,S_y\,S_x}$$

$$= \frac{809.38}{15(14.97)(3.77)}$$

$$= \frac{809.38}{846.55} = .9560923$$

$$\approx .96$$

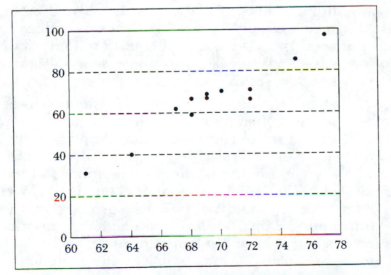

Figure 6.4: Scatterplot for Data in Table 6.3

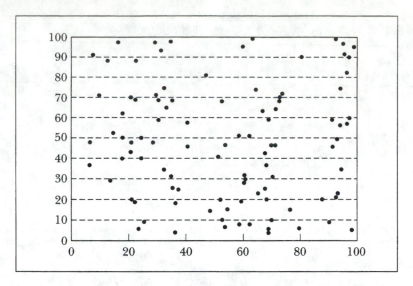

Figure 6.5: Scatterplot for Two Sets of Random Numbers

Statistical Significance

If I were to line up 100 completely random numbers in one column and 100 others in a second column, I could calculate a correlation coefficient and plot the relationship. What would it look like? Figure 6.5 shows a scatterplot of the relationship between 100 pairs of random numbers. Clearly, Figure 6.5 shows no linear relationship between the two sets of numbers because fitting a straight line to the data would be impossible. Thus, by visual inspection alone, I can fairly safely say that there is no relationship between these two sets of numbers. Yet a correlation coefficient of $r_{xy} = -.0442$ was calculated for these data, so some degree of correlation, or relationship, seems to exist. How is this possible?

It turns out that calculating correlation coefficients between sets of random numbers will most often result in non-zero values by chance alone. In other words, even random numbers may haphazardly produce correlation coefficients of some magnitude. Examples of such spurious coefficients are shown in Table 6.4, where correlation coefficients were calculated on the basis of repeated sets of random numbers. Notice that the first column of the table gives the Trial (the first correlation calculated, the second, the third, and so on), while the other four columns give the correlations for differing sizes of random number sets—that is, for sets of 100 pairs of numbers, 50 pairs, 10 pairs, and five pairs of random numbers.

Table 6.4: Correlation Coefficients
from Random Numbers

Trial	$N = 100$	$N = 50$	$N = 10$	$N = 5$
1	−.0517	+.0755	−.3319	+.9281
2	+.1150	+.0185	+.4787	+.5879
3	+.1762	+.2191	−.1488	+.8543
4	+.0384	+.0273	−.2828	+.9032
5	−.1448	+.2192	−.2969	+.3692
6	+.1259	−.0637	+.6394	+.6441
7	−.0216	−.0306	−.0757	+.2468
8	+.0373	−.1658	+.3567	−.8413
9	+.0133	+.0817	−.3801	−.5772
10	−.0442	+.1232	+.4890	−.6933

Notice also that none of the correlation coefficients is exactly zero and that as the size of the number sets decreases the distances that the coefficients vary from zero seem to increase. In the column with samples of 100, the highest chance correlation is +.1762; in the 50s column, it is +.2192; in the 10s column, it is +.6394; and in the fives column, it is +.9281. This may be fairly astounding to most readers, but these results really happened, and similar results will happen again if I replicate these trials. (Should the reader decide to do this by hand, be sure to set aside the better part of a week.) Notice also in Table 6.4 that the results for 100 pairs and 50 pairs are not too different, but the very small sample sizes of 10 and five seem to produce, respectively, high and very high correlation coefficients by chance alone. The message that should come through loud and clear is that testers should avoid using small numbers of students, when doing correlational analysis, because such groups can produce very large correlation coefficients by chance alone.

In interpreting any correlation coefficient, then, one important issue is whether the results could have occurred by chance alone. Fortunately, statisticians have worked out a strategy to help teachers determine the probability that a correlation coefficient occurred by chance. The strategy compares any calculated correlation coefficient, called an *observed correlation*, with the appropriate *critical correlation*, as shown in Table 6.5. If the observed coefficient is larger than the critical value, a high and specific probability exists that the observed correlation coefficient did not occur by chance alone. The trick is to decide which coefficient in the table is the correct one to refer to.

To decide which is the appropriate critical value in Table 6.5, I first decide whether any sound logical or theoretical reasons exist for expecting

Table 6.5: Critical Values of the Pearson Product-Moment
Correlation Coefficient*

(N-2)	Directional Decision: Sound reasons to expect either a positive or a negative correlation		Non-directional Decision: Do not know which direction correlation might be	
	95% Certainty $p < .05$	99% Certainty $p < .01$	95% Certainty $p < .05$	99% Certainty $p < .01$
1	.9877	.9995	.9969	1.0000
2	.9000	.9800	.9500	.9900
3	.8054	.9343	.8783	.9587
4	.7293	.8822	.8114	.9172
5	.6694	.8329	.7545	.8745
6	.6215	.7887	.7067	.8343
7	.5822	.7498	.6664	.7977
8	.5494	.7155	.6319	.7646
9	.5214	.6851	.6021	.7348
10	.4973	.6581	.5760	.7079
11	.4762	.6339	.5529	.6835
12	.4575	.6120	.5324	.6614
13	.4409	.5923	.5139	.6411
14	.4259	.5742	.4973	.6226
15	.4124	.5577	.4821	.6055
20	.3598	.4921	.4227	.5368
25	.3233	.4451	.3809	.4869
30	.2960	.4093	.3494	.4487
35	.2746	.3810	.3246	.4182
40	.2573	.3578	.3044	.3932
45	.2428	.3384	.2875	.3721
50	.2306	.3218	.2732	.3541
60	.2108	.2948	.2500	.3248
70	.1954	.2737	.2319	.3017
80	.1829	.2565	.2172	.2830
90	.1726	.2422	.2050	.2673
100	.1638	.2301	.1946	.2540

*Adapted from Fisher and Yates 1963.

the correlation to be either positive or negative. Such reasons are usually based on an existing theory, or previous research findings, or both. If such reasons exist, I use a *directional decision*, as shown in the second and third columns of the table. In contrast, if I have no way of knowing which way the relationship might go, I would be making a *non-directional decision* and need to examine the fourth and fifth columns in the table. In other words, my expectations before calculating the coefficient are related to the probabilities of a coefficient occurring by chance alone. So I should begin by using the sets of columns, directional or non-directional, that best describe those expectations.

Next, I must decide the degree to which I want to be sure of my results. Since I can never be 100% sure, I will probably want to settle for one of the traditional levels. In language testing, such decisions are traditionally set at 95% or 99%. If I decide that I want the 95% level, only a 5% chance exists, or less than .05 probability ($p < .05$), that I will be wrong in deciding that my correlation coefficient occurred for other than chance reasons. In other words, with this certainty level, I can be 95% sure that I am right in rejecting the notion that my observed correlation coefficient is really .00 (or due to chance alone). I would be safer yet if I set that level at $p < .01$, thereby ensuring that only a 1% chance exists, or less than .01 probability, that I will be wrong in deciding that my observed correlation coefficient occurred for other than chance reasons. In other words, I can set my certainty level so that I can be 99% sure that I am right in rejecting the idea that my observed correlation coefficient is really .00 (or due to chance alone). Therefore, after deciding whether the directional or non-directional columns apply to my decision, I also need to decide on whether I want to use the 95% or 99% certainty column to find my critical value.

As shown in Table 6.4, the degree to which the number of random numbers used in the calculation of correlation coefficients can affect the fluctuations in chance correlations. Hence, the number of students involved also has a bearing on the critical value, as shown in the leftmost column of Table 6.4. To find the correct number that applies to my correlation coefficient, I must subtract two from the number of students who took the two tests (that is, the number of pairs of scores involved in my calculations, minus 2) and move down the left-hand column to the correct number ($N - 2$). Moving across that row, I must then find the correct column for my chosen probability level (.01 or .05) within the directional or non-directional column. The value that is in the place where that row and column intersect is the critical value that my observed correlation must exceed (regardless of its sign, + or −) to be considered **statistically significant**, or due to factors other than chance with the appropriate degree of certainty (that is, 95% or 99%).

For example, the correlation obtained in Table 6.2 of .78 would be worth checking for statistical significance. Say I have sound reasons for expecting any correlation calculated between these two tests to be positive. Perhaps they are both very similar multiple-choice tests of French grammar and therefore, if there is any relationship at all, I would expect it to be positive. This means that I will use a directional decision and must only choose between columns 2 and 3 in Table 6.5. Because of my cautious nature and the importance of being correct in this case, I decide that I want to be correct with 99% certainty. Hence, my decision is further narrowed in that my critical value must be somewhere in the third column. Next, I must go back to the data and check the number of students, in this case $N = 16$. Therefore, $N - 2 = 16 - 2 = 14$. Moving down the left column until I reach the number 14, I have found the correct row. Moving to the right in that row until I reach the correct column (column 3: directional at 99% certainty), I then find the critical value, .5742. Since the magnitude (regardless of sign) of the observed correlation coefficient, .78, is larger than the critical value, .5742 (that is .7800 > .5742), I know that the correlation coefficient is statistically significant at $p < .01$. In other words, there is only a 1% probability that this correlation coefficient occurred by chance alone. Put another way, I can be 99% sure that the correlation coefficient occurred for reasons other than chance.

I would also like to consider another example that will logically turn out to be due to chance. Most (that is, 95%) of the correlations shown in Table 6.4 should reasonably turn out to be due to chance alone. Let's take the coefficient furthest to the right in the last row of Table 6.4. This coefficient is fairly high in magnitude but is negative and is based on only five pairs of scores. In checking this coefficient for statistical significance, I must first decide whether there is any logical reason to expect either a positive or negative correlation in this situation. Since the data are random numbers, I have no reason to expect a positive correlation or a negative correlation. Each correlation in this table could go either way. Thus, I am looking at a non-directional decision. I will also use the relatively liberal .05 probability level because nobody will be hurt if this decision turns out wrong. Looking down the left column until I reach 3 ($N - 2 = 5 - 2 = 3$) for the correct row, I then move to the right in that row until I reach the correct column, non-directional at 95% certainty (fourth column) and find that the critical value is .8783. Since the magnitude (regardless of sign) of the observed correlation coefficient, –.6933, is not larger than the critical value, .8783, I can make no claims about the correlation coefficient being statistically significant at $p < .05$. Hence I must accept that this correlation coefficient could have occurred by chance alone, and it would be safest to accept that it probably does not differ from 0.00 except by chance.

Meaningfulness

The statistical significance of a correlation coefficient is useful to know because the tester can then argue that an observed coefficient probably did not occur by chance, but statistical significance does not imply that the coefficient is "significant" in the sense of meaningful. Instead, statistical significance is a necessary precondition for a meaningful correlation, but it is not sufficient unto itself. A quick look at Table 6.5 reveals that correlations as low as .1638 would be significant if 102 students were taking the tests. But the question would remain as to whether such a low coefficient would be meaningful. *Meaningfulness* is far less probabilistic and absolute than statistical significance because judgment must be used in deciding if the magnitude of a significant coefficient is meaningful.

One statistical tool that aids in making such judgments is called the *coefficient of determination.* Despite its imposing name, this coefficient is very easy to calculate. To get the coefficient of determination, just square the value of the correlation coefficient, which is why the symbol for this statistic is r_{xy}^2. It is simply the correlation coefficient, r_{xy}, squared. The result is a coefficient that directly represents the proportion of overlapping variance between two sets of scores. In other words, this coefficient tells you what proportion of the variance in the two sets of scores is common to both, or the degree to which the two tests are lining up the students in about the same order. Figure 6.6 illustrates what the coefficient of determination means. Consider a correlation coefficient of .80 between Tests X and Y. If I marked that .80 point off on the bottom horizontal line and right vertical line of a square representing Test X (as shown in Figure 6.6), I would be in a position to overlay another square representing Test Y at those two points such that the overlapping variance would be represented by a third smaller square (with diagonal stripes) shared by both measures. To find the area of this smaller square, I would logically multiply the distance along the bottom, .80, times the distance up the right, also .80, and get .64. A quicker way to accomplish the same thing would be to square the value of the correlation coefficient and obtain the area of the overlapping variance.

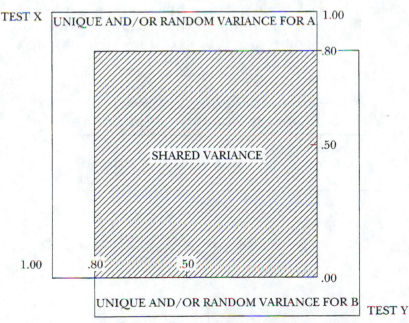

Figure 6.6: Overlapping Variance

The area of overlap can be interpreted as the proportion of variance on one measure that is common to the other measure, and vice versa. Or, by moving the decimal point to the right two places, the coefficient of .64 can be interpreted as a percent. In other words, 64% of the variance in Test X is shared with Test Y. Likewise, 64% of the variance on Test Y is shared with Test X. By extension, the remaining 36% (100% – 64% = 36%) on each test can be said to be unique to that measure and/or totally random in nature.

Table 6.6 illustrates how precipitously the coefficients of determination drop in magnitude when compared with their respective correlation coefficients. For instance, consider the correlations of .90 and .80, which have corresponding squared values of .81 and .64, respectively. Both of these could be said to indicate fairly high percents of overlap (with the 81% being considerably higher than the 64%). A correlation of .70, when squared, yields .49, which indicates that there is less than 50% shared variance between the two sets of scores. A correlation of .60 squared gives .36, which shows that only about one-third of the variance is common to the two sets of scores; .50 squared is .25, which indicates about one-quarter is shared; and .30 squared is .09, or less than one-tenth overlapping variance.

Nonetheless, after all the work of calculating a correlation coefficient and deciding whether or not it is statistically significant, as well as calculating a coefficient of determination, someone must ultimately examine the magnitude of the correlation coefficient to determine if it is meaningful in a particular situation. In some situations, only a very high correlation coefficient makes sense. Other times, a relatively low coefficient will provide useful information. In the next two chapters, on reliability and validity, I demonstrate some of the applications of such correlational analyses.

Table 6.6: Correlation Coefficients
and Corresponding Coefficients of Determination

Correlation Coefficient (r_{xy})	Coefficient of Determination (r_{xy}^2)	Error Variance $(1 - r_{xy}^2)$
1.00	1.00	.00
.90	.81	.19
.80	.64	.36
.70	.49	.51
.60	.36	.64
.50	.25	.75
.40	.16	.84
.30	.09	.91
.20	.04	.96
.10	.01	.99

Correlation Matrixes

Some special problems arise when a number of correlation coefficients must be presented together in one table. One useful way to present a large number of correlation coefficients efficiently is to use a **correlation matrix** like the one shown in Table 6.7a. The correlation coefficients displayed in Table 6.7a are those for four subscales (listening, pronunciation, fluency, and grammar) of an oral interview procedure and overall proficiency scores from Mullen (1980). She no doubt lined up all the subscores and the proficiency scores for her students and calculated correlation coefficients for all possible pairings of these scores. The correlation matrix shown in Table 6.7a is an economical way of displaying this information. To read the table, start with the correlation coefficient between the listening and pronunciation subtest scores, which turns out to be .79 and is found straight across from "1 Listening" at the point just below "2." The "2," "3," "4," and "5" correspond to the numbers to the left of the labels in the first column and are just a shorthand way of doing the labeling across the top of the matrix. Such label abbreviations are common practice. By using the labels in the left column and those across the top as

Table 6.7a: Matrix of Correlation Coefficients

Scale	2	3	4	5
1 Listening	.79	.85	.79	.90
2 Pronunciation		.77	.78	.88
3 Fluency			.80	.89
4 Grammar				.89
5 Overall Proficiency				

Table 6.7b: Matrix of Correlation Coefficients and Coefficients of Determination

Scale	1	2	3	4	5
1 Listening	1.00	79*	85*	.79*	.90*
2 Pronunciation	.62	1.00	.77*	.78*	.88*
3 Fluency	.72	.59	1.00	.80*	.89*
4 Grammar	.62	.61	.64	1.00	.89*
5 Overall Proficiency	.81	.77	.79	.79	1.00

$*p < .01$

coordinates, teachers can isolate the correlation coefficient for any combination of the scales.

Table 6.7b presents an elaboration of Mullen's basic matrix. This second table is provided simply to illustrate some of the other features that might occur in such a correlation matrix. Notice that the table contains the same correlation coefficients. The asterisks for these correlation coefficients refer to the $p < .01$ below the table, which means that all these coefficients were statistically significant at the .01 level. Such labeling is not particularly important in this case because all the coefficients were significant, and that fact could probably have been handled more efficiently in the text that explains the table. However, when only some of the coefficients are significant, this system of asterisks is commonly used to indicate which coefficients are significant.

Notice also that a series of 1.00s runs diagonally across the table. These 1.00s represent the correlation between the scores on each of the subtests and themselves. Of course, any set of numbers should correlate perfectly with themselves, so this makes sense. The main function of these 1.00s (collectively called **the diagonal**) is to divide the correlations above the diagonal from the numbers below it. The new numbers below the diagonal are the coefficients of determination for the same correlations found above the diagonal. In other words, they are the squared values of the corresponding correlation coefficients above the diagonal. For instance, the correlation coefficient of .90 in the upper right corner (between "1 Listening" and "5"), when it is squared equals .81, which is found in the lower left corner (between "5 Overall Proficiency" and "1"). Remember, the coefficient of determination can usefully be interpreted as the percent of shared, or overlapping, variance between the two sets of scores. A correlation matrix, then, is one way to present a great deal of information in a small amount of space.

POTENTIAL PROBLEMS WITH CORRELATIONAL ANALYSIS

There are a number of ways in which interpretations of results can go awry in applying correlational analysis to the problems of test development. Three potential pitfalls may occur: restriction of range, skewedness, and causality.

Restriction of Range

If a tester chooses to base a correlational analysis on a sample that is made up of fairly homogeneous language proficiency levels (perhaps students from one semester level out of the six available in a high-school German program), the sample itself can have dramatic effects on the analysis. Without realizing it, the range of talent may have been restricted, and such restriction tends to make any resulting correlation coefficients much lower. I discuss this issue more in Chapter 8, where I actually demonstrate the effects of restrictions in range on correlation coefficients when they are used to analyze the reliability and validity of tests. For the moment, I only stress that restrictions in the range of students taking the tests involved in a correlation coefficient may be one reason for mediocre or low correlation coefficients. Put another way, if a tester wants to maximize the possibilities of finding a strong correlation, if indeed a strong relationship exists, then the widest possible range of abilities that is logical should be included in the group of students taking the two measures.

Skewedness

Skewed distributions also depress the values of correlation coefficients. This effect occurs if either or both of the tests is skewed and is the reason why the assumption of normality is so important for correlational analysis. Remember, anyone can detect such skewing by examining graphs (histograms, bar graphs, or frequency polygons) of the distributions, or the descriptive statistics for each of the tests, as was discussed previously. Most importantly, remember that skewedness tends to depress correlation coefficients and should therefore be avoided so that the results do not end up being lower, or even much lower, than the actual degree of relationship that may exist between the two sets of scores.

Causality

Another major error that novices make in interpreting even a high correlation between the scores on one test with those on another is in thinking that it indicates a causal relationship. One test, though highly related to another, cannot be said to be "causing" it. This is easily illustrated by considering that there is probably a strong relationship, or correlation, between the number of fires per year in each city in the United States and the number of firemen working in those cities. Yet fairness would never allow anyone to say either that the firemen cause fires or that fires cause the firemen. Yes, a relationship exists, but not a causal one. So it is wisest to avoid entirely making causal statements based on correlational evidence alone.

OTHER TYPES OF CORRELATION COEFFICIENTS

The Pearson r is a very useful statistic for investigating the degree of relationship between two sets of interval or ratio scale numbers. Since most sets of test scores are considered interval scales, the Pearson r is most often appropriate. However, occasions may arise when teachers want to explore the degree of relationship between two sets of numbers that are not interval scales. Statisticians have developed a number of alternative procedures for analyzing different types of scales. The two that most commonly appear are the Spearman rank-order correlation coefficient and the point-biserial correlation coefficient. The Spearman rank-order correlation coefficient helps teachers to analyze two sets of ordinal scale scores, and the point-biserial correlation coefficient aids in the estimation of the degree of relationship between a nominal scale and an interval scale. Each of these two new correlation coefficients is derived from and designed to estimate the Pearson *r*. Therefore, in most ways, the interpretation of these statistics is the same as the interpretation of Pearson *r*.

Spearman Rank-Order Correlation Coefficient

Consider a situation in which I need to compare two sets of ordinal scales. Perhaps I am interested in the degree of relationship between students' ranks (1st, 2nd, 3rd, and so on) on each of two tests (perhaps Spanish proficiency and SAT verbal scores). In such a situation, I would need to apply the ***Spearman rank-order correlation coefficient***. Luckily, the Spearman coefficient was developed to provide an estimate of the Pearson product-moment coefficient, but based on ordinal data rather than the interval or ratio data required for the Pearson coefficient. The Spearman coefficient is usually symbolized as either the Greek letter ρ or as the same letter spelled out as *rho*. Calculation of Spearman ρ is easier than Pearson *r* and is presented in a straightforward, step-by-step manner.

The process begins with lining up the two sets of ranks for a group of students. The pairs of ranks should be lined up in columns like those shown in the second and third columns of Table 6.8. The important thing to remember is that two ordinal scale numbers are necessary for each student, and there can be no *missing data*. Once the data are properly in their columns with no missing data, the formula for the Spearman ρ coefficient works as follows:

$$\rho = 1 - \frac{6 \times \Sigma D^2}{N(N^2 - 1)}$$

where ρ = Spearman rank-order correlation coefficient

D = difference between ranks in each pair

N = number of students for whom you have pairs of ranks

Σ = sum

6 = a constant

Table 6.8: Calculating Spearman *rho*

Column 1	2		3		4	5	6
Student	Ranks on Test A		Ranks on Test B		D	D^2	Calculations
Robert	1	–	4	=	−3	9	
Millie	2	–	3	=	−1	1	
Iliana	3	–	2	=	1	1	$\rho = 1 - \dfrac{6 \times \Sigma D^2}{N(N^2 - 1)}$
Dean	4	–	1	=	3	9	
Cuny	5	–	5	=	0	0	$= 1 - \dfrac{6 \times 40}{9(81 - 1)}$
Bill	6	–	9	=	−3	9	
Corky	7	–	8	=	−1	1	$= 1 - \dfrac{240}{720}$
Randy	8	–	7	=	1	1	$= 1 - .33$
Monique	9	–	6	=	3	9	$= .67$

$^*p < .05$ (with $N = 9$) $\qquad\qquad\qquad\qquad \Sigma D^2 = 40$

Notice that the formula has few elements that are completely unfamiliar. D is the only completely new symbol, and it represents the difference between ranks in each pair. Given this information, calculating the Spearman ρ correlation coefficient is simple.

Table 6.8 shows the calculations for a hypothetical set of ranks:

1. The data are lined up such that the ranks of each student are listed in rows. Their ranks on Test A are shown in column 2 and the corresponding ranks for Test B are given in column 3. For example, Robert was ranked first on Test A, but he was only fourth on Test B. The ranks of the other students are similarly arrayed.

2. For each student, the rank for Test B is then subtracted from the rank on Test A to indicate the difference, (D), which is then put in column 4. In Robert's case, this means that his rank of 4 on Test B is subtracted from his rank of 1 on Test A, and the result of −3 is placed in column 4.

3. The results of each subtraction are then squared, and the outcomes are placed in column 5, labeled D^2.

4. The differences squared for all the students (column 5) are then summed (added up), as shown at the bottom of column 5. This results in a value for ΣD^2, which yields 40 in this example.

5. Turning next to the formula for ρ (column 6), the sum of the differences squared ($\Sigma D^2 = 40$) is substituted into the formula in the numerator and multiplied by 6 (which is a constant determined to be appropriate by

Spearman), which turns out to be $40 \times 6 = 240$. In the denominator, N (which is 9 in the example) is multiplied by $(N^2 - 1)$, which is $(81 - 1) = 80$, to yield $9 \times 80 = 720$. Dividing the numerator of 240 by 720, the result is $240 \div 720 = .33$. The last step is to subtract the outcome of this division from 1, and the result of .67 is the ρ, or *rho*, coefficient for these two sets of ordinal scale data.

Once calculated, I would check the coefficient's statistical significance by using a strategy similar to the one described previously for the Pearson product-moment correlation coefficient. Again, the observed correlation coefficient will be compared with the appropriate *critical value*. For ρ, the critical values are shown in Table 6.9. If the observed coefficient is larger than the critical value, a high and specific probability exists that the coefficient did not occur by chance alone. Again, the trick is to decide which critical value in the table is the correct one.

Looking at Table 6.9, I must first decide whether I want to be 95% or 99% certain so that I can decide which column to use. I next need to find the correct N that applies to my correlation coefficient. In this table, I do not need to subtract 2 from the sample size. In other words, N will be directly interpreted as the number of pairs of scores involved in my calculations. Moving down that column to the correct number (N) and then over to the correct column for whatever level of certainty I want, I find the critical value that my observed correlation must exceed (regardless of its sign, + or −) to be considered *statistically significant,* or due to other than chance factors with the appropriate degree of certainty (that is, 95% or 99%).

For example, the correlation of .67 obtained in Table 6.8 is worth checking for statistical significance. Because the decision is not a crucial one, I decide that I only need to be correct with 95% certainty. Hence, my critical value is somewhere in the middle column. Next, I check the sample size and find that I have nine pairs of ranks, so $N = 9$. I then move to the right in the row for $N = 9$ until I reach the middle column (for 95% certainty) and find the critical value, .600. Since the magnitude (regardless of sign) of the observed correlation coefficient, .67, is larger than the critical value, .600 (that is, .670 > .600), I can make the claim that the observed correlation coefficient is statistically significant at $p < .05$. In other words, there is only a 5% probability that this correlation coefficient occurred by chance alone. Put another way, I can be 95 percent sure that the correlation coefficient occurred for other than chance reasons. Notice, however, that this coefficient would not have been significant if I had chosen the $p < .01$ level instead.

The interpretation of ρ is otherwise much like that for Pearson r except that it is not appropriate to square ρ to get a coefficient of determination. In addition, ρ must be interpreted very carefully because it is generally

Table 6.9: Critical Values for ρ*

	Directional Decision: Sound reasons to expect either a positive or a negative correlation	
(N)	**95% Certainty** $p < .05$	**99% Certainty** $p < .01$
5	.900	1.000
6	.829	.943
7	.714	.893
8	.643	.833
9	.600	.783
10	.564	.746
12	.506	.712
14	.456	.645
16	.425	.601
18	.399	.564
20	.377	.534
22	.359	.508
24	.343	.485
26	.329	.465
28	.317	.448
30	.306	.432

*Adapted from Dixon and Massey 1951.

Table 6.10: Hypothetical Ranks
and Spearman *rho*[†]

Ranks A		**Ranks B**	
1		4	
2		3	
3		2	$\rho = -1.0$
4		1	
5		5	
6	$\rho = .67$*	9	
7		8	
8		7	$\rho = -1.0$
9		6	

*$p < .05$ (with $N = 9$)
[†]From Brown 1983b.

considered only a weak estimate of the tendency of two ranks to be similar. As pointed out in Brown 1983b, such coefficients can be fairly misleading. Consider the "significant" coefficient of .67 that was calculated in Table 6.8 as it is displayed in Table 6.10. Notice that the degree of relationship expressed in the .67 coefficient is largely due to the fact that ranks 4–1 are at the top in both sets and ranks 9–6 are at the bottom. Looking at just the top four ranks and then at just the bottom four, notice that two negative correlations (labeled in Table 6.10) are being masked in the overall correlation coefficient. I am not arguing that ρ should not be used but rather that it should be used, very cautiously along with other careful inspection of the data.

Point-biserial Correlation Coefficient

Under certain conditions, I might also find myself needing to compare a nominal scale with an interval scale in terms of the degree of relationship. For instance, I might be interested in the degree of relationship between being male or female and language aptitude scores as measured by the *Modern Language Aptitude Test,* also known as the MLAT (Carroll & Sapon 1958). Do you think that there would be any relationship between students' gender and their performance on such a test? The point-biserial correlation coefficient could help me find out.

More likely, I would be interested in the degree to which individual items on one of my tests are related to total test scores. Such item-to-whole-test correlations are often used to estimate the item discrimination. In fact, it was just such correlation coefficients that were reported in Table 3.12 (p. 91) in place of item discrimination indexes. In such a situation, I am comparing a dichotomous nominal scale (the correct or incorrect answer on each item usually coded as 1 or 0) with an interval scale (total scores on the test). The appropriate statistic to apply (when examining the relationship between a nominal and an interval scale) is the ***point-biserial correlation coefficient***. This coefficient is usually symbolized as r_{pbi}.

The data in Table 6.11 are set up to illustrate calculations of r_{pbi} between items and total scores. Notice that the items have been coded 1 for correct and 0 for incorrect just as they were in item analyses in Chapter 3. The table presents exactly the same item responses and total scores that were used in Table 3.5 (p. 65). To calculate the r_{pbi} for each item, use the following formula:

$$r_{\text{pbi}} = \frac{\overline{X}_p - \overline{X}_q}{S_t} \sqrt{pq}$$

where: r_{pbi} = point-biserial correlation coefficient

$\overline{X}_p$ = mean on the whole test for those students who answered correctly (i.e., are coded as 1s)

$\overline{X}_q$ = mean on the whole test for those students who answered incorrectly (i.e., are coded as 0s)

S_t = standard deviation for whole test

p = proportion of students who answered correctly on the whole test (i.e., those coded as 1s) (note: $p =$ IF)

q = proportion of students who answered incorrectly on the whole test (i.e., those coded as 0s)

Notice that the formula has no elements that are completely new. Hence, the reader should be able to calculate a point-biserial correlation coefficient on the basis of this formula alone. But again, an example might help. Consider Item 1 from Table 6.11, and look at its correlation with the total scores:

$$r_{pbi} = \frac{\overline{X}_p - \overline{X}_q}{S_t}\sqrt{pq} = \frac{69.53 - 61}{3.87}\sqrt{.94 \times .06} = \frac{8.53}{3.87}\sqrt{.0564} =$$
$$= 2.2041 \times .2375 = .5235 \approx .52$$

Notice that the mean of the total scores for those students who answered item 1 correctly ($\overline{X}_p$ of those coded as 1) was 69.53, as shown in the first row below the item response table, while the mean for those students who answered incorrectly ($\overline{X}_q$ of those coded as 0) was 61.00, as shown in the

Table 6.11: Item–Total Score Data (from Tables 3.5 and 3.6 Item Analysis)

| Names | \multicolumn{10}{c}{Items} | Total |
	1	2	3	4	5	6	7	8	9	10	
Robert	1	1	1	1	1	1	0	1	1	0	77
Millie	1	0	1	1	1	1	0	1	0	0	75
Dean	1	0	0	1	1	1	0	1	0	0	72
Shenan	1	1	0	1	1	1	0	0	0	0	72
Cuny	1	1	1	1	1	0	0	1	0	0	70
Bill	1	1	0	1	1	0	1	1	1	0	70
Corky	1	0	1	1	1	1	0	1	0	0	69
Randy	1	1	0	1	1	0	0	1	0	0	69
Monique	1	0	1	0	1	0	1	1	0	0	69
Wendy	1	1	0	0	1	1	0	0	1	0	69
Henk	1	0	1	0	1	0	1	0	0	0	68
Elisabeth	1	1	0	0	1	1	1	1	1	0	68
Jeanne	1	1	0	0	1	0	1	0	1	0	67
Iliana	1	1	1	0	1	0	1	0	0	0	64
Archie	1	0	0	0	1	0	1	0	1	0	64
Lindsey	0	0	0	0	1	0	1	1	0	0	61
$\overline{X}_p$	69.53	69.56	70.29	71.75	69.00	71.71	66.38	70.00	69.17	0.00	
$\overline{X}_q$	61.00	68.29	68.00	66.25	0.00	66.89	71.63	67.33	68.90	69.00	
p	0.94	0.56	0.44	0.50	1.00	0.44	0.50	0.63	0.38	0.00	
q	0.06	0.44	0.56	0.50	0.00	0.56	0.50	0.38	0.63	1.00	
r_{pbi}	.52*	0.16	0.28	0.69*	0.00	0.60*	−0.66*	0.32	0.03	0.00	
ID	.20	.00	.40	1.00	.00	.60	−1.00	.40	−.40	.00	

*$p < .05$

second row below the main table. In addition, the standard deviation for the total scores (given in Table 4.6, p. 108) was 3.87. The proportion of students in the p group is 15 out of 16, or .94 (as shown in the third row below the main table), so the proportion in the q group is .06 (as shown in the fourth row below the table). Substituting all these values into the formula for Item 1 and solving it as shown, the correlation turns out to be .52. The same processes led to the r_{pbi} values for items 2–10 in Table 6.11.

The formula for the point-biserial correlation coefficient is generalizable to any situation wherein the degree of relationship between a dichotomous nominal scale and an interval scale is of interest. However, language testers most commonly use r_{pbi} to calculate the item–total score correlation as another, more accurate, way of estimating item discrimination. For examples of other uses for this statistic, see Guilford and Fruchter 1973.

The strategy used for interpreting r_{pbi} is very similar to the one described previously for the Pearson product-moment correlation coefficient. Table 6.5 is even appropriate for determining if the observed correlation is statistically significant. Again the comparison is between the observed correlation coefficient and the critical value. If the observed coefficient is larger than the critical value, a high and specific probability exists that the coefficient did not occur by chance alone. Again, the trick is to decide which coefficient in the table is the correct one to use.

Notice in Table 6.11 that asterisks indicate that four of these correlation coefficients were indeed significant at the .05 level, indicating that there is a 95% chance that they occurred for reasons other than chance. Notice also that the item discrimination values (ID) from Table 3.6 (p. 68) are added in the last row at the bottom of Table 6.11 so that readers can compare the results obtained by using ID with the results gotten by using r_{pbi}. In both cases, the goal is to estimate how well each item is separating the better students on the whole test from the weaker students. Clearly, the two different methods do not produce exactly the same results. Items 4 and 6 appear to be effective as "discriminators" using either method, and Items 2, 5, 7, 9, and 10 appear to be ineffective "discriminators" using either method. However, the r_{pbi} seems to indicate that Item 1 is a good discriminator when ID does not so indicate, and the reverse appears to be true for Items 3 and 8. Part of the discrepancy between ID and r_{pbi} results is probably due to the small number of students involved in this example.

In any case, item analysis statistics are only tools to aid in selecting the best items. If a tester has both ID and r_{pbi} available, both statistics can help in making decisions about which items to keep in a revised version of a norm-referenced test. More importantly, the statistics should never take the tester far from the common sense notions involved in developing sound language test items.

SUMMARY

In this chapter, I examined a number of concepts related to the correlational analysis of test results. I provided a definition of correlation and explained what a correlation coefficient is. I demonstrated how two sets of scores can covary and how high or low correlation coefficients can be. I explained how to calculate a Pearson product-moment correlation coefficient and discussed the one design requirement (both scales must be interval or ratio scales) and the three assumptions (scales must be independent, normally distributed, and linearly related) that must be met for the statistic to be applied properly. I also showed how random numbers can be correlated to some degree and how this fact is related to determining whether or not a particular correlation coefficient is statistically significant—that is, whether or not it probably occurred by chance. I also noted that, in interpreting results, the statistical significance is one issue and the meaningfulness of the correlation coefficient is another issue. The coefficient of determination (i.e., the squared value of Pearson r) is one way of determining the meaningfulness of a relationship by thinking of it in terms of the percent of shared, or overlapping, variance. After looking at the use of matrixes for simultaneously displaying many correlation coefficients, I turned to problems that may arise in interpreting correlation coefficients: restriction of range, skewedness, and causality. I ended the chapter with explanations of two other useful correlation coefficients: the Spearman rank-order correlation coefficient (for two ordinal scales) and the point-biserial correlation coefficient (for one dichotomous nominal scale and one interval scale).

TERMS AND SYMBOLS

coefficient of determination (r_{xy}^2)

correlation

correlation coefficient

correlation matrix

correlational analyses

covary

critical correlation (value)

cross-product

curvilinear

the diagonal

directional decision

independence

linear

meaningfulness

missing data

non-directional decision

normally distributed (interval scale)

observed correlation (value)

outlier

Pearson product-moment correlation coefficient (r, r_{xy})

point-biserial correlation coefficient (r_{pbi})

scatterplot

Spearman rank-order correlation coefficient (ρ, or *rho*)

statistically significant

REVIEW QUESTIONS

1. What is correlational analysis? What is a correlation coefficient? If I say that two sets of scores covary, what do I mean?

2. How high and how low can a correlation coefficient go? Near what value would you expect a correlation coefficient to be if absolutely no relationship exists between two sets of numbers?

3. What are the one design requirement and three assumptions underlying the Pearson product-moment correlation coefficient? What does each assumption require, and how would you check to see if each has been met?

4. What is a linear relationship between two sets of numbers? What would a scatterplot of such a relationship look like? What would some of the possible scatterplots for curvilinear relationships look like?

5. How do you know whether a correlation coefficient that you have calculated is statistically significant? What are the steps involved in finding this out? Once you know that a correlation coefficient is significant at $p <$ .05, what does that mean?

6. Can sets of random numbers produce correlation coefficients that turn out to be statistically significant in a small percent of the trials? Why, or why not?

7. Does the fact that a correlation coefficient is statistically significant mean that it is necessarily meaningful?

8. How do you calculate the coefficient of determination, and what does it mean in terms of percents and interpreting the degree of overlap between two sets of test scores?

9. What is the Spearman rank-order correlation coefficient used for, and under what conditions might you find yourself using it?

10. What is the point-biserial correlation coefficient used for, and how is it commonly used in item analysis?

APPLICATION EXERCISES

A. Table 6.12 shows the raw scores for Tests Z and Y in the second and third columns. The descriptive statistics for each are just below the table. Based on these scores and statistics, calculate a Pearson *r* correlation coefficient.

Table 6.12: Data for Application
Exercises on Pearson *r* and Spearman ρ

Students	Test Z Scores	Test Y Scores	Test Z Ranks	Test Y Ranks
Robert	87	77	1.0	1.0
Millie	75	75	2.0	2.0
Iliana	72	64	3.0	14.5
Dean	61	72	4.0	3.5
Cuny	60	70	5.5	5.5
Bill	60	70	5.5	5.5
Corky	59	69	7.0	8.5
Randy	58	69	8.0	8.5
Monique	57	69	10.0	8.5
Wendy	57	69	10.0	8.5
Henk	57	68	10.0	11.5
Shenan	56	72	12.0	3.5
Jeanne	52	67	13.0	13.0
Elisabeth	49	68.	14.0	11.5
Archie	30	64	15.0	14.5
Lindsey	21	61	16.0	16.0
N	16	16		
Mean	56.94	69.00		
S	15.01	3.87		
Range	67	17		

B. Table 6.12 also shows the ranks of each student on Tests Z and Y in the fourth and fifth columns. Based on these ranks, calculate a Spearman *rho* correlation coefficient.

C. Table 6.13 contains data from six students on a dichotomous scale (0 or 1) for items and an interval scale (0–100) for Total Scores. Calculate the r_{pbi} for each of the four items. Notice that the mean and standard deviation for the Total Scores are given below the table. You will need some of this information to calculate r_{pbi}.

Table 6.13: Item–Total Score Data for Application
Exercise C. on r_{pbi}

Student Name	Items					Total* Scores
	1	2	3	4 ...	etc.	
Robert	1	0	1	0 ...		90
Monique	1	0	1	0 ...		80
Randy	1	0	1	0 ...		70
Fred	0	1	1	0 ...		65
Henk	0	1	1	0 ...		60
Corky	0	1	1	0 ...		55

*$\overline{X}_t = 70$; $S_t = 10$

CHAPTER 7

TEST RELIABILITY

A test, like any other type of instrument used to measure, should give the same results every time it measures (if it is used under the same conditions), should measure exactly what it is supposed to measure (not something else), and should be practical to use. If my son uses a tape measure to measure my height and finds that I am 178 centimeters tall one time, I would expect to be about the same height if he measures me again 30 minutes later. In addition, I would reasonably assume that the scale that he is using to measure me was designed to measure height and does not turn out to be measuring weight. Finally, the instrument that he is using must be practical so that it is not too inconvenient or difficult for him to use. In language testing terms, these considerations are called *reliability*, *validity*, and *usability*. I discussed the usability, or practicality, issues in some depth in Chapter 2. I cover test reliability and related concepts in this chapter, and test validity is the subject of the next chapter.

The fundamental problem that I tackle in this chapter is that a certain amount of error exists whenever measurements take place. Even in measuring on relatively stable scales like meters, liters, and kilograms, nobody can count on the results being exactly the same every time because the measurement instruments inevitably have small flaws that cause inaccuracies or because the person using the instruments makes small almost imperceptible errors. Because measurements are error-prone and because measurements are often very important, many countries have established some equivalent to the U.S. Bureau of Weights and Standards to watch over the consistency and accuracy of measuring devices.

In testing language, the problem is that measuring for language proficiency, placement, achievement, diagnosis, or other mental traits of human beings is much harder to do consistently than measuring the heights or weights of those same people. The very difficulty of measuring mental traits explains why consistency is of particular concern to language testers. In this chapter, I explain the numerous strategies that language testers use to deal with the problem of consistency in measurement. For NRTs, testers use reliability coefficients and the standard error of measurement to examine the consistency of measurement. For CRTs, testers use quite different strategies to demonstrate test dependability or consistency. To construct tests that measure consistently, language testers must first understand the potential sources of consistent and inconsistent test score variance.

SOURCES OF VARIANCE

The performances of students on any test will tend to vary from each other, but their performances can vary for a variety of reasons. In the best of all possible worlds, all the variance in test scores would be directly related to the purposes of the test. For example, consider a relatively straightforward test of the spelling rules of English. At first glance, teachers might think that the variance in students' performances on such a test could be attributed entirely to their knowledge of the spelling rules of English. Unfortunately, reality is not quite that simple and clear. Many other factors may be potential sources of score variance on this spelling test. These variables fall into two general sources of variance: (1) those creating variance related to the purposes of the test (called *meaningful variance* here), and (2) those generating variance due to other extraneous sources (called *measurement error*, or *error variance*).

In order for the meaningful variance to be most informative, the concept being tested must be very carefully defined and thought through so that the items are a straightforward reflection of the purpose for which the test was designed. For instance, a spelling test could be carefully designed to assess specific spelling rules. However, if exactly the same spelling words are used on the test that were used in classroom exercises, the variance in scores may be due partly to knowledge of the spelling rules, but also partly to remembering the spelling words. Some students may answer items correctly because they know the spelling rules, while others get them right because they memorized the isolated spelling words. This type of ambiguity can cause serious problems because, in most cases, a test should have a clearly defined purpose that is not confounded with other sources of variance.

In language testing, many purposes exist for testing students. The **meaningful variance** on a test is defined here as that variance which is directly attributable to the testing purposes. (This is essentially a test validity issue, which I discuss at more length in Chapter 8.) A number of issues were covered in Chapters 1 and 2 that can help teachers to think through the purposes of various types of tests. Once those purposes are clear, thinking about the meaningful variance on any test should be relatively easy.

Bachman (1990) provided an outline of the components of language competence (see Table 7.1)—an outline that may prove helpful in thinking about these issues. Based on earlier work by Canale and Swain (1980), Bachman and Palmer (1982), and Canale (1983), this outline includes many of the important factors that teachers should consider in defining the purpose of a given test. For instance, in designing part of the listening comprehension section of the ELI Placement Test at the University of Hawaii,

Table 7.1: Potential Sources of Meaningful Test Variance

Components of Language Competence:

Organizational Competence
   Grammatical Competence
      Vocabulary
      Morphology
      Syntax
      Phonology/graphemes
   Textual Competence
      Cohesion
      Rhetorical organization

Pragmatic Competence
   Illocutionary Competence
      Ideational functions
      Manipulative functions
      Heuristic functions
      Imaginative functions
   Sociolinguistic Competence
      Sensitivity to differences in dialect or variety
      Sensitivity to differences in register
      Sensitivity to naturalness
      Ability to interpret cultural references and figures of speech

we referred to Bachman's organizational framework, and we decided to include a component to assess the students' comprehension of cohesion in academic lectures (see Table 7.1, under Textual Competence within *Organizational Competence*). Thus, the Bachman framework helped us to define and include a purpose that we might not otherwise have thought of.

Naturally, other models of language learning exist that may prove useful in defining meaningful variance on a test, especially as the field of language learning and teaching continues to develop new ways of looking at these issues. Consider for instance how the types of syllabuses, or organizational frameworks, used in a curriculum could affect the purposes of the tests that would result (see Brown 1995 for more on syllabuses). A group of elementary-school ESL teachers might prefer to organize their curriculum and testing purposes around a structural syllabus going from the simple structures of English to more difficult structures. Another group of high-school Spanish teachers might prefer to organize their curriculum and testing purposes around various language functions as in a functional syllabus. Yet another group of adult-education EFL teachers in Amsterdam might want to develop curriculum and testing purposes centered on tasks that the students must perform in the language. The point is that, regardless of how teachers decide on the purpose of a given test, they must clearly define that purpose so that they know what sources of meaningful variance they should be focusing on.

Unfortunately, other factors, unrelated to the purpose of the test, almost inevitably enter into the performances of the students. For instance, in a set of scores from a spelling test, other potential sources of score variance might include: variables in the environment like noise, heat, etc.; the adequacy of administration procedures; factors like health and motivation in the examinees themselves; the nature and correctness of scoring procedures; or even the characteristics of the set of items selected for this particular test. All these factors might be contributing to the success or failure of individual students on the test—factors that are not directly related to the students' knowledge of spelling rules.

Measurement Error

Measurement error (also sometimes called *error variance*) is a term that describes the variance in scores on a test that is not directly related to the purpose of the test. Thorndike (1951), Lord and Novick (1968), Cronbach et al. (1970), Stanley (1971), and Feldt and Brennan (1989) all discuss these sources of variance at some length and from a variety of perspectives. For the purposes of this book, the summary provided in Table 7.2 will suffice to clarify the types of issues that are generally associated in the testing literature with measurement error.

Variance due to environment. The first potential source of measurement error shown in Table 7.2 is the environment in which the test is administered. The very location of the test administration can be one source of measurement error if it affects the performance of the students. Consider for instance the possible effects of administering a test to a group of students in a quiet library with other people in it, as opposed to administering it in a quiet auditorium that contains only examinees and proctors. Clearly, the difference in surroundings could cause some variance in test scores that is not related to the purpose of the test. Similarly, the amount of space available to each student can become a factor. And noise can be a factor that will affect the performance of students, particularly on a listening comprehension test, but also on other types of tests if the noise distracts the students from the items at hand. Indeed, lighting, ventilation, weather, or any other environmental factors can serve as potential sources of measurement error if they affect the students' performances on a test. Hence, the checklist in Table 2.2 (p. 43) should be used when setting up a test administration so the effects of environment as a source of measurement error can be minimized.

Variance due to administration procedures. Another potential source of measurement error involves the procedures that are used to administer the test. For instance, if the directions for filling out the answer sheets or for

Table 7.2: Checklist for Potential Sources of Error Variance

- ❑ Variance due to environment
  - ❑ location
  - ❑ space
  - ❑ ventilation
  - ❑ noise
  - ❑ lighting
  - ❑ weather
- ❑ Variance due to administration procedures
  - ❑ directions
  - ❑ equipmen
  - ❑ timing
  - ❑ mechanics of testing
- ❑ Variance attributable to examinees
  - ❑ health
  - ❑ fatigue
  - ❑ physical characteristics
  - ❑ motivation
  - ❑ emotion
  - ❑ memory
  - ❑ concentration
  - ❑ forgetfulness
  - ❑ impulsiveness
  - ❑ carelessness
  - ❑ testwiseness
  - ❑ comprehension of directions
  - ❑ guessing
  - ❑ task performance speed
  - ❑ chance knowledge of item content
- ❑ Variance due to scoring procedures
  - ❑ errors in scoring
  - ❑ subjectivity
  - ❑ evaluator biases
  - ❑ evaluator idiosyncracies
- ❑ Variance attributable to the test and test items
  - ❑ test booklet clarity
  - ❑ answer sheet format
  - ❑ particular sample of items
  - ❑ item types
  - ❑ number of items
  - ❑ item quality
  - ❑ test security

doing the actual test are not clear, score variance may be created that has nothing to do with the purpose of the test. If the results from several administrations are to be combined and the directions are inconsistent from administration to administration, another source of measurement error will exist. Likewise, if the quality of the equipment or the timing are not the same each time a test is administered, sources of measurement error are being created. Consider, for instance, a situation in which the students take a 6-minute taped dictation test (three readings, the second with pauses so that students have time to write) played to them on a small cassette recorder, as compared to another group that takes the same dictation read aloud from a script by a teacher, who reads a bit louder, clearer, and more slowly than the cassette tape. If all other factors are held constant, which group do you think will do best? The second group with the teacher reading louder, clearer, and slower, right? Thus, equipment and timing can create error variance that is not related to the central purpose of the test? Indeed, any issues related to the mechanics of testing may inadvertently become sources of measurement error. Hence, error variance may be caused by factors such as differences in the helpfulness of the proctors, the speed with which the directions are delivered, the attitudes of the proctors toward the students, the anxiety level of the proctors, and so forth. Again, careful attention to the checklist shown in Table 2.2 (p. 43) should help to minimize the effects of administration procedures as a source of error variance.

Variance attributable to examinees. A large number of potential sources of error variance are directly related to the condition of the students when they take the test. The sources include *physical* characteristics like differences among students in their fatigue, health, hearing, or vision. For example, if five students in a class are coming down with the flu at the time that they are taking a test, their poor physical health may be a variable that should be considered as a potential source of measurement error. Depending on the tasks involved on a test, color blindness or other more serious physical differences could also become important sources of measurement error.

Other factors, which would more appropriately be termed *psychological factors*, include differences among students (or in individual students over time) in motivation, emotional state, memory, concentration, forgetfulness, impulsiveness, carelessness, and so forth.

The experience of students with regard to test taking can also affect their performances. This experience, sometimes termed **testwiseness**, includes the ability to comprehend easily almost any test directions, or knowledge of guessing strategies (developed by some students to an art form), or strategies for maximizing the speed of task performance.

Just by chance, through classes or life experience, some of the students may have topic knowledge that will help them with certain questions on a test in a way that is not related to the purpose of the test. By and large, the issues related to the condition of the students are the responsibility of the students themselves; however, testers must be aware that they are potential sources of measurement error and must attempt to minimize their effects.

Variance due to scoring procedures. Factors over which testers have considerably more control are related to the scoring procedures used. Human errors in doing the scoring are one common source of measurement error. Another source is variance in judgments that may occur in any of the more subjective types of tests (for example, in composition and interview ratings). The problem is that the subjective nature of the scoring procedures can lead to evaluator inconsistencies or biases having an effect on the students scores. For instance, if a rater is affected positively or negatively by the sex, race, age, or personality of the interviewee, these biases can contribute to measurement error. An evaluator may also simply have certain idiosyncrasies that contribute to measurement error. Perhaps one composition rater is simply tougher than the others. Then a student's score is affected by whether or not the rating is done by this particular rater. Careful adherence to the checklists provided in Tables 2.1 and 2.2 (p. 39 and 43) should help to minimize scoring procedures as a source of measurement error.

Variance attributable to the test and test items. The last general source of measurement error is the test itself and its items. For instance, the clarity of the test booklet may become a factor if some of the booklets were smudged in the printing process, or the format of the answer sheets may be an issue if some of the students are familiar with the format while others are not. Item selection may also become an issue if the particular sample of items chosen is for some reason odd or unrepresentative of the purpose of the test. The type of items chosen can also be an issue if that type is new to some of the students or is a mismatch with the purpose of the test. The number of items used on a test is also a potential source of measurement error. If only a small number of items is used, it is known that the measurement will not be as accurate as for a larger number of items. For instance, a 30-item, multiple-choice test will clearly measure more accurately than a 1-item test. Once that premise is accepted, differences in the accuracy of measurement for other numbers of items simply become a matter of degrees. The quality of the items can also become a source of measurement error, if that quality is poor or uneven. Lastly, test security can become an issue, particularly if some of the students have managed to get a copy of the test beforehand and prepared for that particular set of questions. To minimize the effects of the test itself and the test items on measurement error, testers should use Tables 2.1, 2.2, and 3.1–3.3 (pp. 39, 43, 51, 54, and 58) as carefully as possible.

All the foregoing sources of measurement error could affect students' scores on any given test. Such effects are undesirable because they are creating variance in the students' scores that is unrelated to the purpose(s) of the test. Therefore, every effort must be made to minimize these effects.

Many of the procedures and checklists previously described in this book were designed to do just that: minimize the sources of error variance in a test and its administration.

In the remainder of this chapter, I cover ways of estimating the effects of error variance on the overall variance in a set of test scores. As Cronbach (1970) pointed out, "Test theory shows how to estimate the effects of unwanted influences and permits judgments about the relation between the actual score and the score that could be obtained by thorough measurement." This is an important issue because, if I know the degree to which error variance is affecting test scores (that is, the unreliability of a test), I can also determine the degree to which error variance is NOT affecting test scores (that is, the reliability of a test). Knowing about the relative reliability of a test can help me to decide the degree to which I should be concerned about all the potential sources of measurement error presented in Table 7.2.

RELIABILITY OF NRTs

In general, the *test reliability* is defined as the extent to which the results can be considered consistent or stable. For example, if teachers administer a placement test to their students on one occasion, they would like the scores to be very much the same if they were to administer the same test again one week later. Such consistency is desirable because they do not want to base their placement decisions on an unreliable (inconsistent) test, which might produce wildly different scores if the students were to take it again and again. Placement decisions are important decisions that can make big differences in the lives of the students involved in terms of the amounts of time, money, and effort that they will have to invest in learning the language. Since most language teachers are responsible language professionals, they want the placement of their students to be as accurate and consistent as possible so that they can responsibly serve the students' needs.

The degree to which a test is consistent, or reliable, can be estimated by calculating a *reliability coefficient* ($r_{xx'}$). A reliability coefficient is like a correlation coefficient in that it can go as high as +1.0 for a perfectly reliable test. But the reliability coefficient is also different from a correlation coefficient in that it can only go as low as 0 because a test cannot logically have less than no reliability. In cases where testers find negative values for the reliability of a test, they should first go back and check their arithmetic for errors; then if the calculations are all correct, they should round their negative result upward to 0 and accept that the results on the test had zero reliability (that is, they were totally unreliable).

Reliability coefficients, or *estimates* as they are also called, can be interpreted as the percent of systematic, or consistent, or reliable variance in the scores on a test. For instance, if the scores on a test have a reliability coefficient of $r_{xx'} = .91$, by moving the decimal two places to the right, the tester can say that the scores are 91% consistent, or reliable, with 9% measurement error (100% − 91% = 9), or random variance. If $r_{xx'} = .40$, the variance on the test is only 40% systematic and 60% measurement error.

As I explain next, language testers use three basic strategies to estimate the reliability of most tests: the test–retest, equivalent-forms, and internal-consistency strategies. I also show how certain types of productive language tests (like compositions and oral interviews) necessitate estimating the reliability of ratings or judgments.

Test–retest Reliability

Of the three basic reliability strategies, *test–retest reliability* is the one most appropriate for estimating the stability of a test over time. The first step in this strategy is to administer whatever test is involved two times to a group of students. The testing sessions should be far enough apart so that students are not likely to remember the items on the test, yet close enough together so that the students have not changed in any fundamental way (like learning more language). Once the tests are administered twice and the pairs of scores for each student are lined up in two columns, simply calculate a Pearson product-moment correlation coefficient between the two sets of scores. The correlation coefficient will provide a *conservative estimate* (that is, a low estimate, or underestimate) of the reliability of the test over time. This reliability estimate can then be interpreted as the percent of reliable variance on the test.

Admittedly, administering a test two times to the same group of students is not a very attractive proposition for the teachers or the students—clearly a major drawback for this reliability strategy. However, situations do occur in which the test–retest strategy is the most logical and practical alternative for estimating reliability.

Equivalent-forms Reliability

Equivalent-forms reliability (sometimes called *parallel-forms reliability*) is similar to test–retest reliability. However, instead of administering the same test twice, the tester administers two different but equivalent tests (for example, Forms A and B) to a single group of students. Then the tester calculates a correlation coefficient between the two sets of scores, and that indicates the degree of relationship between the scores on the two forms.

The resulting equivalent-forms reliability coefficient can be directly interpreted as the percent of reliable, or consistent, variance on either form of the test. However, note that this strategy provides an estimate of the consistency of scores across forms rather than over time, as was the case with test–retest reliability.

One question that always arises in discussing equivalent-forms reliability is the issue of what constitutes equivalence between two forms. Of course, writing parallel items for each form will aid in the creation of equivalent or parallel forms. At least, the items on the two forms should be similar because the goal is to make the two forms as similar as possible. The number of items on each test should be the same as well. From a strict statistical point of view, equivalent (or parallel) forms produce scores that have equal means, equal standard deviations, and equal correlations with some third measure of the same knowledge or skills. So establishing the equivalence of two forms could be done by simply showing that the means and standard deviations that students produce are quite similar and that the two forms correlate about equally with some third measure.

Clearly, however, developing two forms, establishing their equivalence, administering the two forms to a hapless group of students, and calculating the correlation coefficient between the scores is a fairly cumbersome way to go about estimating the reliability of each form. However, conceptually it is correct, and sometimes this strategy is useful.

Internal-consistency Reliability

To avoid the work and complexity involved in the test–retest or equivalent-forms strategies, testers most often use internal-consistency strategies to estimate *internal-consistency reliability*. As the name implies, internal-consistency strategies have the advantage of estimating the reliability of a test with only one form and only one administration of that form.

Split-half reliability. The easiest internal-consistency strategy to understand conceptually is called the *split-half method*. This approach is very similar to the equivalent-forms technique except that, in this case, the "equivalent forms" are created from the single test being analyzed by dividing it into two equal parts. The test is usually split on the basis of odd- and even-numbered items. The odd-numbered and even-numbered items on the test are scored separately as though they were two different forms. A correlation coefficient is then calculated for the two sets of scores. The tester could then interpret this coefficient as a reliability estimate except that it represents the degree of reliability for only half of the test—either half, but still just half of the test. If all other things are held constant, a longer test is usually more reliable than a short one, and the correlation calculated between the odd-numbered and even-numbered items must be adjusted so that it can be interpreted as full-test reliability. This adjustment of the half-test correlation to estimate the full-test reliability is accomplished by using the **Spearman-Brown Prophecy formula** (yes, that is the real name). The applicable formula is:

$$r_{xx'} = \frac{n \times r}{(n-1)r + 1}$$

where: $r_{xx'}$ = full-test reliability

r = correlation between two test parts

n = number of times the test length is to be increased

Once the half-test correlation coefficient is calculated between the even-numbered and odd-numbered items, this formula is easy to apply. For example, if the half-test correlation is .60, simply insert that .60 value into the two places in the formula where r appears. Since the full test is twice as long as the half-tests, the adjustment is for a test that is twice as long. Hence, n will be 2. The calculations are then carried out as follows:

$$r_{xx'} = \frac{n \times r}{(n-1)r + 1} = \frac{2 \times .60}{(2-1).60 + 1} = \frac{1.20}{1.60} = .75$$

So the adjusted full-test reliability is .75, and that is the value that the tester should report as the split-half reliability (adjusted).

Table 7.3 shows a more realistic set of data (previously used to illustrate item analysis techniques in Table 3.11, p. 90). Note in Table 7.3 that the odd-numbered items have been scored separately from the even-numbered ones and that they have been lined up into two columns representing the two scores for each student. The Pearson r calculated for these two sets of scores turned out to be .66. Since this is the half-test correlation between the even-numbered and odd-numbered items, it is labeled r. The Spearman-Brown formula should then be used to provide an estimate of what the full-test reliability is. Inserting the .66 half-test correlation value into the formula where r appears, and 2 where n appears, the necessary calculations are simple:

$$r_{xx'} = \frac{n \times r}{(n-1)r + 1} = \frac{2 \times .66}{(2-1).66 + 1} = \frac{1.32}{1.66} = .7952 \approx .80$$

The result, $r_{xx'}$, is an internal-consistency reliability estimate calculated using the split-half method on the data from a single administration of a single test. This result was made possible by separately scoring the odd-numbered and even-numbered items on the test and treating them as if they were two

Table 7.3: Split-half Reliability
for Data in Table 3.11

Odd	Even
13	14
13	14
12	14
14	12
12	12
11	10
12	9
11	9
12	7
10	8
9	9
10	8
11	7
11	7
9	8
9	8
8	8
8	8
9	7
9	6
5	9
8	6
8	6
6	7
6	7
9	3
7	5
6	5
3	7
5	3

Odd	Even	Total	Stat
15	15	30	k
9.20	8.10	17.30	$\bar{X}$
2.66	2.80	4.97	S

$r_{\text{odd-even}} = .66$

forms. The half-test reliability was then adjusted to full-test magnitude, and the result was an estimate of the reliability, or consistency, of the test.

Cronbach alpha. Conceptually, the split-half method is the easiest of the internal consistency procedures to understand. However, others are easier to calculate. For instance, Cronbach (1970) offers an alternative procedure for calculating the split-half reliability, which will give very similar results. This coefficient is one variant of his *alpha coefficient* (α) and is much easier to calculate than the split-half procedures described above. The formula is as follows:

$$\alpha = 2 \, (1 - \frac{S^2_{odd} + S^2_{even}}{S^2_t})$$

where: α = split-half reliability for the full test

  S_{odd} = standard deviation for the odd-numbered items

  S_{even} = standard deviation for the even-numbered items

  S_t = standard deviation for the total test scores

Referring once again to Table 7.3, find the values for the half- and whole-test standard deviations given at the bottom of the table. Substitute these into Cronbach's formula and solve for α as follows:

$$\alpha = 2 \, (1 - \frac{S^2_{odd} + S^2_{even}}{S^2_t}) = 2 \, (1 - \frac{2.66^2 + 2.80^2}{4.97^2})$$

$$= 2 \, (1 - \frac{7.0756 + 7.8400}{24.7009}) = 2 \, (1 - \frac{14.9156}{24.7009})$$

$$= 2 \, (1 - .6038484) = 2 \, (.3961516) = .7923031 \approx .79$$

Notice that the .79 **Cronbach alpha** (α) value obtained here is very similar to the .80 value calculated using the split-half (adjusted) method, but also note that the Cronbach α is much easier to calculate.

Kuder-Richardson formulas. Among the many other variations of internal-consistency reliability, the most commonly reported are the Kuder-Richardson formula 20 (K-R20) and formula 21 (K-R21) (Kuder & Richardson 1937). I would like to discuss these formulas in reverse order by beginning with the **Kuder-Richardson formula 21**. The easiest internal-consistency estimate to calculate is that produced by the K-R21 formula:

$$\text{K-R21} = \frac{k}{k-1} \, (1 - \frac{\overline{X}(k - \overline{X})}{kS^2})$$

where   K-R21 = Kuder-Richardson formula 21

  k = number of items

  $\overline{X}$ = mean of the test scores

  S = standard deviation of the test scores

To calculate K-R21, a tester only needs to know the number of items, the mean, and the standard deviation on a test. The tester does not have to administer the test twice or develop and administer two equivalent forms;

the tester does not have to score the odd-numbered and even-numbered items separately; and the tester does not have to calculate a correlation coefficient. Hence, the K-R21 formula is relatively easy in those situations where it can be applied.

For instance, perhaps I have a 100-item hypothetical test with a mean of 50 and a standard deviation of 10. To calculate K-R21, I only need to substitute the number of items, the mean, and the standard deviation into the K-R21 formula and solve for the result, as follows:

$$
\begin{aligned}
\text{K-R21} &= \frac{k}{k-1}(1 - \frac{\overline{X}(k - \overline{X})}{kS^2}) \\
&= \frac{100}{99}(1 - \frac{50\,(100 - 50)}{100 \times 10^2}) \\
&= 1.01\,(1 - \frac{2500}{10000}) = 1.01\,(1 - .25) \\
&= 1.01 \times .75 = .7575 \approx .76
\end{aligned}
$$

Applying the same formula to the data used in Table 7.3, I begin by marshalling my information, which means I have to look below the table for the mean (17.30), standard deviation (4.97), and number of items (30). Again I need to substitute the values into the formula and solve for the K-R21 reliability estimate, as follows:

$$
\begin{aligned}
\text{K-R21} &= \frac{k}{k-1}\,(1 - \frac{\overline{X}(k - \overline{X})}{kS^2}) \\
&= \frac{30}{29}\,(1 - \frac{17.30(30 - 17.30)}{30 \times 4.97^2}) \\
&= 1.0345\,(1 - \frac{219.71}{741.03}) \\
&= 1.0345\,(1 - .2965) = 1.0345 \times .7035 \\
&= .7278 \approx .73
\end{aligned}
$$

While this method of calculating reliability appears relatively simple, new language testers must understand one thing about calculating K-R21 for real language tests. Notice that the .73 result of the K-R21 formula is considerably lower (even though it is based on the same data) than the .79 result obtained by the Cronbach α strategy. This difference is due to the fact that the K-R21 is a conservative estimate of the reliability of a test, which is to say that, if it is in error, the error will always be one of underestimation for the reliability of the test. In other words, K-R21 should never overestimate the reliability of a test, but it may seriously underestimate the reliability. In

Table 7.4: K-R21 Estimates for Cloze Procedure (Brown 1983a)

Reliability Estimate	EX scoring		AC scoring	
	GP 1	GP 2	GP 1	GP 2
Cronbach alpha	.66	.61	.67	.67
K-R20	.64	.60	.67	.67
Split-half adjusted by Spearman-Brown prophecy formula	.67	.63	.61	.67
Flanagan's coefficient	.66	.63	.61	.67
Rulon's coefficient	.66	.63	.61	.67
K-R21	.48	.36	.56	.55

my experience, the K-R21 usually does not give a very serious underestimate for multiple-choice language tests. However, for some types of tests, like the cloze procedure, the K-R21 may produce a very serious underestimate, as compared to other approaches for estimating internal-consistency reliability.

Since the data in Table 7.3 are derived from a cloze test, I am not surprised that a fairly large difference exists in the reliability estimates produced for this test by the Cronbach α strategy and the K-R21 strategy. While the difference between .79 and .73 may not seem too large, I have found far more substantial K-R21 underestimates of cloze reliability in other previous studies (Brown 1983a, 1984b). The results of one of these studies are shown in Table 7.4. Notice how very much lower the K-R21 estimates are in comparison to the other estimates.

The ***Kuder-Richardson formula 20*** (K-R20) appears to avoid the problem of underestimating the reliability of certain language tests. Although it is marginally more difficult to calculate, K-R20 is also considered a much more accurate estimate of reliability than the K-R21. K-R20 is estimated using the following formula:

$$\text{K-R20} = \frac{k}{k-1} \left(1 - \frac{\Sigma \text{ IV}}{S_t^2}\right)$$

where K-R20 = Kuder-Richardson formula 20

k = number of items

IV = item variance

S_t^2 = variance for the whole test (that is, the standard deviation of the test scores squared)

This formula contains some elements that may not be familiar to the reader. The first of these is the sum of the item variances, symbolized by Σ IV. These ***item variance*** values are derived from the concept of item facility (see

Table 7.5). As shown in Table 7.6, begin by lining up the IF values for each item. Recall that these represent the proportion of students who answered each item correctly. Next, 1 − IF must be calculated for each item. Subtracting the IF from 1.00 yields the proportion of students who answered each item incorrectly. These results must then be lined up with their corresponding IF values as shown in Table 7.6. The next step is to multiply the IF times (1 − IF), which yields the item variance, or IV = IF (1 − IF). In other words, the item variance for each item is equal to the proportion of students who answered correctly times the proportion who answered incorrectly. As shown in Table 7.6, these item variance values for each item are then lined up in their own column, which in turn is summed for all the items. This sum is substituted into the numerator of the second fraction in the K-R20 formula.

The other element of the K-R20 formula that is probably unfamiliar is the one symbolized by S_i^2. This is just a new label for an old concept: S_i^2 represents the variance for the whole test—that is, the standard deviation of the test scores squared.

Consider the example data once again. Based on the information provided in Table 7.6, the test variance (4.97^2), sum of the item variances (4.62), and number of items (30) can be substituted into the formula to calculate K-R20 as follows:

$$\text{K-R20} = \frac{k}{k-1}\left(1 - \frac{\Sigma\,IV}{S_i^2}\right) = \frac{30}{29}\left(1 - \frac{4.62}{4.97^2}\right)$$

$$= 1.0345\left(1 - \frac{4.62}{24.70}\right) = 1.0345\,(1 - .1870)$$

$$= 1.0345 \times .8130 = .8410485 \approx .84$$

Notice that the result of these calculations, though based on the same data as those above for the split-half, Cronbach α, and K-R21 reliabilities, is a considerably higher estimate (at .84) than any of the others, which were .80, .79, and .73, respectively.

Which estimate is the correct one? Because all these estimates are underestimates of the true reliability of the test, they are all correct but lower than the true state of affairs. In other words, none will overestimate the actual state of reliability in the test being analyzed, so they can all be safely interpreted. However, the single most accurate of these estimates is the K-R20 strategy. Nevertheless, the other three approaches have advantages that sometimes outweigh the need for accuracy. For instance, the split-half version makes more sense conceptually than any other

Table 7.5: Item variance data (from Table 3.11) for Calculating K-R20

Student score summary (ID Number sorted by Total Scores):

ID Number	Total Scores	Proportion Scores
1	27	.9000
2	27	.9000
20	26	.8667
29	26	.8667
12	24	.8000
5	21	.7000
4	21	.7000
3	20	.6667
16	19	.6333
30	18	.6000
17	18	.6000
6	18	.6000
27	18	.6000
18	18	.6000
19	17	.5667
9	17	.5667
22	16	.5333
8	16	.5333
24	16	.5333
21	15	.5000
14	14	.4667
10	14	.4667
25	14	.4667
15	13	.4333
26	13	.4333
23	12	.4000
11	12	.4000
7	11	.3667
13	10	.3333
28	8	.2667

Summary statistics:

	Total Scores	Proportion Scores
Mean	17.30	.5766667
S	4.97	.1656667

Item statistics (Item Number 1–30):

Item	IF	ID
1	.5667	.2000
2	.7667	.4000
3	.2000	.5000
4	.8667	.4000
5	.8000	.5000
6	.8333	.2000
7	.8000	.6000
8	.8667	.4000
9	.9000	.3000
10	.9333	.1000
11	.6667	.6000
12	.2333	.3000
13	.4667	.4000
14	.2333	.4000
15	.7333	.3000
16	.1333	.4000
17	.4333	.5000
18	.0667	.2000
19	.9333	.2000
20	.9333	.2000
21	.9000	.3000
22	.1333	.3000
23	.8333	.2000
24	.3000	.6000
25	.2000	.4000
26	.7000	.6000
27	.7000	.6000
28	.7333	.1000
29	.0667	.1000
30	.3667	.5000

Table 7.6: Calculating Item Variances

Item Number	IF	1 - IF	IF(1 - IF)	Test Statistics	
1	0.5667	0.4333	0.2456	17.30	Mean
2	0.7667	0.2333	0.1789	4.97	S
3	0.2000	0.8000	0.1600		
4	0.8667	0.1333	0.1156		
5	0.8000	0.2000	0.1600		
6	0.8333	0.1667	0.1389		
7	0.8000	0.2000	0.1600		
8	0.8667	0.1333	0.1156		
9	0.9000	0.1000	0.0900		
10	0.9333	0.0667	0.0622		
11	0.6667	0.3333	0.2222		
12	0.2333	0.7667	0.1789		
13	0.4667	0.5333	0.2489		
14	0.2333	0.7667	0.1789		
15	0.7333	0.2667	0.1956		
16	0.1333	0.8667	0.1156		
17	0.4333	0.5667	0.2456		
18	0.0667	0.9333	0.0622		
19	0.9333	0.0667	0.0622		
20	0.9333	0.0667	0.0622		
21	0.9000	0.1000	0.0900		
22	0.1333	0.8667	0.1156		
23	0.8333	0.1667	0.1389		
24	0.3000	0.7000	0.2100		
25	0.2000	0.8000	0.1600		
26	0.7000	0.3000	0.2100		
27	0.7000	0.3000	0.2100		
28	0.7333	0.2667	0.1956		
29	0.0667	0.9333	0.0622		
30	0.3667	0.6333	0.2322		

$$\Sigma \text{ IV} = 4.6200 = \text{Sum of item variances}$$

estimate for explaining how internal-consistency reliability works. In addition to the fact that it gives a fairly accurate estimate of the reliability of a test, it is useful for teaching about reliability, as I am trying to do in this book. So there may be reasons why you would want to use the split-half variety of reliability estimate. The K-R21 formula has the advantage of being quick and easy to calculate. So, for situations where a quick, rough estimate of the reliability is sufficient, this may be the formula of choice. If the items on a test are weighted in some sense, like two points for each item in one section and only one point each in another, then Cronbach α might be the statistic of choice because it can be applied to tests with weighted items, it is easy to calculate, and it is reasonably accurate, whereas the K-R20 can only be applied when the items are scored correct/incorrect with no weighting scheme of any kind. If accuracy is the main concern, then the K-R20 formula clearly should be used if at all possible.

However, in all cases, remember that the error will be in the direction of an underestimate of the actual reliability of the test. All these statistics are conservative in the sense that they should never overestimate the existing state of affairs. Testers simply have to decide how much of an underestimate they are willing to accept in terms of the amount of work involved, the accuracy of the estimate, and whether a weighting scheme was used in scoring the test.

This coverage of internal-consistency reliability has necessarily been brief. Numerous other strategies exist for estimating internal consistency, some of which appeared in Table 7.4. (For more information on Flanagan's coefficient, Rulon's coefficient, or others like the Guttman coefficient, which are not mentioned in Table 7.4, refer to Cronbach 1970, Guilford 1954, or Stanley 1971.) The strategies chosen for presentation here were selected on the basis of their conceptual clarity, ease of calculation, accuracy of results, and frequency of appearance in the language testing literature. In most cases, these strategies should provide all the necessary tools for calculating internal-consistency reliability in most language programs. Remember, internal-consistency estimates are the ones most often reported by language testers because they have the distinct advantages of being estimable from a single form of a test administered only once.

Reliability of Rater Judgments

Two other types of reliability may be necessary in language testing situations where raters make judgments of the language produced by students. Raters usually are necessary when testing students' productive skills (speaking and writing) as in composition, oral interview, or role-play situations. Testers most often rely on interrater and intrarater reliabilities in such situations.

Interrater reliability is essentially a variation of the equivalent-forms type of reliability in that the scores are usually produced by two raters, the scores are lined up in columns, and a correlation coefficient is calculated between them. The resulting coefficient is an estimate of the interrater reliability of the judgments being made in either set of ratings. A real-world example of this application is shown in Table 7.7, in which three scores (in columns) are shown for each of 55 students (in rows). These are the three ratings assigned by three different teachers to each student's composition on the ELIPT in one small Spring semester administration in 1989.

Table 7.8 gives the correlation coefficients between each of the three possible pairings of ratings. These are estimates of the reliabilities for each set of ratings as they were assigned by the raters in this test administration. They are not as high as I would like. However, recall that the number of items (or number of ratings in this case) can have a dramatic effect on the

Table 7.7: Three Ratings for Each of 55 Compositions
(Writing Sample subtest of the ELIPT in Spring 1989)

Student ID Number	R1	R2	R3	Student ID Number	R1	R2	R3
A1	66	66	72	A51	80	67	74
A2	84	72	67	A52	82	78	74
A3	62	66	56	B2	63	65	67
A5	79	90	68	B3	60	57	69
A6	73	67	67	B5	60	73	65
A8	76	78	71	B6	73	71	69
A9	72	82	64	B9	64	77	82
A11	63	54	57	B10	68	74	61
A13	57	62	71	B11	65	62	66
A16	58	76	81	B13	84	78	82
A19	72	71	70	B14	41	46	37
A20	61	63	71	B17	87	91	81
A25	68	79	62	B18	71	68	77
A30	62	87	78	B20	69	63	54
A31	61	67	72	B21	61	59	58
A32	73	87	78	B23	66	74	67
A36	70	76	63	B24	65	70	64
A37	70	71	68	C2	67	77	70
A38	95	80	89	C3	67	67	57
A40	67	81	71	C4	53	66	65
A41	76	75	77	C5	88	87	90
A43	68	53	55	C6	83	90	67
A44	75	64	69	C9	59	69	62
A46	87	85	75	C11	68	72	66
A47	64	69	61	C12	59	75	71
A48	73	60	65	C13	68	72	75
A49	63	60	69	C14	87	93	90
				C15	64	64	65

Table 7.8: Interrater Correlations for Writing
Sample ($N = 55$)

R1	1.000		
R2	0.632	1.000	
R3	0.571	0.662	1.000
	R1	R2	R3

magnitude of the reliability coefficient. Since these estimates are for the reliability of each single set of ratings, and since two or three sets of ratings are likely to be higher in reliability when taken together, adjusting to find the reliability of larger numbers of ratings taken together would be logical, possible, and advisable.

The Spearman-Brown Prophecy formula (explained in the discussion of split-half reliability, p. 194-196) can be used for just this purpose (see

Guilford 1954, p. 397, for more on this point). Remember that the formula for this adjustment was:

$$r_{xx'} = \frac{n \times r}{(n-1)r + 1}$$

where $r_{xx'}$ = full-test reliability

r = correlation between test parts

n = number of times the test length is to be increased

I could apply the adjustment to any one of the coefficients reported in Table 7.8, but my naturally careful approach to all statistics leads me to use the lowest estimate, .571 in this case. Adjusted for two ratings ($n = 2$) from this single set estimate, the Spearman-Brown prophecy formula is applied as follows:

$$r_{xx'} = \frac{n \times r}{(n-1)r + 1} = \frac{2 \times .571}{(2-1).571 + 1} = \frac{1.142}{1.571}$$

$$= .7269255 \approx .73$$

However, since the actual decisions in this case are based on three sets of ratings, a more appropriate adjustment is for three ratings ($n = 3$), as follows:

$$r_{xx'} = \frac{n \times r}{(n-1)r + 1} = \frac{3 \times .571}{(3-1).571 + 1} = \frac{1.713}{2.142}$$

$$= .7997198 \approx .80$$

This result gives a conservative reliability estimate (that is, it is safe and not likely to be an overestimate) for the rating procedure as it is applied to writing samples in the ELI at UHM (that is, with three ratings on each composition written during the ELIPT in Spring 1989). (See Chaudron, Crookes, and Long 1988 for more on the problems associated with the reliability of ratings in second-language classroom research.)

Intrarater reliability is most closely related to the test–retest strategy discussed previously in that two sets of scores are produced by the same rater on two separate occasions, say about 2 weeks apart, for the same group of students, and a correlation coefficient is calculated. The resulting coefficient is an estimate of the intrarater reliability of the judgments being made by the rater on two occasions. Thus, intrarater reliability is an estimate of the consistency of judgments over time. Hence, the results may be confounded by the raters' remembering, on the second occasion, their ratings from the first occasion. Perhaps as a result of this potential problem, or as a result of the slightly more complex logistics involved, this form of reliability estimate is not reported as often in language testing as the interrater type.

Interpreting Reliability Estimates

Reporting the degree to which a test is reliable is often necessary in the process of developing and defending a new language test. I have shown a number of alternatives from which teachers can choose to estimate the reliability of their non-referenced tests. However, regardless of the type of reliability involved, the interpretation of the coefficients is about the same. The central concern is with how consistent the test is in terms of the percent of variance in the scores that is reliable and the percent that is attributable to measurement error. If $r_{xx'} = .33$, then 33% of the variance is reliable, and the remaining 67% is measurement error. Hence, a reliability estimate of .33 indicates that the test is not very reliable and that the test should either be seriously revised or replaced entirely.

Remember that reliability estimates are derived from the performances of a particular group of people. Hence, the estimate is linked to that group. In other words, the tester can only make claims about the reliability of a test with reference to a particular group of students; or perhaps very cautiously, claims can be made about the probable level of reliability when the test is administered to a *very similar* group of students with about the same range of abilities.

Standard Error of Measurement

Reliability coefficients are just one useful way of looking at the issue of norm-referenced test consistency. Such coefficients can, indeed, be used to estimate how reliable the test is in percentage terms. Another, perhaps more concrete, way of looking at the consistency of a set of test scores is called the *standard error of measurement* (SEM). Conceptually, this statistic is used to determine a band around a student's score within which that student's score would probably fall if the test were administered to him or her repeatedly. Based on the percentages in a normal distribution (discussed in Chapter 4), the SEM can also be used to estimate the probability with which the tester can expect those scores to fall within the band.

Consider Test A, a 100-item test administered in the Kalihi-Palama Adult Education Program, for which the standard error of measurement is 5 (that is, SEM = 5). I can conclude from this SEM that a particular student, Xiao

Lao, who scored 80, would score within a band of one SEM plus (80 + 5 = 85) or minus (80 − 5 = 75) 68% of the time if she were to take the test over and over many times. I base this interpretation on the notion that a standard deviation would exist for the hypothetical distribution of Xiao Lao's many test scores. The deviation of these scores with regard to her particular score of 80 is an estimate of measurement error. The purpose of the SEM is to estimate a sort of average of the distribution of error deviations across all the students who took the test. On the basis of this estimate, a tester can estimate with certain amounts of probability how far students' scores would vary by chance alone if the students were to take the test repeatedly. Using this information, the tester can be fairly sure that, for any student, error alone can cause the scores to vary within a band of plus or minus one SEM (±1 SEM, or ±5 points in this case) 68% of the time. For Xiao Lao, whose score was 80, this SEM would indicate that, by chance alone, her scores could vary between 75 and 85 points 68% of the time if she were to take the test repeatedly. If the tester wanted to be even more sure of this band, he or she could extend it out further to two SEMs (5 + 5 = 10) plus (80 + 10 = 90) or minus (80 − 10 = 70) on either side of the observed raw score. The tester would then be relatively sure that Xiao Lao's score would consistently fall between 70 and 90, (95% of the time, based on the percents under the normal distribution).

To calculate the SEM, I must have the standard deviation of the test under analysis and any of the reliability coefficients discussed previously. The formula for calculating this statistic is relatively simple:

$$SEM = S\sqrt{1 - r_{xx'}}$$

where   SEM = standard error of measurement

S = standard deviation on the test

$r_{xx'}$ = reliability estimate for the test

I apply this formula to the data shown in Tables 7.3, 7.5, and 7.6, for which S = 4.97 and $r_{xx'}$ = .84. The reliability coefficient chosen here is the K-R20 because it is considered the most accurate available. The resulting SEM based on this formula is:

$$SEM = S\sqrt{1 - r_{xx'}}$$
$$= 4.97\sqrt{1 - .84} = 4.97\sqrt{.16} = 4.97 \times .40$$
$$= 1.988 \approx 2.0$$

This is a much lower figure than the SEM calculated for Xiao Lao; therefore, the band of chance fluctuations in students' scores will be narrower. However, as with all statistics, this one is relative to other factors that must be considered at the same time. In comparing the SEM found here with the one produced by the test that Xiao Lao took, note that this test only had 30 items while Xiao Lao's test had 100 items. Nevertheless, in this case, the SEM of 2.0 indicates that there would only be relatively small chance fluctuations in the students' scores if they were to take the test repeatedly.

A corollary to all this is that the narrower the SEM is, the narrower the band of possible fluctuations will be, or the more consistently the raw scores represent the students' actual abilities. Thus, with all other factors held constant, a test that has a small SEM is more consistent than one with a large SEM. In a sense, the SEM is easier to interpret than a reliability coefficient because it is expressed in terms of raw score bands rather than the more abstract percent interpretations typically used with reliability estimates.

This difference extends to the use of these statistics for real-life, decision-making purposes, where the SEM is often far more important than any reliability coefficient. The SEM is especially useful in deciding the "fate" of students who are on the borderline for some decision that can affect their lives in important ways. For example, perhaps the test that Xiao Lao took was for purposes of placement into adult-education English courses. This decision is a fairly important one for Xiao Lao. After all, if the test inaccurately places her into a level below her true ability, it would unjustly cost her extra terms of studying and extra money if tuition fees are involved. In such a situation, most language professionals would like placement to be as accurate and fair as possible.

Unfortunately, our hapless Xiao Lao scored 80, and the cut-point between the second and third levels of ESL study was 82 points. Into which course should she be placed? She is clearly within one SEM (5 points) of the cut-point, so she might score into the third level if she were to take the test again, yet her actual score indicates that she should be placed into the second level. A responsible decision about Xiao Lao, or any student in a similar situation, would probably involve getting more information about her proficiency (for example, an additional composition or oral interview) before making the decision about which way she should be placed. Clearly then, the SEM can be a very important way to apply the concept of reliability in a very practical sense to the actual decision making in a language program. The standard error of measurement should be considered, therefore, and reported right along with the reliability coefficients for any norm-referenced test.

Factors Affecting the Reliability of NRTs

To sum up briefly, a number of factors may affect the reliability of any test (see Table 7.1). Some of these factors are more directly within the control of testers than are other factors. However, language test developers and users must realize that, if all other factors are held constant, the following is usually true:

1. a longer test tends to be more reliable than a short one

2. a well-designed and carefully written test tends to be more reliable than a shoddy one

3. a test made up of items that assess similar language material tends to be more reliable than a test that assesses a wide variety of material

4. a test with items that discriminate well tends to be more reliable than a test with items that do not discriminate well

5. a test that is well-centered and disperses the scores efficiently (that is, a test that produces normally distributed scores) tends to be more reliable than a test that has a skewed distribution

6. a test that is administered to a group of students with a wide range of abilities tends to be more reliable than a test administered to a group of students with a narrow range of abilities

In other words, if a tester wants to maximize the possibility that a test designed for NRT purposes will be reliable, he or she should make sure that it is as long as possible, is well-designed and carefully written, assesses relatively homogeneous material, has items that discriminate well, is normally distributed, and is administered to a group of students whose abilities are as wide as logically possible within the context.

CONSISTENCY ESTIMATES FOR CRTS

As noted previously (particularly in Chapters 1 and 5), CRTs will not necessarily produce normal distributions even if they are functioning correctly. On some occasions, such as at the beginning of instruction, CRTs may produce normal distributions, but the tester cannot count on the normal distribution as part of the strategy for demonstrating the reliability of a test. If all the students have learned all the material, the tester would like them all to score near 100 percent on the end-of-course achievement CRT. Hence, a CRT that produces little variance in scores is an ideal that testers seek in developing CRTs. In other words, a low standard deviation on the posttest may actually be a byproduct of developing a sound CRT. This is quite the opposite of the goals and results when developing a good NRT.

Popham and Husek (1969) were the first to question the appropriateness of using correlational strategies for estimating the reliability of CRTs, which all depend in one way or another on a large standard deviation. Consider the test–retest and equivalent-forms strategies. In both cases, a correlation coefficient is calculated. Since correlation coefficients are designed to estimate the degree to which two sets of numbers go together, scores that are very tightly grouped (that is, have a low standard deviation) will probably *not* line the students up in a similar manner. As that standard deviation approaches zero, so do any associated correlation coefficients. Correlation coefficients used for estimating interrater and intrarater reliability are similarly affected. A quick glance back at the K-R20 and K-R21 formulas also indicates that as the standard deviation goes down relative to all other factors, so do these internal-consistency estimates. In short, all the strategies for reliability discussed in this chapter are fine for NRTs because they are very sensitive to the magnitude of the standard deviation, and a relatively high standard deviation is one result of developing a norm-referenced test that spreads students out well.

However, those same reliability strategies may be quite inappropriate for CRTs because CRTs are not developed for the purpose of producing variance in scores. However, many other strategies have been worked out for demonstrating their consistency—strategies that do not depend on a high standard deviation; in general, they fall into three categories (Berk 1984b, p. 235): threshold loss agreement, squared-error loss agreement, and domain score dependability. These three strategies have been developed specifically for CRT consistency estimation. Note that these strategies provide tools for analyzing CRTs that have only recently become available to language testers. So, like all statistics, they should be used with caution and interpreted carefully as just what they are: *estimates* of **test consistency**.

Notice in the previous paragraph that the terms *agreement* and *dependability* are used with reference to CRTs in lieu of the term reliability. In this book, the terms **agreement** and **dependability** are used rather arbitrarily for estimates of the consistency of CRTs, while the term **test reliability** is reserved for NRT consistency estimates. This distinction helps teachers to keep the notions of NRT reliability separate from the ideas of CRT agreement and dependability.

Threshold Loss Agreement Approaches

As shown in Brown (1990), two of the **threshold loss agreement** statistics that are prominent in the literature are also straightforward enough mathematically to be calculated in most language teaching situations. These two statistics are the agreement coefficient (Subkoviak 1980) and the kappa coefficient (Cohen 1960). Both of these coefficients measure the consistency of master/non-master classifications as they were defined in Chapter 3. Recall that a master is a student who knows the material or has the skill being tested, while a non-master is a student who does not. These two threshold loss agreement approaches are sometimes called *decision consistency* estimates because they gauge the degree to which decisions that classify students as masters or non-masters are consistent. In principle, these estimates require the administration of a test on two occasions. I base my conceptual explanations on this relatively impractical strategy. Then I cover some strategies that Subkoviak (1988) recently reported for estimating the agreement and kappa coefficients from the data of a single test administration.

Agreement coefficient. The *agreement coefficient* (p_o) is an estimate of the proportion of students who have been consistently classified as masters and non-masters on two administrations of a CRT. To apply this approach, the test should be administered twice such that enough time has been allowed between administrations for the students to forget the test but not so much time that they have learned any substantial amount. Using a predetermined cut-point, the students are then classified on the basis of their scores into the master or non-master groups on each test administration. The cut-points are usually determined by the purpose of the test. On an achievement test, for instance, a passing score might be considered 60% or higher. If this achievement test were administered twice near the end of a term of instruction, the tester would need to tally the number of students who passed (masters) and those who failed (non-masters) on the two administrations.

Figure 7.1 shows a way of categorizing the results on the two tests in order to calculate p_o. In some cases, classifications agree between the two

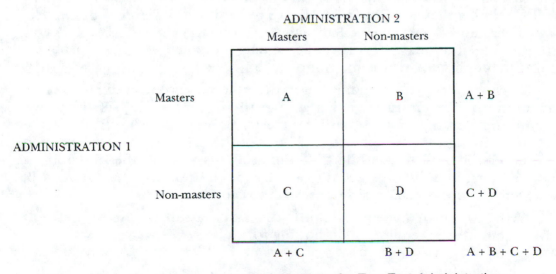

Figure 7.1: Master/Non-master Classifications for Two Test Administrations

ADMINISTRATION 2

	Masters	Non-masters

		Masters	Non-masters	
	Masters	77	6	83
ADMINISTRATION 1				
	Non-masters	6	21	27
		83	27	110

Figure 7.2:   Example Master/Non-master Classifications for Two Test Administrations

tests. Thus, when students are classified as masters on both administrations of the test, the tester should count them up and record the number in cell A in Figure 7.1. Similarly, the number of students classified as non-masters by both tests should go in cell D. In other cases, the classifications disagree between the two administrations. Some students may be classified as masters on the first administration and non-masters on the second. This number should appear in cell B, while those students classified as non-masters on the first administration and masters on the second should go in cell C. Notice that A + B and C + D are totaled to the right of the figure, and A + C and B + D are totaled below it. Note also that A + B + C + D is shown in the bottom right corner. These data are called *marginals* (probably because they appear in the margins of such figures).

Consider a contrived example for the sake of understanding how the agreement coefficient works: A group of 110 students take two administrations of a posttest, and the master/non-master classifications are as shown in Figure 7.2. Notice that 77 out of the 110 students are classified as masters by both tests, while 21 other students are classified by both as non-masters. In addition, 12 students (12 = 6 + 6 students in cells C and B, respectively) are classified differently by the two tests.

With this information in hand, the calculation of the agreement coefficient merely requires the following formula:

$$p_o = \frac{A + D}{N}$$

where p_o = agreement coefficient

  A = number of students in cell A

  D = number of students in cell D

  N = total number of students

Substituting the values found in Figure 7.2, the calculations turn out as follows:

$$p_o = \frac{A + D}{N} = \frac{77 + 21}{110} = \frac{98}{110} = .89$$

This indicates that the test classified the students in the same manner with about 89% agreement. Thus, the decision consistency is about 89% and this CRT appears to be very consistent.

Notice that, if all the students were classified in exactly the same way by both administrations, the coefficient would be 1.00 [for example, $(A + D)/N = (80 + 30)/110 = 1.00$, or $(99 + 11)/110 = 1.00$]. Thus, 1.00 is the maximum value that this coefficient can have. However, unlike the reliability coefficients discussed previously for NRTs, the agreement coefficient can logically be no lower than the value that would result from a chance distribution across the four cells. For 120 students, you might reasonably find 30 students per cell by chance alone. This would result in a coefficient of .50 [$(A + D)/N = (30 + 30)/120 = 60/120 = .50$]. Thus, for all two-way classifications like that shown in Figure 7.2, the agreement coefficient can logically be no lower than what would occur by chance alone. This is very different from NRT reliability estimates, which can have a logical lower limit of .00.

Kappa coefficient. The *kappa coefficient* (κ) adjusts for this problem of a chance lower limit by adjusting to the proportion of consistency in classifications beyond that which would occur by chance alone. The adjustment is given in the following formula:

$$\kappa = \frac{(p_o - p_{chance})}{(1 - p_{chance})}$$

where p_o = agreement coefficient

  p_{chance} = proportion classification agreement that could occur by chance alone = $[(A + B)(A + C) + (C + D)(B + D)]/N^2$

As mentioned above, two-way classifications like those shown in the example, will always have a certain p_{chance} level. Hence, before calculating the κ value, a tester must calculate p_{chance} for the particular classification table involved. These levels will differ, of course, depending on the score used as a cut-point in making the absolute decision. For the example data, the calculations would be as follows:

$$p_{chance} = [(A + B)(A + C) + (C + D)(B + D)] / N^2$$
$$= [(83)(83) + (27)(27)] / 12100$$
$$= [6889 + 729] / 12100 = 7618 / 12100$$
$$= .6296 \approx .63$$

$$\kappa = \frac{(p_o - p_{chance})}{(1 - p_{chance})}$$
$$= \frac{.89 - .63}{1 - .63} = \frac{.26}{.37} = .7027 \approx .70$$

The kappa coefficient is an estimate of the classification agreement that occurred beyond what would be expected by chance alone and can be interpreted as a percentage of that agreement by moving the decimal two places to the right. Since kappa represents the percentage of classification agreement beyond chance, it is usually lower than the agreement coefficient. Like the agreement coefficient, it has an upper limit of 1.00, but unlike the agreement coefficient with its chance lower limit, the kappa coefficient has the more familiar lower limit of .00

Estimating threshold loss agreement from a single administration. Because administering a test twice is cumbersome and hard on everyone involved, many approaches have been worked out to estimate threshold agreement from one administration (see, for instance, Huynh 1976, Marshall 1976, and Subkoviak 1980). Historically, these approaches have been far too complex for practical application by anyone but a statistician. Recently, however, Subkoviak (1988) presented practical approaches for approximating both the agreement and kappa coefficients. In order to approximate either of these coefficients from a single test administration, a tester needs two values. The first is a value for the cut-point score converted to a standard score. This is calculated using the following formula:

$$z = \frac{(c - .5 - \overline{X})}{S}$$

where z = standardized cut-point score

c = raw cut-point score

$\overline{X}$ = mean

S = standard deviation

The second is one of the NRT internal-consistency reliability estimates (Split-half adjusted, Cronbach α, or K-R20). Once the tester has the standardized cut-point score and an internal-consistency reliability estimate in hand, he or she simply checks the appropriate table (Table 7.9 or 7.10) and looks in the first column for the z value (regardless of sign, + or −) closest to the obtained value and looks across the first row for the r_{xx} closest to the obtained reliability estimate. Where the row for the z value meets the column for the reliability coefficient, an approximate value is given for the threshold agreement of the CRT in question. Table 7.9 gives the approximations for agreement coefficients, and Table 7.10 gives the same information for kappa coefficients.

For instance, perhaps a CRT posttest had a mean of 58.47, a cut-point of 60 out of 100, a standard deviation of 6.10, and a K-R20 reliability estimate of .86. To obtain the standardized cut-point score, the tester would first need the following formula:

$$z = \frac{(c - .5 - \overline{X})}{S}$$

$$= \frac{(60 - .5 - 58.47)}{6.10} = \frac{1.03}{6.10}$$

$$= .1689 \approx .17$$

To approximate the agreement coefficient, the tester would check Table 7.9 at the row for z that is the closest to .17 (.20 in this case) and then look across the top for the reliability closest to .86 (.90 in this case). Where the identified row and column meet, the tester finds a value of .86 for the approximate agreement coefficient. Following the same steps in Table 7.10 yields an estimate for the kappa coefficient, $\kappa = .71$ in this case.

These approximations of the agreement and kappa coefficients are underestimates of the values that would be obtained using two test administrations. Thus, they are safe estimates but will always be on the low side of what the tester would obtain in a two-administration situation. Hence, these approximations should only be used to give an idea, or rough approximation, of the decision consistency of a test. If they are high, great. However, if they are low, the tester might want to double-check the consistency of the test by using other approaches. Using a variety of approaches is a good idea in any case.

Squared-error Loss Agreement Approaches

Threshold loss agreement coefficients focus on the degree to which classifications in clear-cut categories (master or non-master) are consistent.

Table 7.9: Approximate Values of the Agreement Coefficient*

	Reliability (r)								
z	.10	.20	.30	.40	.50	.60	.70	.80	.90
.00	.53	.56	.60	.63	.67	.70	.75	.80	.86
.10	.53	.57	.60	.63	.67	.71	.75	.80	.86
.20	.54	.57	.61	.64	.67	.71	.75	.80	.86
.30	.56	.59	.62	.65	.68	.72	.76	.80	.86
.40	.58	.60	.63	.66	.69	.73	.77	.81	.87
.50	.60	.62	.65	.68	.71	.74	.78	.82	.87
.60	.62	.65	.67	.70	.73	.76	.79	.83	.88
.70	.65	.67	.70	.72	.75	.77	.80	.84	.89
.80	.68	.70	.72	.74	.77	.79	.82	.85	.90
.90	.71	.73	.75	.77	.79	.81	.84	.87	.90
1.00	.75	.76	.77	.77	.81	.83	.85	.88	.91
1.10	.78	.79	.80	.81	.83	.85	.87	.89	.92
1.20	.80	.81	.82	.84	.85	.86	.88	.90	.93
1.30	.83	.84	.85	.86	.87	.88	.90	.91	.94
1.40	.86	.86	.87	.88	.89	.90	.91	.93	.95
1.50	.88	.88	.89	.90	.90	.91	.92	.94	.95
1.60	.90	.90	.91	.91	.92	.93	.93	.95	.96
1.70	.92	.92	.92	.93	.93	.94	.95	.95	.97
1.80	.93	.93	.94	.94	.94	.95	.95	.96	.97
1.90	.95	.95	.95	.95	.95	.96	.96	.97	.98
2.00	.96	.96	.96	.96	.96	.97	.97	.97	.98

*Adapted fom Subkoviak 1988.

Squared-error loss agreement strategies also do this, but they do so with "sensitivity to the degrees of mastery and nonmastery along the score continuum" (Berk 1984b, p. 246). Thus, squared-error loss agreement approaches attempt to account for the distances that students are from the cut-point—that is, the degree of mastery and non-mastery rather than just the dichotomous categorization.

I present only the *phi (lambda) dependability index* (Brennan 1980, 1984) because it is the only squared-error loss agreement index that can be estimated using one test administration, and because Brennan has provided a short-cut formula for calculating this index that can be based on raw score test statistics. Adapted to the symbols of this book, the formula is as follows:

$$\Phi(\lambda) = 1 - \frac{1}{k-1} \left[\frac{\overline{X}_p (1 - \overline{X}_p) - S_p^2}{(\overline{X}_p - \lambda)^2 + S_p^2} \right]$$

where $\Phi(\lambda)$ = phi (lambda) dependability index

Table 7.10: Approximate Values of the Kappa Coefficient*

					Reliability (r)				
z	.10	.20	.30	.40	.50	.60	.70	.80	.90
.00	.06	.13	.19	.26	.33	.41	.49	.59	.71
.10	.06	.13	.19	.26	.33	.41	.49	.59	.71
.20	.06	.13	.19	.26	.33	.41	.49	.59	.71
.30	.06	.12	.19	.26	.33	.40	.49	.59	.71
.40	.06	.12	.19	.25	.32	.40	.48	.58	.71
.50	.06	.12	.18	.25	.32	.40	.48	.58	.70
.60	.06	.12	.18	.24	.31	.39	.47	.57	.70
.70	.05	.11	.17	.24	.31	.38	.47	.57	.70
.80	.05	.11	.17	.23	.30	.37	.46	.56	.69
.90	.05	.10	.16	.22	.29	.36	.45	.55	.68
1.00	.05	.10	.15	.21	.28	.35	.44	.54	.68
1.10	.04	.09	.14	.20	.27	.34	.43	.53	.67
1.20	.04	.08	.14	.19	.26	.33	.42	.52	.66
1.30	.04	.08	.13	.18	.25	.32	.41	.51	.65
1.40	.03	.07	.12	.17	.23	.31	.39	.50	.64
1.50	.03	.07	.11	.16	.22	.29	.38	.49	.63
1.60	.03	.06	.10	.15	.21	.28	.37	.47	.62
1.70	.02	.05	.09	.14	.20	.27	.35	.46	.61
1.80	.02	.05	.08	.13	.18	.25	.34	.45	.60
1.90	.02	.04	.08	.12	.17	.24	.32	.43	.59
2.00	.02	.04	.07	.11	.16	.22	.31	.42	.58

*Adapted fom Subkoviak 1988.

λ = cut-point expressed as a proportion

k = number of items

$\overline{X}_p$ = mean of proportion scores

S_p = standard deviation of proportion scores

Consider once again the example shown in Table 7.5 as though it were a CRT. Notice that the proportion scores given in the column furthest to the right in the table are the raw scores divided by the total possible. The mean (.5766667) and standard deviation (.1656667) of these proportion scores are the $\overline{X}_p$ and S_p, respectively, shown in the formula for the $\Phi(\lambda)$ coefficient. The k indicates the total number of items, or 30 in this case, and the λ is the cut-point expressed as a proportion. For the example, the cut-point for mastery has been set at 70% (or .70 if expressed as a proportion). Substituting all these values into Brennan's formula:

$$\Phi(\lambda) = \Phi(.70) = 1 - \frac{1}{k-1}\left[\frac{\overline{X}_p(1-\overline{X}_p) - S_p^2}{(\overline{X}_p - \lambda)^2 + S_p^2}\right]$$

$$= 1 - \frac{1}{30-1}\left[\frac{.5766667\,(1-.5766667) - .1656667^2}{(.5766667 - .70)^2 + .1656667^2}\right]$$

$$= 1 - \frac{1}{29}\left[\frac{.2441222 - .0274454}{.0152111 + .0274454}\right]$$

$$= 1 - .0344828\left[\frac{.2166768}{.0426565}\right]$$

$$= 1 - (.0344828 \times 5.0795728)$$

$$= 1 - .1751578 = .8248422 \approx .82$$

Remember that this is a short-cut index of dependability that takes into account the distances of students from the cut-point for the master/non-master classification. The full-blown version of this analysis is better overall, but such analyses are beyond the scope of this volume (see Brennan 1984 for more on this topic).

Domain Score Dependability

All the threshold loss and squared-error loss agreement coefficients described previously have been criticized because they are dependent in one way or another on the cut-score. Alternative approaches, called the *domain score estimates of dependability*, have the advantage of being independent of the cut-score. However, they apply to domain-referenced interpretations rather than to all criterion-referenced interpretations. **Domain-referenced tests** (DRTs) are defined here as a type of CRT that is distinguished primarily by the way in which items are sampled. For DRTs, the items are sampled from a general, but well-defined, domain of behaviors rather than from individual course objectives as is often the case in what might be called **objectives-referenced tests** (ORTs). The results on a DRT can therefore be used to describe a student's status with regard to that domain in a manner similar to the way in which ORT results are used to describe the student's status on small subtests for each course objective. Thus, the terms domain-referenced and objectives-referenced describe variant sampling techniques within the overall concept of criterion-referenced testing. Since objectives-referenced tests define a domain of their own, but within the scope of the course objectives, I feel that analyses appropriate for DRTs are also appropriate for ORTs. One way of analyzing the consistency of domain-referenced tests (and by extension, objectives-referenced tests) is the *phi coefficient.*

The ***phi dependability index*** (Φ) is also known as the *generalizability coefficient for absolute error* (for more on generalizability theory, see Cronbach et al. 1970; Bolus, Hinofotis, & Bailey 1982; Brown 1984c, forthcoming b; Brown & Bailey 1984; and Brown & Ross forthcoming). Phi is a general-purpose estimate of the domain-referenced dependability of a test. This interpretation assumes that the items are sampled from a well-defined domain and gives no information about the reliability of the individual objectives-based subtests. Nevertheless, phi does provide a handy way to estimate the overall dependability of the scores without reference to a cut-score. The formula that is presented here was derived in Brown (1990) from information provided in Brennan (1980, 1984). The formula for the phi coefficient that resulted is as follows:

$$\Phi = \frac{\dfrac{nS_p^2}{n-1}[K - R20]}{\dfrac{nS_p^2}{n-1}[K - R20] + \dfrac{\overline{X}_p(1 - \overline{X}_p) - S_{p2}}{k-1}}$$

where n = number of persons who took the test

k = number of items

$\overline{X}$ = mean of proportion scores

S_p = standard deviation of proportion scores (using the n formula rather than $n-1$)

K-R20 = Kuder-Richardson formula 20 reliability estimate

All that is necessary for calculating this coefficient of dependability is the number of students, the number of items, the mean of the proportion scores, the standard deviation of the proportion scores, and the K-R20 reliability estimate. Once again using the data in Table 7.5, k is the number of items (or 30 in this case); n is the number of students (30); $\overline{X}_p$ is the mean (.5766667) of the proportion scores; S_p is the standard deviation (.1656667) of the same proportion scores; and K-R20 is the traditional reliability estimate (.8410485) demonstrated previously (p. 200). Substituting all these values into the formula gives the following result:

$$\Phi = \frac{\dfrac{nS_p^2}{n-1}[\mathrm{K-R20}]}{\dfrac{nS_p^2}{n-1}[\mathrm{K-R20}] + \dfrac{\overline{X}_p(1-\overline{X}_p)-S_p^2}{k-1}}$$

$$= \frac{\dfrac{30\times(.1656667)^2}{30-1}[.8410485]}{\dfrac{30\times(.1656667)^2}{30-1}[.8410485] + \dfrac{.5766667(1-.5766667)-.1656667^2}{30-1}}$$

$$= \frac{\dfrac{.8233620}{29}[.8410485]}{\dfrac{.8233620}{29}[.8410485] + \dfrac{.2166768}{29}}$$

$$= \frac{.0238787}{.0238787+.0074716} = \frac{.0238787}{.0313503} = .7616737 \approx .76$$

It is important to note that this result in calculating phi matches exactly the result obtained in a full set of generalizability procedures (including analysis of variance, estimation of G Study variance components, estimation of D Study variance components and finally calculation of the phi, or G coefficient for absolute error—all which are well beyond the scope of this book). In other words, although the full generalizability study would be clearer conceptually, precisely the same result has been obtained here using only n, k, $\overline{X}_p$, S_p and the K-R20 reliability.

There are several additional points related to these CRT consistency estimates that must be stressed. First, some of the coefficients presented in this chapter are related in rather predictable ways. Second, there are a number of cautions that must be kept in mind when making calculations—particularly for the phi coefficient.

Relationships. Certain predictable relationships exist between some of the NRT reliability coefficients and the phi dependability index. One interesting relationship that Brennan (1984, pp. 315–316) demonstrates is that, for a given test, K-R21 will always be less than Φ, which will in turn be less than K-R20, as follows:

K-R21 < Φ < K-R20

Using the example data in Table 7.5 (where K-R21 = .73; Φ = .76; and K-R20 = .84), it is clear that, indeed:

.73 < .76 < .84

This fact has one important implication: If K-R21 is indeed always lower than Φ, then K-R21 can be used as a conservative "rough and ready" underestimate of the domain-referenced dependability (Φ) of a test (Brennan 1984, pp. 331–332).

Cautions. In doing calculations for the phi or phi (lambda) estimates that I demonstrated in this chapter, three cautions must be observed. First, these formulas are only applicable when the items on the test are dichotomously scored (i.e., right or wrong). Second, the n formula (rather than the $n - 1$ formula) should be used in calculating the means and standard deviations of the proportion scores that are used in the phi and phi(lambda) formulas. Third, as much accuracy as possible should be used when doing all the calculations. In other words, throughout the calculations, as many places should be carried to the right of the decimal point as possible, which means that rounding should be avoided until the final coefficient is estimated.

In addition, the full-blown versions of phi and phi (lambda) coefficients are related to the variance components involved in the test; as Brennan states, "it is strongly recommended that whenever possible one report variance components, and estimate indices of dependability in terms of variance components" (1984, p. 332). Thus, if the resources are available for doing a full-fledged generalizability study, that is the best way to proceed.

Confidence Intervals

I must cover one last statistic in this section on CRT dependability, the *confidence interval* (CI). The CI functions for CRTs in a manner analogous to the standard error of measurement described for NRTs (Brennan 1984). More explicitly, the CI can be used to estimate a band around each student's score (plus or minus one CI) within which they would probably score with 68% probability if they were to take the test again. This thinking can also extend out to two bands plus or minus to obtain a 95% probability, or three bands for 98% probability. Formulaically, the confidence interval is as follows:

$$CI = \sqrt{\frac{\overline{X}_p(1 - \overline{X}_p) - S_p^2}{k - 1}}$$

where k = number of items

$\overline{X}_p$ = mean of proportion scores

S_p = standard deviation of proportion scores (using the N formula rather than $N - 1$)

For the example data shown in Table 7.5, the CI would be calculated as follows:

$$CI = \sqrt{\frac{\overline{X}_p(1 - \overline{X}_p) - S_{p^2}}{k - 1}}$$

$$= \sqrt{\frac{.5766667(1 - .5766667) - .1656667^2}{30 - 1}} = \sqrt{\frac{.2166768}{29}}$$

$$= \sqrt{.0074716} = .0864384 \approx .086$$

In interpreting such CIs, remember that it is a confidence interval for the proportion scores. Thus, the CI of .086 indicates that a student with a proportion score of .70 would score between .614 and .786 (or within a band of one CI plus or minus) 68% of the time if the test was repeatedly administered. In other words, the interpretation of the CI for CRT dependability is very much analogous to the interpretation for the SEM when it is applied to the interpretation of NRT reliability.

Factors Affecting the Consistency of CRTs

As with norm-referenced tests, a number of factors may affect the consistency of a criterion-referenced test. Many of these factors are exactly the same as those listed in Table 7.1. However, some factors are more directly under the control of the test developers than others. If all other factors are held constant, the following is usually true for CRT development:

1. a longer test tends to be more consistent than a short one
2. a well-designed and carefully written test tends to be more consistent than a shoddy one
3. a test made up of items that assess similar language material tends to be more consistent than a test that assesses a wide variety of material
4. a test with items that have relatively high difference indexes, or *B*-indexes, tends to be more consistent than a test with items that have low ones
5. a test that is clearly related to the objectives of instruction tends to be more consistent than a test that is not obviously related to what the students have learned

In other words, to maximize the possibility that a test designed for CRT purposes will be dependable, make sure that it is as long as possible, is well-designed and carefully written, assesses relatively homogeneous material, has items that produce high difference indexes or *B*-indexes, and is clearly related to the instructional objectives of the course or program in which it is used.

SUMMARY

In this chapter, I began by presenting a number of different sources of measurement error, which can be minimized to increase the meaningful variance on a test so that the test will successfully measure what it was designed to measure. I also covered a number of strategies for estimating the reliability of norm-referenced tests, including the test-retest, equivalent-forms, and internal-consistency strategies. The last of these was shown to have many variants, including the split-half (adjusted) strategy, Cronbach α, and the Kuder-Richardson formulas 20 and 21. I also explained interrater and intrarater reliability estimates, which aid in estimating the consistency of ratings of productive language tasks like compositions, role plays, and oral interviews. Then I discussed the SEM, which is used in decision making to identify a band of scores around decision points within which more information should be gathered about students before plunging ahead with a decision that could dramatically affect their lives. I ended the section on NRT reliability with a list of the most important factors to consider in trying to maximize the reliability of NRTs.

Next I explored some of the different options for analyzing the dependability of criterion-referenced tests. These options included the threshold loss agreement and kappa coefficients, the squared-error loss agreement phi (lambda) dependability index, and the domain score phi dependability index. I ended this section with a discussion of confidence intervals and a listing of the most important factors that influence the consistency of CRT scores.

Remember that test consistency is a desirable and necessary quality, but consistency is not sufficient unto itself. The *Test of English as a Foreign Language* (Educational Testing Service 1994) is considered a reliable test of overall ESL proficiency. The reliability coefficients tend to be very high and the SEM relatively low on this test (see Educational Testing Service 1992). If TOEFL were administered to a group of foreign students as a test of mathematical ability, it would probably remain reliable but would obviously not be valid in any logical sense for the purpose of testing mathematical ability. Likewise, if it were administered to a group of native speakers of English to determine their admissibility to college, it might prove reliable, but it would not make any sense to use the test for that purpose. TOEFL would not be valid for that purpose. Hence, test consistency and validity, though related, are quite different test characteristics, as I explain in the next chapter.

TERMS AND SYMBOLS

agreement

agreement coefficient (p_o)

alpha coefficient (α)

confidence interval (CI)

conservative estimate

Cronbach alpha (α)

decision consistency

dependability

domain-referenced tests (DRTs)

equivalent-forms reliability

error variance

internal-consistency reliability

interrater reliability

intrarater reliability

item variance

kappa coefficient (κ)

Kuder-Richardson formula 20 (K-R20)

Kuder-Richardson formula 21 (K-R21)

meaningful variance

measurement error

objectives-referenced tests (ORTs)

parallel-forms reliability

phi dependability index (Φ)

phi (lambda) dependability index $[\Phi(\lambda)]$

reliability coefficient $(r_{xx'})$

Spearman-Brown prophecy formula

split-half method

squared-error loss agreement

standard error of measurement (SEM)

test reliability

test consistency

test–retest reliability

testwiseness

threshold loss agreement

REVIEW QUESTIONS

1. What are some of the sources of measurement error? And how is measurement error related to the meaningful variance on a test?

2. Why are the procedures for NRT reliability estimation different from those for CRT reliability?

3. What are the three basic types of NRT reliability discussed in this chapter? What different statistical estimates are used for each?

4. What are interrater and intrarater reliability? For what types of tests would they be most appropriate?

5. Which of the three types of NRT reliability is the intrarater reliability most similar to? Why? And the interrater approach?

6. What is the standard error of measurement? For decision-making purposes, is it better to have a large or small SEM?

7. What are the factors that affect the dependability of a CRT, and what steps can you take to maximize such reliability?

8. What are the three basic types of CRT dependability discussed in this chapter? What different estimates are used for each?

9. What are the factors that affect the dependability of a CRT, and what steps can you take to maximize such dependability?

10. What are the necessary qualities of a good test? How does reliability/dependability relate to the other qualities? Is reliability/dependability sufficient unto itself?

APPLICATION EXERCISES

A. Table 7.11 shows the item responses for 30 students who took a 20-item NRT. As with Table 3.11 (p. 90), these data are for the Sri Lankan high-school students in Premaratne 1987. Notice that the IF values, 1 − IF, and IV are given at the bottom of the table and that the total scores as well as the odd-numbered and even-numbered scores are given in the columns to the right. In the bottom right corner, you will also find the mean and standard deviation for the total scores, the odd-numbered scores, and the even-numbered scores. Given the information in Table 7.11, calculate each of the following reliability estimates:

A1. Cronbach α =

A2. K-R21 =

A3. K-R20 =

A4. Split-half reliability (remember to use the half-test correlation and Spearman-Brown Prophecy formula) =

B. What do the reliability estimates that you calculated in exercises A1–A4 mean to you in terms of consistency of this test as an NRT?

C. What would the SEM be (based on the K-R20 estimate that you found)?

D. If you had a set of scores assigned by two raters to 30 compositions, you would have two scores for each student. How would you determine the degree to which the scores given by the raters were consistent? What is this type of reliability called? What application of the Spearman-Brown Prophecy formula should you make in calculating interrater reliability?

E. Figure 7.3 shows a hypothetical set of master/non-master classifications for a CRT administered on two occasions 10 days apart. Given the information in Figure 7.3, calculate each of the following CRT reliability estimates:

E1. agreement coefficient =

E2. kappa coefficient =

F. Table 7.12 shows the item responses for 30 students who took a 30-item CRT. Assume that the cut-point is a raw score of 24 (80%), or a proportion of .80 on this CRT and that the K-R20 estimate is .6471832. Notice that the IF values, 1 − IF, and IV are given at the bottom of the table and that the proportion scores are given in the columns to the right. In the bottom right corner, you will also find the mean and standard deviation for the total scores and the proportion scores. Given the information in Table 7.12, calculate each of the following dependability estimates:

F1. agreement coefficient (you will also need to use Table 7.9 to do this) =

F2. kappa coefficient (you will also need to use Table 7.10 to do this) =

F3. phi (lambda) dependability index =

F4. phi dependability index =

Table 7.11: Reliability Application for NRTs

ID Number											Item Number												
	2	3	4	5	7	8	11	12	13	14	15	16	17	21	22	24	25	26	27	30	Total	Odd	Even
2	1	1	1	1	1	1	1	1	1	1	1	1	1	1	1	1	1	1	1	1	20	10	10
20	1	1	1	1	1	1	1	1	1	1	1	1	1	1	1	1	0	1	1	1	19	9	10
1	1	1	1	1	1	1	1	1	1	1	0	1	1	1	1	1	0	1	1	1	18	8	10
29	1	1	1	1	1	1	1	1	1	0	1	0	1	1	0	1	1	1	1	1	17	10	7
12	1	1	1	1	1	1	1	1	1	1	1	0	0	1	0	1	0	1	1	1	15	7	8
17	1	1	1	1	1	1	1	0	1	0	1	0	0	1	0	1	0	1	1	1	13	7	6
4	1	0	1	1	1	1	1	0	1	0	1	0	1	1	0	0	0	1	1	1	13	8	5
5	1	0	1	1	1	1	1	0	1	0	1	0	0	1	0	1	0	1	1	1	13	7	6
16	1	1	1	1	1	1	1	0	1	0	1	0	0	1	0	0	0	1	1	1	12	7	5
3	1	1	1	1	1	1	1	0	1	0	1	0	0	1	0	0	0	1	1	1	12	7	5
18	1	1	1	1	1	1	1	0	0	0	1	0	0	1	0	0	0	1	1	1	11	6	5
19	1	1	1	1	1	1	1	0	1	0	1	0	0	1	0	0	0	1	1	0	11	7	4
27	1	1	1	1	1	1	1	0	1	0	1	0	0	1	0	0	0	1	1	0	11	7	4
30	1	0	1	1	1	1	1	0	0	0	1	0	0	1	0	0	1	1	1	1	11	6	5
6	1	0	1	1	1	1	1	0	0	0	1	0	0	1	0	0	1	1	1	1	11	6	5
8	1	0	1	1	1	1	1	0	0	0	1	0	0	1	0	0	0	1	1	0	10	6	4
24	1	0	1	1	1	1	0	0	0	0	1	0	0	1	0	0	0	1	1	1	10	5	5
9	1	1	1	1	1	1	1	0	0	0	1	0	0	1	0	0	0	1	0	0	10	6	4
21	1	0	1	1	1	1	1	0	0	0	1	0	0	1	0	0	0	1	0	0	9	5	4
22	1	1	1	1	1	1	0	0	0	0	1	0	0	1	0	0	0	1	0	0	9	5	4
14	1	0	1	1	1	1	0	0	0	0	0	0	0	1	0	0	0	1	0	1	8	3	5
15	1	0	1	1	1	1	0	0	0	0	0	0	0	1	0	0	0	1	0	0	7	3	4
10	1	0	1	1	1	1	0	0	0	0	0	0	0	1	0	0	0	1	0	0	7	3	4
23	0	0	1	1	1	1	0	0	0	0	1	0	0	1	0	0	0	0	0	0	6	4	2
13	1	1	1	1	0	1	0	0	0	0	0	0	1	0	0	0	0	0	0	0	6	3	3
25	0	0	1	1	1	0	0	0	0	0	1	0	0	1	0	0	0	0	1	0	6	5	1
28	0	0	1	1	0	1	0	0	0	0	0	0	1	0	0	0	0	1	0	0	5	3	2
7	1	1	0	1	0	1	0	0	0	0	0	0	0	0	0	0	0	0	0	0	5	2	3
26	1	0	0	1	1	0	1	0	0	0	0	0	0	0	0	0	0	0	0	0	5	3	2
11	0	0	0	1	1	0	0	0	0	0	1	0	0	1	0	0	0	0	1	0	5	5	0
IF	.7667	.2000	.8667	.8000	.8000	.8667	.6667	.2333	.4667	.2333	.7333	.1333	.4333	.9000	.1333	.3000	.2000	.7000	.7000	.3667	10.50	5.77	4.73 Mean
1 − IF	.2333	.8000	.1333	.2000	.2000	.1333	.3333	.7667	.5333	.7667	.2667	.8667	.5667	.1000	.8667	.7000	.8000	.3000	.3000	.6333	4.18	2.11	2.39 S
IV	.1789	.1600	.1156	.1600	.1600	.1156	.2222	.1789	.2489	.1789	.1956	.1156	.2456	.0900	.1156	.2100	.1600	.2100	.2100	.2922			

$\Sigma \text{IV} = 3.50$

ADMINISTRATION 2

	Masters	Non-masters	
Masters	51	10	61
Non-masters	15	24	39
	66	34	100

ADMINISTRATION 1

Figure 7.3:   Application for Hypothetical Master/Non-master Classifications on Two
Administrations of a Test

Table 7.12: Reliability Application for CRTs

ID Number	1	2	3	4	5	6	7	8	9	10	11	12	13	14	15	16	17	18	19	20	21	22	23	24	25	26	27	28	29	30	Total	Prop.
12	1	1	1	1	1	1	1	1	1	1	1	1	1	1	1	1	1	1	1	1	1	1	1	1	1	1	1	1	1	0	29	0.9667
2	1	1	1	1	1	1	1	1	1	1	1	1	1	1	1	1	1	1	1	1	1	1	1	1	1	1	1	1	1	0	29	0.9667
1	0	1	1	1	1	1	1	1	1	1	1	1	1	1	1	1	1	1	1	1	1	1	1	1	1	0	1	1	1	1	28	0.9333
20	1	1	1	1	1	1	1	1	1	1	1	1	1	1	1	1	1	0	1	1	1	1	1	1	1	1	1	1	1	0	28	0.9333
29	1	1	1	1	1	1	1	1	1	1	1	1	0	1	1	1	1	1	1	1	1	1	1	1	1	0	1	1	1	0	27	0.9000
6	1	1	1	1	0	1	1	0	1	1	1	1	1	1	1	1	0	1	1	1	1	1	1	1	1	1	1	1	1	0	26	0.8667
19	1	1	1	1	1	1	1	1	1	0	1	1	1	1	1	1	1	1	0	1	1	1	0	1	1	0	1	1	1	0	25	0.8333
4	1	1	1	1	1	1	1	0	1	1	1	1	1	1	1	1	1	1	0	1	1	1	1	1	1	0	1	0	1	0	25	0.8333
21	1	1	1	1	1	1	1	1	0	1	1	1	1	1	0	0	1	1	1	1	1	1	1	0	1	1	1	0	0	1	24	0.8000
18	1	1	1	1	1	1	1	1	1	1	1	1	1	1	0	1	1	1	1	0	1	1	0	1	1	1	1	0	0	0	24	0.8000
27	1	1	1	1	1	1	1	1	1	1	1	1	1	1	0	1	1	1	1	0	1	1	1	1	1	1	0	0	0	0	24	0.8000
13	1	1	1	1	1	1	1	0	1	1	1	1	1	0	1	0	0	1	0	0	1	1	1	1	1	1	1	1	1	0	23	0.7667
7	1	1	1	1	0	1	1	0	1	1	1	1	1	1	1	0	0	1	0	0	1	1	1	1	1	1	1	1	1	0	23	0.7667
30	1	1	0	1	1	1	0	1	1	0	0	1	1	1	1	0	1	0	1	1	1	1	1	1	1	1	1	1	1	0	23	0.7667
3	1	1	1	1	0	1	1	1	1	1	1	1	1	1	0	0	1	1	1	0	1	1	1	1	1	1	1	0	0	0	23	0.7667
9	1	1	1	1	1	1	1	0	1	1	1	1	1	0	1	0	0	1	0	0	1	1	1	1	1	1	1	1	1	0	23	0.7667
25	1	1	0	0	1	1	1	1	0	0	1	1	1	1	1	0	1	1	1	0	1	1	1	1	1	1	0	1	1	0	22	0.7333
15	1	1	0	1	1	1	1	1	0	0	0	0	1	1	1	0	1	1	1	0	1	1	1	1	1	1	1	1	1	0	22	0.7333
24	1	1	0	1	1	0	1	1	0	0	0	1	1	1	1	0	1	1	1	0	1	1	1	0	1	1	1	1	1	0	21	0.7000
22	1	1	1	1	1	0	0	0	0	1	1	1	1	1	1	0	0	1	1	0	1	1	1	0	1	1	1	1	1	0	21	0.7000
8	1	1	0	1	1	0	0	1	0	0	1	1	1	0	1	0	1	1	1	0	1	1	1	1	1	1	1	1	1	0	21	0.7000
14	1	1	0	1	1	0	0	1	0	1	1	0	1	1	1	0	0	1	1	0	1	1	1	1	1	1	1	1	1	0	21	0.7000
26	1	1	0	1	1	0	1	1	0	0	0	1	1	1	1	0	1	1	1	0	1	1	1	1	1	1	0	1	1	0	21	0.7000
16	1	1	1	0	1	0	0	1	0	1	0	0	1	1	1	0	1	1	1	0	1	1	1	1	0	1	1	1	0	0	19	0.6333
28	1	1	1	0	1	0	0	1	0	1	0	1	0	1	1	0	1	1	1	0	1	1	1	1	0	1	1	1	0	0	19	0.6333
5	1	1	1	0	0	0	0	1	0	1	0	1	1	1	1	0	1	1	1	0	1	1	1	1	0	1	1	1	0	0	19	0.6333
23	1	1	1	0	1	0	0	1	0	1	0	1	1	1	0	0	1	1	1	0	1	1	1	1	1	0	1	0	0	0	18	0.6000
17	1	1	1	0	1	0	0	1	0	1	0	1	1	1	0	0	1	1	0	0	1	1	0	1	0	1	1	1	1	0	18	0.6000
11	1	1	1	0	1	0	0	1	0	1	0	1	1	0	0	0	1	1	0	0	1	1	1	1	0	1	1	1	1	0	18	0.6000
10	1	0	1	0	1	0	0	0	0	1	0	1	1	1	0	0	0	1	0	0	1	1	1	1	1	1	1	1	1	0	17	0.5667
IF	.9667	.9667	.7667	.7333	.8667	.6000	.6333	.7667	.5000	.7667	.6333	.9000	.9333	.8667	.7333	.3333	.7667	.9333	.7333	.3333	1.0000	1.0000	.9000	.9000	.8333	.8333	.9000	.8000	.7333	.0667		
1 – IF	.0333	.0333	.2333	.2667	.1333	.4000	.3667	.2333	.5000	.2333	.3667	.1000	.0667	.1333	.2667	.6667	.2333	.0667	.2667	.6667	.0000	.0000	.1000	.1000	.1667	.1667	.1000	.2000	.2667	.9333		
IV	.0322	.0322	.1789	.1956	.1156	.2400	.2322	.1789	.2500	.1789	.2322	.0900	.0622	.1156	.1956	.2222	.1789	.0622	.1956	.2222	.0000	.0000	.0900	.0900	.1389	.1389	.0900	.1600	.1956	.0622		

Σ IV = 4.1767

Total: Mean 22.7000, S 3.3481

Prop.: Mean 0.7566667, S 0.1116033

CHAPTER 8

TEST VALIDITY AND STANDARDS SETTING

In the previous chapter, I argued that consistency is a necessary and important quality that should be monitored in tests; however, consistency is not sufficient unto itself for claiming that a test is doing a good job. For example, the *Test of English as a Foreign Language* is considered a reliable test of EFL proficiency. The reliability coefficients reported in the *TOEFL Test and Score Manual: 1992–93 Edition* (Educational Testing Service 1992) were as follows: Listening Comprehension = .89, Structure and Written Expression = .86, Vocabulary and Reading Comprehension = .90, and Total Scores = .95. The corresponding SEM values were reported to be fairly low at 2.2, 2.8, 2.3, and 14.1, respectively. Thus, focusing solely on reliability, this test could only be described as a very good measure.

However, validity is a separate but equally important issue. For instance, if the TOEFL were administered to a group of foreign students as a test of their abilities in mathematics, the reliability would be high because the test would spread the students out rather consistently along a continuum of scores. However, as discussed at the end of the previous chapter, the TOEFL is clearly not valid for the purpose of testing mathematical ability. This is not to say that anyone ever claimed that TOEFL should be used to test mathematics or that TOEFL is not valid for measuring proficiency in EFL. The point is that, a test can be reliable without being valid. In other words, a test can consistently measure something other than that for which it was designed. Hence, test reliability and validity, though related, are different test characteristics. In fact, reliability is a precondition for validity but not sufficient for purposes of judging overall test quality. Validity must also be carefully examined.

Test validity is defined here as the degree to which a test measures what it claims, or purports, to be measuring. (Note that "Measurement people don't find too many occasions to use the word *purport*, hence they love to employ it when defining validity" Popham 1981, p. 98). If a test claims to measure Indonesian speaking proficiency, then the test should measure the ability to speak Indonesian. If another test purports to assess proficiency in German listening comprehension, that is just what it should assess. Validity is especially important for all the decisions that teachers regularly make about their students. Teachers certainly want to base their admissions, placement, achievement, and diagnostic decisions on tests that are actually testing what they claim to test. Adopting, developing, and adapting tests for such decisions is difficult enough without having to worry about whether the tests are measuring the wrong student characteristics, abilities, proficiencies, and so on. Hence, in all cases, after ensuring that a test is practical and reliable, teachers should consider its validity.

Three main strategies exist for investigating the validity of a test: content validity, construct validity, and criterion-related validity. Once again, it is necessary to distinguish between NRTs and CRTs in terms of how the results are analyzed. Recall that NRTs are designed to produce a normal distribution with relatively high variance among the scores. In contrast, CRTs are designed to measure what has been learned and therefore cannot be expected to necessarily produce variance among scores (for instance, if all the students know all the material).

Only the content and construct validity strategies are applicable for analyzing the validity of CRTs because these two strategies do not depend on the magnitude of the variance in the test scores. The third strategy, criterion-related validity, does not lend itself to investigating the validity of CRTs because it is based on correlational analysis. Since the distributions of scores on CRTs may be skewed, especially when they are working well, the assumption of normal distribution, which underlies correlational analysis, is not met. Hence, the results of a criterion-related validity study for a CRT would be difficult, if not impossible, to interpret. NRTs, on the other hand, can be analyzed from all three perspectives: content, construct, and criterion-related.

Regardless of which strategy testers decide to use to demonstrate and defend the validity of a test, the strongest arguments are built around at least two, or (for NRTs) all three, of these perspectives. Notice that I am advocating that test developers "defend" and build "arguments" for the validity of their tests. I strongly feel that test developers are responsible for convincing test users that their product is testing what it claims to measure.

As mentioned earlier, the content and construct validity strategies are each appropriate for investigating the validity of both NRTs and CRTs. Content and construct validity are therefore covered here under one major heading. The third approach, criterion-related validity, which depends rather heavily on test score variance, is suitable primarily for NRTs, so criterion-related validity is covered in a section of its own, followed by a discussion of a naturally related issue: the matter of setting standards, or cut-points, on a test.

VALIDITY STRATEGIES APPLICABLE TO BOTH NRTS AND CRTS

Content Validity

In order to investigate *content validity*, testers must decide whether the test is a representative sample of the content of whatever the test was designed to measure. To address this issue, testers or some of their colleagues usually end up making some sort of judgments. To maximize the efficiency of these judgments, the testers may need to focus particularly on the organization of the different types of items that they include on the test and on the specifications for each of those item types. This content validation process may take many forms, depending on the particular language teaching situation and staff, but the goal should always be to establish an argument that the test is a representative sample of the content that the test claims to measure.

Overall strategy for establishing content validity. Consider the problems involved in adopting, developing, or adapting a Tagalog listening comprehension proficiency test. The first step might be to decide what the test should be designed to measure—that is, what it will actually be claiming to measure. Going back to the test's original purpose, the test will be designed to measure Tagalog listening proficiency. That purpose is all well and good, but what is Tagalog listening proficiency? To figure out the nature of Tagalog listening proficiency, it may help to analyze it into its component parts. Perhaps such analysis will lead those responsible for putting a test in place to decide that Tagalog listening proficiency is made up of distinguishing minimal pairs, understanding vocabulary in context, listening for facts, listening for inference, listening for gist, listening for main ideas, among a number of other testing objectives. The testers might then want to talk to their teaching colleagues to get their ideas on the components of Tagalog listening proficiency. Thus, thinking about the validity of a test may initially involve defining what it is that the testers wanted to measure in the first place. If they cannot define what they wanted to assess, how can they possibly determine the degree to which the test is measuring it?

Assuming that the testers and their teaching colleagues reach a consensus on what they want to test, they might find that no such measure exists and that they will either have to compromise what they want to test or develop a test of their own. Being uncompromisingly professional and ethical, they all decide to develop a new test that will be valid for the purpose of testing Tagalog listening proficiency, as defined by their group of teachers. They would then want to outline and organize the different types of items that they have identified as important and decide how many of each they want to end up with on the final version of the test.

The test developers should also write out item specifications if at all possible for each of the testing objectives that they have collectively identified as components of Tagalog listening proficiency. As explained in Chapter 3, item specifications include a general description, a sample item, stimulus attributes, response attributes, and supplemental lists. Recall also that the purpose of each item specification is to make it possible for any item writer to produce items that test about the same thing. Thus, clear item specifications can help to make items much more consistent and also more valid in the sense that, when specifications are used, the items are more likely to match those specifications, which in turn match the objectives of the test. Also note that this match between the items and the specifications can be verified and incorporated as part of the argument for the content validity of the test.

Whether or not testers use formal item specifications, they will probably want to get together with the other teachers and write items for each of the testing objectives that they feel are important to Tagalog listening proficiency. They will need to write enough items (50–100% more than they need in the final version of the test) so they can throw some of them out in the revision process. In the end, they must have enough items left so each testing objective can be adequately represented on the test.

Once they have administered the test and revised the test using the appropriate item analysis strategies, they will want to examine the descriptive statistics, calculate a reliability coefficient or two, and look at the SEM. At that point, they will be in a position to explore the content validity of their new test. One way to do this would be to convene a panel of Tagalog listening comprehension experts to judge the degree to which the items on their new test actually do represent the testing objectives of Tagalog listening proficiency.

If those experts disagree as to whether the items represent the proficiency in question and its underlying elements, the testers may have to return to the drawing board for at least some portions of the test. If, on the other hand, the experts agree that the test is representative of Tagalog listening proficiency, the testers would have built at least one argument for the content validity of their test for purposes of testing Tagalog listening proficiency as defined by them and their colleagues and confirmed by experts. Unfortunately, this procedure is only accurate to the extent that the biases of the experts do not interfere with their judgments. Hence, test developers may wish to take certain steps to ensure that the experts' judgments are as unclouded as possible.

First, the testers should ensure that the experts really are experts and that, at least to a degree, the experts share the kinds of professional viewpoints that the testers and their colleagues have. In other words, if the group developing the test favors the *ACTFL Proficiency Guidelines* (American Council on the Teaching of Foreign Languages 1986) as the way of defining language proficiency, they probably should not bring in experts who have written articles criticizing those guidelines (for example, Savignon 1985; or Bachman & Savignon 1986). Similarly, if the testers favor a communicative approach to language teaching, they would be foolish to invite experts who believe firmly in teaching structures, structures, and more structures. On the other hand, testers will probably never find experts who agree 100% with their definition and categories of items for Tagalog listening proficiency. This is fine. After all, the testers and their colleagues may be able to learn something from the activity of having experts look at their test items. If nothing else, the experts may provide insights or points of view that the testers never would have considered. In short, sometimes an outsider's fresh perspective can help.

Second, the test developers must recognize that judgments of the quality of individual items may not be absolutely clear-cut and black-and-white. An item may be a 70% or 80% match with what the test developers want to test. In other words, such judgments are sometimes a matter of degrees rather than a pure and simple thumbs up or thumbs down. Therefore, the test developers may want to provide the experts with some sort of rating scale. Such a scale should be designed to help them focus in on each item to make as objective a judgment as possible. At the same time, the particular scale that test developers use will depend on the type of information and the amount of detail that they need. For instance, testers might have a need for each item to be judged on a scale from 1–5 that represents a continuum from "bad item" to "good item." In another situation, testers might benefit more from a rating sheet that simply asks the expert to estimate the percent of match to the testing goals. Or, perhaps, a group of testers needs even more information and therefore decides to have three 1–5 scales for each item: one for the form of the item, a second for the content, and a third for match to the overall goals of the course.

Table 8.1 shows one such scale, which was developed for judging the validity of a Tagalog listening proficiency test developed at UHM (Brown et al. 1990, 1991) Notice that the overall layout of the rating sheet focuses the expert's attention on the individual test questions. The stems are given in capital letters because they were actually heard on audiotape by the students (rather than written above the options). However, the students are asked to read the four options as shown and select the one that makes the

Table 8.1: Content Validity Judgment Scale[†]

SEASSI Proficiency Examination Listening Comprehension Subtest	Name_____				
	Match to ACTFL Guidelines				
	No Match				**Perfect Match**

Intermediate–Low

13) MAGKANO MO IPINAGBIBILI ANG TELEBISYONG ITO?
  A. Opo, ang mahal.
  B. Isa po.
  K. P6,000.00 po.*
  D. Cash lang po.
	1	2	3	4	5

14) NASAAN KA NITONG NAKARAANG SABADO AT LINGGO?
  A. Noong Linggo.
  B. Nasa Baguio po.*
  K. Dalawang araw po sa isang linggo.
  D. Tanghali na po akong gumising noong Linggo.
	1	2	3	4	5

15) PAPASOK KA BA SA ESKUWELAHAN BUKAS?
  A. Opo, dahil kailangang pumasok.*
  B. Opo, pumasok po ako.
  K. Bukas po ang pasok sa eskuwela.
  D. May pasok po.
	1	2	3	4	5

16) ANO ANG GINAGAWA NIYA SA KANYANG LIBRENG ORAS?
  A. Wala rin po siyang gaanong pera.
  B. Nagtratrabaho po siya mula 8:00 hanggang 5:00.
  K. Nagbibihis na po siya ngayon.
  D. Lumalangoy po siya.*
	1	2	3	4	5

17) ANO ANG KAPITAL NG KANLURANG ALEMANYA, BONN
O BERLIN?
  A. Bonn o Berlin po lamang.
  B. Bonn po.*
  K. Opo, iyon nga.
  D. Opo, ang mga iyon nga.
	1	2	3	4	5

18) ILANG WIKA ANG SINASALITA MO?
  A. Bansang Hapon po lamang.
  B. Napakahusay po.
  K. Dalawa po lamang.*
  D. Opo, pero hindi mahusay.
	1	2	3	4	5

19) NASISIYAHAN KA BA SA BAGO MONG KOTSE?
  A. Opo, ang husay ng takbo.*
  B. Opo, ang pangit. [Yes, it's ugly.]
  K. Meron po akong bagong kotse.
  D. Hindi po, ang galing.
	1	2	3	4	5

20) MAS MATANDA BA SA IYO ANG KAPATID MONG BABAE?
  A. Hindi po, mas matanda siya.
  B. Hindi po, mas bata siya.*
  K. Hindi po, bata siya.
  D. Hindi po, matanda siya.
	1	2	3	4	5

*Correct answer.
[†]From Brown, Ramos, Cook, & Lockhart 1990.

most sense as a response to the taped utterance. Notice that the items are being rated on a scale that asks for the expert to rate the degree to which the item matches the ACTFL Guidelines. Since the items had originally been developed to match the nine different levels described for listening comprehension proficiency in the *ACTFL Proficiency Guidelines*, that scale was considered appropriate for experts to use in rating each item on a scale of 1–5 for the degree of match to those descriptions. Handled as a separate but related issue was whether or not the items (and indirectly the ACTFL descriptions) were an adequate reflection of what they expected of their students at each level.

Naturally, this example is not perfect. For one thing, the experts were being asked to judge the degree of match between an item and a description that itself may have some serious problems (see Savignon 1985; or Bachman & Savignon 1986). This scale nevertheless provided us with useful and interesting information about our new listening test.

The reader may have noticed that Table 8.1 is very similar to Table 3.8 (p. 78) in the chapter on item analysis. That is correct. All of what was presented about item quality (including Tables 3.1–3.3, pp. 51, 54, and 58) and content analysis (including Table 3.8) has direct bearing on content validity. The discussion in Chapter 3 was simply focused on the single item level, whereas this discussion covers the overall validity of a group of items taken together as a test or subtest. That overall validity will nevertheless be highly related to the individual item validities.

An example of the importance of item planning. In the process of developing a test like the one described above, good planning can aid in creating a sound test as well as in building a strong argument for the content validity of that test. Sound planning involves working out a rational blueprint for what to include in the test and in approximately what proportions. Thus, test developers should be very careful about planning the test objectives and specifying the types and proportions of items that will appear.

Consider the following plan, which was used to develop items for tests designed to measure non-native speakers in their engineering-English reading and listening abilities (described in more detail in Brown 1984c, 1988b; or Erickson & Molloy 1983). In 1979, a group of seven graduate students at UCLA (including myself) set out to develop tests for this purpose. We were breaking new ground with this test development project, and we soon discovered that nobody had any idea what the components of engineering-English reading ability might be. After consulting with engineering professors and examining the literature on English for specific purposes (ESP), we decided to test as broad a spectrum of item types as we could and, in the process, discovered that our perspectives as linguists were quite different from those of the engineering professors. As a result, we found that two distinct categories of item types emerged in our plan: one that we labeled linguistic factors and another that we called engineering factors. The individual item types for each category were as follows:

I. Linguistic factors
  A. Cohesion (after Halliday and Hasan 1976)
    1. Reference items
    2. Substitution items
    3. Lexical cohesion items
    4. Conjunction items
  B. Non-technical vocabulary items

II. Engineering factors
  A. Fact items
  B. Inference items
  C. Lexis (after Cowan 1974; and Inman 1978)
    1. Subtechnical vocabulary items
    2. Technical vocabulary items
  D. Scientific rhetorical function items (after Lackstrom, Selinker, & Trimble 1973; and Selinker, Todd-Trimble, & Trimble 1976, 1978)

Two sets of tests were developed in this project: three for reading comprehension and three for lecture listening. The three reading comprehension tests were developed from three reading passages taken from sophomore-level engineering textbooks. For each of the three reading passages, we wrote three to five items for each of the item types in the plan outlined above. The lecture listening tests were similarly developed from three videotapes of engineering lectures with the same overall item organization plan. Because we were trying to produce a new type of test for which there were no precedents, we had necessarily planned very carefully, basing our selection of item types on the best available information in ESP and on the insights of engineering professors who knew the material. Since we were also trying to create three reading and three lecture listening tests that were more or less parallel, we felt the need to lay out our item plan very clearly before charging ahead. The net result was that we developed the tests, and the item plan became part of the argument for the validity of the tests.

Content validity and other types of validity. One problem that may arise in looking exclusively at the content validity of a test is that the performance of the particular group of students who took the test can be overlooked. In the same sense that a test can only be said to be reliable for a particular group of students (or very similar students), a test can only be said to be valid for testing a particular kind of student. Put another way, in language testing, the students who are tested in development process on a test become part of the definition of that purpose because language tests must be designed with particular students in mind, based on ability levels, language backgrounds, nationalities, educational levels, and so forth. As a result, a test can only be considered reliable and valid for a particular context (or for contexts that are very similar), and context is defined by the type of decision involved and the type of students involved, as well as by the testing objectives.

The effectiveness of a content validity strategy can be enhanced by making sure that the experts are truly experts in the appropriate field and that they have adequate and appropriate tools in the form of rating scales so that their judgments can be sound and focused. However, testers should never rest on their laurels. Once they have established that a test has adequate content validity, they must immediately explore other kinds of validity arguments (construct or criterion-related) so that they can assess the validity of the test in terms related to the specific performances of the types of students for whom the test was designed in the first place.

Construct Validity

An understanding of the concept of a psychological construct is prerequisite to understanding *construct validity*. A *psychological construct* is an attribute, proficiency, ability, or skill defined in psychological theories. Consider, for example, "love." Love is a name for a very complex emotion that goes on in human beings. Everyone knows about it, and everyone accepts that it exists. Yet love goes on largely inside the individuals involved and is therefore very difficult to observe (except for the well-known and highly observable tendency among those in love to bump into walls). Nevertheless, love is an example of a psychological construct. It goes on; it is accepted; yet it is hard to observe because it goes on inside of the head. Some other psychological constructs that are more pertinent to the topic at hand are language aptitude, intelligence, Thai speaking proficiency, overall English as a second language proficiency, and so forth.

Since these constructs occur inside the brain, they must be observed indirectly if they are to be observed at all. This job often falls to the language tester because only through tests (broadly defined) can such constructs be measured efficiently. In terms of test validity, the major problem with psychological constructs is that testers cannot take a construct out of the students' brains and show that a test is in fact measuring it. The only recourse is to demonstrate indirectly through some kind of experiment that a given test is measuring a particular construct. Since such demonstrations are always indirect, the results must be interpreted very carefully. Nonetheless, such experiments are the most straightforward strategy available to testers for establishing the construct validity of a test. The experiment may take numerous forms, but the easiest to understand initially are the differential-group and intervention types of studies.

Differential-groups studies. Sometimes studies are designed to compare the performances of two groups on a test. Such studies are called *differential-groups studies* because, in conducting such a study, the tester is trying to show that the test differentiates between groups: one group that obviously has the construct being measured, and another that clearly does not have it (much like what I explained in Chapter 3 about the difference index). For instance, consider the Tagalog listening proficiency construct discussed previously. If I wanted to demonstrate the construct validity of that test, I might locate two groups of students who are similar in all ways except that one group has no Tagalog listening comprehension ability, while the other group has the ability. I could, of course, compare the performance of native Tagalog speakers with the performance of individuals who had never heard a single word of Tagalog, but this would be illogical and would load the results in favor of finding that my test is valid. Such a strategy would be illogical because the purpose of the Tagalog listening proficiency test would never be to separate the native speakers of Tagalog from absolute non-speakers of the language. The purpose would more likely be to spread out students who are studying Tagalog as a foreign language along a continuum of abilities from beginner to very advanced. Since "purpose" is what validity is all about, I would probably want to set up my differential-groups study so that I could demonstrate that the test is indeed differentiating among students who range from beginners to very advanced students of Tagalog as a foreign language.

To do this, I could find a group of second-year Tagalog students, a group of first-year Tagalog students, and perhaps another group of first-semester students. I could then administer the Tagalog listening test to all these students and analyze the results. If the second-year students scored high on the test, while the first-year students scored relatively low, and the first-semester students scored lowest of all, I would have a fairly strong argument for the construct validity of the test. In other words, I would have shown that the test differentiates between students who have a great deal of the Tagalog listening proficiency construct (second-year Tagalog students) and those who have little of the construct (first-year students); I would have further demonstrated that the test differentiates between those who have a little of the construct (first-year students) and those who have *very* little of it (first-semester students). Especially when coupled with evidence of content and/or criterion-related validity, this line of reasoning forms a convincing argument that the test is measuring the construct that it was designed to measure.

A more concrete example of a construct validity study is provided by the engineering-English testing project described above. The three engineering-English reading tests were analyzed and revised to form a single three-passage test with 20 items for each passage and 60 items altogether. The next step was to establish the validity of the new 60-item reading test. We had already contributed to the necessary arguments for the test validity by carefully planning with engineering professors and defining various theoretical categories of item types that we wanted to pilot. The next step was to administer the test and find out how well we had measured what we thought we were assessing.

To this end, a differential-groups experiment was set up to address the validity question both at the total test score level and at the individual item type level. The question was whether our test was valid for purposes of measuring overall engineering-English reading ability for norm-referenced decisions about foreign engineering students who wanted to study in English-speaking countries. All the students in this differential-groups study were graduate students and were studying either at UCLA or at Zhongshan University in the People's Republic of China (PRC). Two nationalities were tested: native speakers of English who were Americans, and non-native speakers of English who were Chinese from the PRC. Two academic majors were also involved: engineers and non-engineers (all humanities students in the sense that they had varied backgrounds at the undergraduate level but were currently doing graduate work in TESL/TEFL). Four groups were formed in this differential-groups study based on their majors and nationalities (see Figure 8.1): (a) American engineers, (b) American TESL/TEFL, (c) Chinese engineers, and (d) Chinese TESL/TEFL. There were 29 students in each of these groups.

After the test was administered to these four groups of students and the reliability was investigated (K-R20 was .85 for the targeted foreign students), descriptive statistics were calculated as shown in Figure 8.1. Not surprisingly, the American engineers scored highest with a mean of 50.52 out of 60, and the Chinese non-engineers (TESL/TEFL) scored lowest with a mean of 27.38. In addition, all engineers together had a mean of 43.74, thereby outscoring the TESL/TEFL students, who had a combined mean of 36.09. This alone would lend credence to our validity argument in the sense that the test was clearly tapping something related to engineering reading ability. Since our focus was on the foreign students, the construct validity of the test was further supported by the fact that the Chinese engineers also

	MAJOR		
	Engineer	TESL/TEFL	
American	$\overline{X} = 50.52$ $n = 29$	$\overline{X} = 44.79$ $n = 29$	$\overline{X} = 47.66$ $n = 58$
NATIONALITY			
Chinese	$\overline{X} = 36.97$ $n = 29$	$\overline{X} = 27.38$ $n = 29$	$\overline{X} = 32.17$ $n = 58$
	$\overline{X} = 43.74$ $n = 58$	$\overline{X} = 36.09$ $n = 58$	

Figure 8.1: Means and Marginals for Differential Groups (in Brown 1984c)

outscored their non-engineer countrymen, with means of 36.97 and 27.38, respectively.

Using analysis of variance procedures (ANOVA), the mean differences between nationalities and between majors were found to be statistically significant at $p < .01$, as shown in Table 8.2. A full explanation of ANOVA is well beyond the scope of this book (for more on the topic, see Brown 1988a; Butler 1985; Hatch & Farhady 1982; Hatch & Lazaraton 1990; Woods, Fletcher, & Hughes 1986). However, notice that "Source" in an ANOVA table (like that shown in Table 8.2) refers to the *source* of variance measured. In this case, both academic major (engineers versus TESL/TEFL students) and nationality (Americans versus Chinese) are contributing to significant differences among the means of the four groups. In other words, ANOVA is used to investigate whether differences among group means are significantly different from each other, in the same sense that correlation coefficients can be shown to be significantly different from zero (as I explained in Chapter 6). The particular ANOVA used here indicates that I can be 99% sure ($p < .01$) that the mean differences observed between engineers and TESL/TEFL students (Major), as well as between Americans and Chinese (Nationality) are due to factors other than chance. In short, the test appears to differentiate between engineers and non-engineers, as well as between natives and non-natives, for other than chances reasons. Hence, this differential-groups study can be used to argue for the construct validity of our test for purposes of measuring engineering-English reading proficiency.

An intriguing question that remained was why the native TESL/TEFL students (non-engineers), who had a mean of 44.79, outscored by nearly eight points the Chinese engineers, who had a mean of 36.97. Was it possible that engineering-English reading ability as measured in this test was more reliant on language ability than on engineering factors?

Table 8.2: Results of Two-way ANOVA[†]

Source	SS	df	MS	F
Major	1699.45	1	1699.45	35.88*
Nationality	6951.76	1	6951.76	146.75*
Major × Nationality	108.14	1	108.14	2.28
Residual (error)	5305.65	112	47.37	
Total	14064.99	115	122.30	

*p < .01
[†]From Brown 1984c.

To investigate this question, omega squared analysis was performed. Again, a full explanation of this form of statistical analysis is beyond the scope of this book (see Guilford & Fruchter 1973 for a clear description of this procedure). In a nutshell, this type of analysis is derived from the results of an ANOVA—in this case, the ANOVA shown in Table 8.2. Omega squared analysis is a way of estimating the percent of variance among scores in the ANOVA design that is attributable to each of the factors involved. As shown in Table 8.3, the Nationality factor in this study apparently accounted for about 49% of the variance in scores, while the Major factor explained about 12% of that variance. In other words, knowledge of the language, at least in terms of native/non-native differences, appears to be a much more important factor in explaining score variation than is Major in terms of engineering/non-engineering differences. From a validity point of view, the interaction between the Major and Nationality factors (Major × Nationality) in this study did not contribute significantly to the score variance, so it was ignored. However, the Residual, or error (that is, variance not explained by the factors included in this study), is more worrisome. The residual in Table 8.3 indicates that 39% of the variance among scores was not accounted for by Major or Nationality. Hence, 39% of the variance can only be considered random until further study can identify more systematic sources. Nevertheless, for a new test designed to measure an entirely new area of language proficiency, these results are encouraging from a construct validity perspective insofar as they indicate that roughly 61% (Major + Nationality = 11.71 + 48.93 = 60.64 ≈ 61) of the variance in the scores on the test is attributable to something related to engineering knowledge or English language reading ability.

One other benefit can be derived from having both a clear item plan to defend the content validity of a test and a differential-groups study to defend the construct validity of that test. Both strategies can be combined to provide useful insights and information about different item types. Consider the analysis of the engineering-English reading test that is shown

Table 8.3: Results of Omega Squared Analysis*

Source	Omega Squared	Percent of Variance
Major	.1171	11.71
Nationality	.4893	48.93
Major × Nationality	.0041	.41
Residual (error)	.3894	38.94
Total	.9999	99.99

*From Brown 1984c.

in Table 8.4. Observe that percent scores are provided in the body of the table for each of the groups (labeled across the top) and for each of the item types (labeled in the left column). Notice that the same pattern of performances exists in this table that appeared in Figure 8.1—that is, the American engineers performed best on each item type, just as they did on the overall test mean. Their performance is followed in order by the American TESL students, Chinese engineers, and Chinese TEFL students. This pattern holds true for each item type, as the reader can see by reading each line from left to right across Table 8.4. Notice also that some item types appear to have been easier than others and that in general the linguistic items appear to be easier than the engineering items for all the groups involved in this validity study.

This more detailed look at the content and construct validity of the test led me to conclude (Brown 1988b, p. 198) that the table indicates:

> that the engineering items are more efficient than the linguistic ones. There are only 34 percentage points between high and low group scores (American engineers and Chinese TEFL) for the linguistic items, while the same figure for the engineering items is 49 points. Using only the engineering items might also be more justified, from a theoretical standpoint, as more "authentic" engineering tasks after Widdowson's (1978, p. 80) distinction between "genuine" and "authentic."

Such additional information proved useful in further exploring the degree to which the test was measuring the construct in question, what that construct might be, and what content might most efficiently assess the construct. In other words, the study of the validity of a test can cause the test developer to take a long, hard look at what is being measured and how that construct should be defined—both theoretically and practically.

The results of this study are typical in that validity is never absolute; rather, validity is a relative quality that can be demonstrated experimentally to exist but only in probabilistic terms. Interestingly, in the process of investigating the degree to which this engineering reading test assessed the construct involved, something about the construct was also learned. Engineering-

Table 8.4: Performance of Differential Groups on each Content Type

Item Type	Americans		Chinese	
	Engineers %	TESL %	Engineers %	TESL %
Linguistic Factors				
Reference	82	67	60	52
Substitution	100	79	77	41
Lexical cohesion	94	64	63	55
Conjunction	85	80	66	65
Non-technical vocabulary	97	95	78	72
Engineering Factors				
Fact	89	81	62	48
Inference	90	69	59	36
Subtechnical vocabulary	71	65	59	28
Technical vocabulary	80	52	42	21
Rhetorical functions	92	91	81	50

*From Brown 1988b.

English reading ability, *as measured by this test,* relies more on language ability than on factors related to engineering itself. Thus, this validation study helped us to understand the degree to which the test was assessing the engineering-English reading ability construct (see Brown 1984c), and it also helped us to discern which of the components of the engineering-English reading ability construct might be most important (see Brown 1988b).

The general strategy for establishing test validity involves the marshalling of evidence from a variety of sources and perspectives, and then arranging that evidence into logical arguments. Thus, in the case of the engineering-English reading test, the argument is based both on showing the content validity through description of careful item planning and on demonstrating the degree of construct validity through a differential-groups experiment. The combined evidence supports the claim that the test measures overall engineering-English reading ability for NRT decisions about foreign students—at least for the groups involved in this validation study. The evidence and arguments may or may not be convincing to potential test users. Test developers are responsible for convincing test users of the validity of a test. From a common-sense point of view, if a potential test user is not convinced of the practicality, reliability, and validity of our engineering-English reading test, they do not have to use it. So, as in any marketplace, the best rule is *Caveat emptor!*

Intervention studies. Another way to address the same set of validity problems is to set up intervention studies. *Intervention studies* are similar to differential-groups studies but are conducted with only one group of students. In order to do an intervention study for the engineering-English reading test, we could administer the test at the beginning of a course for students studying English for engineering reading. We could then readminister the test at the end of their course. If they perform much better on the second administration than on the first, we have built an argument for the construct validity of the test.

This intervention strategy is often the one that makes the most sense in classroom teaching situations and is particularly suited to criterion-referenced testing where the purpose is to assess learning. Since CRT item analysis also works best in this pretest–posttest design, testers can accumulate the validity information they need in the process of gathering item analysis data. Using an intervention study in support of the construct validity of a CRT turns out to be quite a natural process.

Of course, the logic of the decision to run an intervention study is based on the assumption that students actually do learn something (engineering-English reading in the example above). A problem could arise, however, if the students all skipped classes constantly or if the teacher taught general grammar instead of engineering reading. In such a case, differences in pretest–posttest scores on the engineering-English reading test might be small or nonexistent. Obviously, such results would not necessarily indicate a problem with the validity of the test. Fortunately, students usually attend classes regularly, and teachers typically address the general goals of the course. So intervention studies often make a good deal of sense, especially when used to investigate the construct validity of a CRT.

Numerous other approaches exist for demonstrating the construct validity of a test. Occasionally in our field, multitrait–multimethod studies have been done (for instance, Bachman & Palmer 1981, 1983) or factor analytic techniques (for example, Bachman & Palmer 1983; Hinofotis 1983) have been used to defend the validity of a given test. Neither of these is particularly practical in most classroom testing situations so they are not explained here.

Regardless of the techniques used, the basic strategy in demonstrating construct validity is always the same. The tester conducts an experiment to investigate the degree to which the test is measuring the construct for which it was designed. Such construct validation will be strongest and most convincing if it is a cumulative process of gathering evidence based on a variety of experiments.

CRITERION-RELATED VALIDITY: A STRATEGY FOR NRTS

The concept of *criterion-related validity* (not to be confused with criterion-referenced tests) is basically a subset of the ideas discussed under construct validity. Demonstration of criterion-related validity usually entails designing an experiment, too, but in this case, one group of students takes two tests: the new test that testers are developing, and another test that is already a well-established measure of the construct involved. For instance, to demonstrate the criterion-related validity of a new test called the Test of Overall ESL Proficiency (TOESLP), I might administer it to a group of foreign students wishing to study English in the United States. As a ***criterion measure***, I might also administer the *Test of English as a Foreign Language*. I would choose this particular test to administer because it is a well-established test of the construct under investigation. Once the two tests are administered to a group (preferably a large group representative of the new test's target population), I can calculate a correlation coefficient for the two sets of scores and determine the degree to which the scores on the two tests go together, or overlap. For example, a ***correlation coefficient***, also called a ***validity coefficient*** in this context, of $r_{xy} = .95$ would indicate a very strong relationship between the two sets of scores. In fact, the scores on the two tests would appear to be spreading the students out in almost exactly the same way.

Based on this correlation, I could argue that, since the TOESLP appears to produce a distribution of scores very similar to the TOEFL scores, the TOESLP provides results that are virtually the same as TOEFL results. If this is true, and if the TOEFL is indeed a well-established measure of overall ESL proficiency, it follows that the TOESLP is a valid test of overall ESL proficiency (as that construct is measured by TOEFL). In short, I would have demonstrated the criterion-related validity of the TOESLP. If test users believe that the criterion measure, in this case TOEFL, is a valid measure of overall ESL proficiency, then they really must believe that the TOESLP is also valid for that purpose.

To make this even clearer, recall that the squared value of a correlation coefficient can be directly interpreted as the percentage of overlap between the two measures. Since the criterion-related validity estimate is a correlation coefficient, the squared value of a validity coefficient can also be directly interpreted as the percentage of overlap between the two measures—one the new test, and the other the well-accepted criterion measure. For example, if the scores on the TOESLP were correlated at $r_{xy} = .95$ with the scores on TOEFL, I could simply say that this magnitude shows a very strong relationship—that is, .95 is much closer to the perfect correlation of 1.00 than it is to zero. If, on the other hand, I square the .95 value ($r_{xy}^2 = .95^2 = .9025 \approx .90$), I can make the claim that the variance in the TOESLP scores overlaps about 90% with the variance of the TOEFL scores. This squared value, as you may recall, is called the ***coefficient of determination***.

One source of confusion that arises from reports about criterion-related validity studies is that it is sometimes called *concurrent* or *predictive validity*. These two labels are just variations on the same theme. ***Concurrent validity*** is criterion-related validity but indicates that both measures were administered at about the same time, as in the TOESLP example. ***Predictive validity*** is also a variant of criterion-related validity, but this time the two sets of numbers are collected at different times. In fact, for predictive validity, the purpose of the test should logically be "predictive." Imagine that I have administered a French aptitude test and want to interpret the scores in terms of how well they predict students' French course grades after one semester. A correlation coefficient between scores on the test and course grades would be an indication of how well the test predicts grades—that is, an indication of its predictive validity for purposes of testing French aptitude.

Restrictions of Range and NRT Validity

Remember, as discussed in Chapter 6, that a tester generally should avoid restricting the range of talent in any groups being tested unless they have a very good reason for doing so. If a tester chooses to base a correlational analysis on a sample with fairly homogeneous language proficiency, the sample itself can have dramatic effects on the analysis. For example, if I chose to test only students at the lowest level of study in a particular language program, I would unwittingly be restricting the range of talent, which would tend to make any resulting correlation coefficients lower. An example of the degree to which this can affect results is shown in Table 8.5. In this table, I present a number of sets of testing statistics. The results are systematically arranged from the group with the widest range of talent at the top to narrower and narrower ranges of ability as one moves down the table.

Notice that the ranges of talent are generally reflected in both the standard deviation and the range. Both statistics get much smaller as one moves down the columns. Notice also the rather dramatic relationship between this systematic restriction of range and both the reliability and validity coefficients. The startling thing about this table is that these results are based on exactly the same cloze test administered to different samples of students with different ranges of overall language abilities. In this example, the effect of restriction of range is so great that the particular cloze test involved here may appear to be the most highly reliable and valid cloze test ever created or a hands-down loser as the worst. This difference depends almost entirely on differences in the ranges of talent among the samples. The message here is that descriptive statistics should always be examined whenever such analyses are conducted. And testers should look not only at the reliability and validity coefficients but also at the amount of dispersion in the scores as indicated by the range and standard deviation. By doing so, testers may notice things that they would otherwise miss—things that can change how they interpret their results and how they view the validity of their test.

Table 8.5: Ranges of Talent in Relationship
to Reliability and Validity of a Cloze Test*

Sample	S	Range	$r_{xx'}$	r_{xy}
1978A	12.45	46	.95	.90
1978B	8.56	33	.90	.88
1981A	6.71	29	.83	.79
1981B	5.59	22	.73	.74
1982A	4.84	22	.68	.59
1982B	4.48	20	.66	.51
1982C	4.07	21	.53	.40
1982D	3.38	14	.31	.43

*Adapted from Brown 1984b.

STANDARDS SETTING METHODS

Since the purpose of most language tests is to make decisions about students, the validity of a test is often linked to the degree to which the test is accurate for decision making. As discussed in the previous chapter, the accuracy of a decision is a test consistency issue and can be enhanced by using the standard error of measurement as part of the decision-making process—especially for students who fall near cut-points. On the other hand, the appropriateness of a cut-point (and the decisions that result) is a test validity issue.

This whole area of concern is called *standards setting*. **Standards setting** is defined here as the process of deciding where and how to make cut-points. In all language programs, many decisions must be made at least partially on the basis of test scores. In order to make such decisions, standards must be set. Basically, five types of decisions require setting standards of performance; teachers and administrators must often decide whether a student should be: (a) admitted into an institution, (b) placed in the elementary, intermediate, or advanced level of a program, (c) diagnosed as knowing certain objectives and not knowing others, (d) passed to the next level of study, or (e) certified as having successfully achieved the objectives of a course or program. Thus, *standards* might be defined as the levels of performance set for any of the above five types of decisions.

In order to establish standards, teachers and administrators must determine the appropriate cut-point for a given decision and a given set of test scores. I define a *cut-point* as that score at or above which students will be classified one way and below which they will be classified differently. Such a cut-point may separate students who will be admitted into an institution from those who will not, or separate students who are placed into contiguous levels of study, or indicate the level at which students are considered to have mastered material or skills for diagnostic decisions, promotion decisions, or achievement decisions.

In the field of educational measurement, standards setting has been an important issue for several decades (for overviews, see Berk 1986; Burton 1978; Busch & Jaeger 1990; Jaeger 1989a & b; Koffler 1980; Linn 1978; Livingston & Zieky 1982; Popham 1978; Sheppard 1980 & 1984; and Skakun & Kling 1980; for a sound but negative review, see Glass 1978; for a light-hearted view, see Rowley 1982). In the language testing field, the ideas involved in standards setting are not entirely new (see Powers & Stansfield 1982; Moy unpublished ms.). However, standards are not commonly discussed even though they are often the basis for making important decisions that may strongly affect students' lives and well-being.

I was first introduced to the notion of standards and cut-points when I was put in charge of the ESL Placement Examination at UCLA as a graduate student. I supervised the duplication, administration, and scoring of over 800 tests, and everything was going surprisingly well. Then the time came for making decisions about which of the four levels of ESL study each student should be assigned to, or whether they should be exempt. The results on the test formed a classic normal distribution, as would be expected on such a norm-referenced test. In addition, the reliability statistics were very impressive. I had just one problem: I could not decide where to draw the lines that would divide the students into the four levels of study and exempt categories.

So I turned to a distinguished and very experienced senior professor of ESL for guidance. His solution was to count up the number of sections we needed at each level, and, based on a figure of about 20 students for each section, draw the cut-points working from the lower end of the distribution. Thus, in this case, the cut-points were decided on the basis of the department's logistical needs rather than on the basis of students' abilities, or on the content of the test, or on the curriculum taught in the courses. Later I realized that this type of thinking might have lead to the mismatch that I found between ESL Placement Examination results at UCLA and the ESL curriculum that was being taught (Brown 1981).

This anecdote highlights the necessarily arbitrary nature of such decisions. As Glass (1978, p. 258) pointed out "every attempt to derive a criterion score is either blatantly arbitrary or derives from a set of arbitrary premises." However, such arbitrariness is not necessarily bad, as pointed out by Popham (1978, p. 169):

> To have someone snag a performance standard "off the wall," with little or no thinking involved, is truly arbitrary with all the negative connotations that the term deserves. To go about the task of standard setting seriously,

relying on decent collateral data, wide-ranging input from concerned parties, and systematic efforts to make sense out of relevant performance and judgmental data is not capriciously arbitrary. Rather, it represents the efforts of human beings to bring their best analytic powers to bear on important decisions.

Whether language teachers like it or not, relatively arbitrary decisions must often be made about their students, particularly for purposes of admissions, placement, diagnosis, and achievement. As should be abundantly clear by now, the first two of these types of decisions should typically be made using norm-referenced tests. For admissions decisions and placement, people are categorized in relationship to each other, and different actions must be taken based on test scores. For diagnostic and achievement decisions, criterion-referenced tests will prove more useful. Until all types of admissions, placement, diagnosis, and achievement decisions are abandoned in human societies, standards will be appropriate and necessary.

Clearly, then, standards are here to stay. Because such decisions are important to the lives of the language students involved, testers must use the best available techniques to establish standards. In other words, well-considered (though necessarily imperfect) standards are better than no standards at all (Hambleton 1978; Popham 1978; and Scriven 1978).

In the educational testing literature, a variety of methods have been proposed for rationally setting standards. These methods include state mastery and continuum methods, as well as test-centered methods and student-centered methods.

State Mastery

Some of the early methods for standards setting were what would now be considered state mastery methods (see Emrick 1971 and Macready & Dayton 1977 for further description). These methods assume that the trait being measured on a test is dichotomous—that is, either the students have mastered the material or they have not mastered it. Since their inception, state mastery methods have received serious criticism (see Sheppard 1984 and Jaeger 1989b, for summaries). The central problem is that, as argued by Meskauskas (1976), state mastery methods contain an implicit expectation that students will master the material 100%, or be non-masters at 0%.

Such an approach can be particularly problematic in language teaching because so much of what is tested may turn out to be a question of degrees rather than an all-or-nothing proposition. For instance, the article system of English and prepositions are both taught early in most students' ESL/EFL learning careers. Yet these systems are among the last aspects of English that most students completely master. How, then, can teachers reasonably expect students to have mastered the article or preposition systems 100%. In short, the state mastery methods for standards setting might work with some very clearly defined subject areas, but they do not seem reasonable for testing and making decisions in language learning and teaching. Thus, as in the main body of the literature on standards setting (see Shepard 1984; Jaeger 1989b), these state mastery methods are only touched on here because of their historical interest.

An additional problem that some scholars found with the state mastery methods was that they attempted to dichotomize learning into 100% mastery or 0% categories based on a set of scores. Since test scores, by their very nature, are continuous in nature, it was felt that methods which acknowledged this continuous nature would be superior. Thus, a series of standards setting methods were developed. These methods have come to be known as *continuum methods*. A number of continuum methods have come into existence. They will be described here in briefly two categories: test-centered methods and student-centered methods (after Jaeger's 1989b distinction among continuum methods).

Continuum Methods: Test-centered

All current methods for standards setting are based on judgments made by appropriate experts in the field. However, as I show soon, test-centered methods for standards setting require various types of judgments that are focused on the test content itself, whereas student-centered methods require judgments that are focused on student performance. The four key test-centered methods for standard setting are the Nedelsky, Anghoff, Ebel, and Jaeger methods.

Nedelsky method. Nedelsky (1954) suggested a standard setting method that relies on judgments of the test design. Unfortunately, his method is only appropriate for multiple-choice tests. To apply Nedelsky's method, the following steps must be taken:

1. Identify a population of appropriate judges, and sample from that population.

2. Judges define and describe a "minimally competent" student.

3. Each judge decides which of the individual options in multiple-choice tests a minimally competent student could eliminate as not plausible.

4. Assuming that the students guess at random from among the plausible options that remain, a minimal pass level is computed for each item based on the predictions (made in the previous step) by calculating the reciprocal

of the plausible options (e.g., if two out of four options are judged to be clearly incorrect for a minimally competent student, $1/(4-2) = \frac{1}{2}$).

5. The standard is computed for any particular judge by summing the minimal pass levels for all the items.

The Nedelsky method has been criticized for a number of reasons. First, students do not necessarily follow a strategy of eliminating implausible options and then guessing from among the remaining plausible ones. After all, they may know the answer. Second, the values obtained from this method tend to be consistently lower than those obtained by other methods. Third, and perhaps most important for language testers, this method is restricted to use with multiple-choice tests, which precludes its use with many productive item language tests.

Anghoff method. Anghoff (1971) proposed a standard setting method that also relies on judgments and focuses on the test design by estimating the probability that competent students will answer correctly. This method is not restricted to use with multiple-choice questions. The following steps should be taken in applying Anghoff's method:

1. Identify a population of appropriate judges, and sample from that population.

2. Judges review the content that the test is supposed to measure and estimate the level of performance that separates students who are acceptably competent from those who are not (as suggested by Livingston & Zieky 1982).

3. For each item, judges estimate the probability that a "minimally acceptable" student will answer correctly. (Anghoff suggests conceptualizing this notion as the proportion of minimally acceptable students in a normal group of students.)

4. The sum of the probability estimates (in the previous step) then form the minimally acceptable score.

One possible disadvantage of this method is that, while it is not restricted to multiple-choice items as is the Nedelsky method, it can be applied readily only to items that are scored dichotomously (that is, either correct or incorrect). However, the Anghoff method is relatively easy to apply and does yield the professional opinions of those judges most interested in the outcomes.

Ebel method. Ebel (1979) suggested a method that begins with judgments about the expected success of test items judged according to their difficulty and relevance. The Ebel method requires the following steps:

1. Identify a population of appropriate judges, and sample from that population.

2. Establish a two-way taxonomy of difficulty and relevance for judging the items on a test; for example, difficulty (with three levels: easy, medium, and hard) could be on one dimension, and relevance (with four levels: essential, important, acceptable, and questionable) could be on the other dimension (see Figure 8.2).

3. Assign each item on the test to one cell of the taxonomy (for instance by assigning item numbers within Figure 8.2).

4. For each cell, judges decide the proportion of items that a borderline passing student (who answered a large number of questions like those assigned to cells in number 3 above) would answer correctly.

5. The standard is computed by calculating a weighted sum of the judges' suggested proportions (that is, the proportion suggested by each judge for each cell would be multiplied by the number of items in that cell, and the results would be summed across all cells; these sums for each judge would then be averaged across all judges).

DIFFICULTY

	Easy	Medium	Hard
Essential			
Important			
Acceptable			
Questionable			

RELEVANCE

Figure 8.2: Two-way Taxonomy for Applying Ebel's Method of Standard Setting

Apparently, in applying Ebel's method, judges often have difficulty keeping the two dimensions separate in their minds (Shepard 1984, p. 176). However, this disadvantage may be outweighed by the advantage gained by having all judges working on a common scale that results in common probability estimates.

Jaeger method. Jaeger's (1982, 1989a & b) method is much more elaborate than the other test-centered methods described above and involves development of consensus through an iterative process. Jaeger's method includes at least the following steps:

1. Identify all populations of judges who have a legitimate interest in the outcomes, and sample from those populations.

2. Judges then examine each item and answer *yes* or *no* with regard to whether or not a student who passes the test should be able to answer the item.

3. Judges are given data on student performance on the test as well as the judgments of their fellow judges.

4. The judges then re-examine each item and answer *yes* or *no* again.

5. Each judge's standard is calculated by summing the *yes* answers; the test standard is set for each sample of judges by calculating the median across judges in the sample; the overall standard is set by comparing the medians for all groups of judges and using the lowest as the standard for passing.

The single greatest disadvantage to applying the Jaeger method for standard setting is its complexity. Because of its iterative nature, this method is clearly the most difficult to set up logistically. However, that disadvantage may be outweighed by the political advantages gained by including all interested groups as judges and by having them discuss, think about, and judge the individual test items.

Continuum Methods: Student-centered

Whereas the test-centered methods require judgments that focus on the test content, the student-centered methods discussed here require judgments focused on the performances of the students. These student-centered standard setting methods fall into one of two types: borderline-group or contrasting-group methods.

Borderline-group method. The borderline-group method suggested by Zieky & Livingston (1977) utilizes judgments about who the borderline cases are in a particular population of students to establish what a typical borderline performance is on the test in question. To do so, these steps are followed:

1. Identify a population of judges who are familiar with the students, and sample from that population.

2. Through discussion, the judges collectively define three categories of performance on the test in question: acceptable, borderline, and inadequate.

3. Based on information other than the test scores, the judges identify any students known to them who they view as borderline cases.

4. The test is administered.

5. The standard that is set is the median of the performances of students who have been identified by the judges as borderline.

One strength of this method is that the observations of teachers in the classroom are usually the basis for establishing the cut-point. Teachers are the judges most likely to know which students are on the borderline. Teachers are an excellent source of information about students' performances, and their judgments are appropriate and relevant if the standard being set is for achievement in the classes they are teaching. This strength is also related to the one drawback of the borderline-group method: This method can only be applied to decisions where teachers have experience with the students (or a pilot group of students) in the classroom. Such experience may not always be available.

Contrasting-groups method. The contrasting-groups method suggested by Zieky and Livingston (1977) is similar to the method just discussed, except that the groups with acceptable and inadequate performance are used to establish the cut-point in the following steps:

1. Identify a population of judges who are familiar with the students, and sample from that population.

2. Through discussion, the judges collectively define three categories of performance on the test in question: acceptable, borderline, and inadequate.

3. Based on information other than the test scores, the judges identify all students known to them as belonging in acceptable, borderline, or inadequate categories.

4. The test is administered.

5. The distributions of the acceptable and inadequate groups of students are then examined, and the standard is set in one of two ways:

   a. Plot the two sets of scores so that they overlap, and set the standard at that point where they intersect (see Figure 8.3a).

   b. Calculate the percentage of students classified as acceptable at each test score, and set the standard at the score value that classifies 50% as acceptable (see Figure 8.3b).

Conceptually, the contrasting-groups method for standards setting is most closely related to the construct validity strategies, which were called intervention and differential-groups studies. Thus, there is a satisfying sense that the use of this method for establishing standards is most closely related to the purpose of the test and therefore supports its validity. However, in practice, the judgments of who falls into the two groups may result in distributions that overlap so much that no rational cut-point can be decided.

a. Overlapping Distributions
   Method

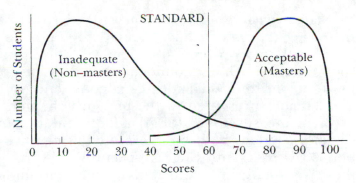

b. Percentage of Acceptable
   Performances

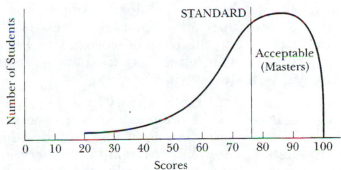

Figure 8.3: Cut-points for Contrasting-groups Method of Standard Setting

Which method should I use? Given unlimited resources and time, I would apply all the methods discussed above to the problem of standards setting and use some combination of the resulting information to decide on cut-points. At the very least, teachers may find it useful to select a few of the methods (those which make the most sense to them and their colleagues) and compare the results of the various methods before deciding on a cut-point.

Hopefully, this section of the chapter has convinced readers that the issues involved in standards setting should be far from the seemingly straightforward line-drawing exercises that I first experienced in making placement decisions at UCLA. Rather, standards setting methods must be rational processes designed to bring the best efforts of expert judges to bear on test content and/or student performance with the goal of deciding what levels of test performance should be used as cut-points.

Reliability, Validity, and Standards Setting

Assuming that teachers have used some rational and thoughtful method for setting the standards on a test, they must recognize that no standard will ever be perfect. As such, it is useful to think about how the existing standard on a particular test is related to both test consistency and validity.

Standards and test consistency. Standards are related to test consistency in that teachers can have a relatively high degree of confidence in a decision based on a cut-point on a highly consistent test, whereas they should have much less confidence in a decision and cut-point on a test with low test consistency. The degree of confidence is directly reflected in two of the statistics presented in the previous chapter. Recall that the standard error of measurement (SEM) and confidence interval (CI) discussed in Chapter 7 could both be interpreted as bands of confidence around cut-points for NRTs and CRTs, respectively. Also recall that, at least in theory, these were bands of scores within which the students' scores were likely to fall repeatedly (with certain degrees of probability) if they were to take the test over and over again. If a given test is a highly reliable NRT (or dependable CRT), this band of scores above and below the cut-point will be relatively narrow. If, on the other hand, the test is not very consistent, the band will be relatively wide.

Remember that the SEM or CI can be used to identify those students who might fall on the other side of a cut-point if they were to take the test again. In other words, students who scored within one SEM below the cut-point might fall above the cut-point if they were to take the test again. Thus, in Chapter 7, I argued that additional information should be gathered at least on those students who fall within one SEM (or one CI) of the cut-point in order to help teachers decide on which side of the cut-point each student belongs.

The strategy of using the SEM or CI in decision making should improve the overall consistency and accuracy of the decisions. This process should probably involve at least the following steps:

1. Set the standard using whatever method is deemed most appropriate in the particular language program.

2. Calculate the SEM or CI, whichever is appropriate for the type of test and decision involved, recognizing that it represents a band of possible decision errors that are normally distributed around the cut-point.

3. Decide whether to consider errors that will work against the student, against the institution, or against both.

4. Isolate those students who scored within one band (for 68% confidence) above or below the cut-point (depending on number 3 above). Gather additional information about these students, and make decisions on the basis of all available information.

5. At some point, use all available test reliability or dependability information, as well as the SEM and CI, to inspect other possibilities and revise the cut-point for future use.

Standards and test validity. Standards are also directly related to test validity in that decisions as to where to put the cut-point will often depend on the purposes of the test. Since validity is also related to the purposes of the test, standards can affect not only the degree to which a test is measuring what it was designed to measure, but also the degree to which a test is being used to make decisions in the way they were intended to be made. Thus, testers should not only be concerned with test validity but also with *decision validity*.

For instance, at University of Hawaii at Manoa, we administer two forms of a criterion-referenced test at the beginning of each course and again at the end in a counterbalanced design so that no student takes the same form twice. When the tests are administered at the beginning of the course, they are meant to be diagnostic. In addition, the scores are used to decide if there are any students who have been misplaced. The cut-points for this type of decision vary from course to course, but, because of the nature of the decision being made, the cut-point tends to fall at about the 90% level. Such high cut-points are valid because we want to identify only students who have been placed too low for their actual abilities. Students who score this high are moved up to the next level of study or exempted from study in the skill area involved. (For political reasons, we decided that we could not move students who had been placed above their actual levels down to a lower level of study.)

When the same tests are administered at the end of the course, the purpose is different. The decision that is being made is whether or not each student should pass the course. Thus, the cut-point is set much lower, usually at 60% or 70%, depending on the course. Teachers are also advised to use additional information on all students, especially for those students who are close to the cut-point (that is, within one CI below the cut-point).

Hence, *decision validity*, as I use that term, should also include what Messick (1988) refers to as the value implications of test interpretation and social consequences of test use. The *value implications* are the "more political and situational sources of social values bearing on testing" (p. 42). So the value implications of test interpretation, though related to test validity and standards, are primarily the ethical responsibility of the test users because only the test users know the special political and pedagogical circumstances surrounding the particular context in which the test is to be used and the decision is to be made. The *social consequences* of test use are also largely the responsibility of test users because they include "the appraisal of the potential social consequences of the proposed use and of the actual consequences when used" (p. 42).

As a result of these value implications and social consequences, language testers must always be aware that decisions made on the basis of test scores are essentially nature of decisions. In this sense, the very purpose and validity of a test can also be considered political rather than pedagogical. For instance, consider an end-of-course achievement test on which the rational cut-point from a judgmental and statistical point of view (including reliability and validity) turns out to be 85%. Such a cut-point would probably make no sense politically because it is "just too high." In other words, the opinions of experts and statisticians are immaterial if those opinions cause the students to riot in the halls because decisions seem unfair.

Standards setting is also nature of standards setting in another way: Decisions can be made to favor one group or another among the interested parties. For instance, in applying the contrasting-groups method, the cut-point could be established as originally described (and illustrated in Figure 8.3a), or it could be fixed at points like those shown in Figures 8.4a and 8.4b. If the purpose for making the decision warrants protecting the institution against mistakes, the cut-point in Figure 8.4a would make most sense. Such a cut-point would protect the institution against what Popham (1981, p. 389) calls *false positives*, or decisions that falsely put students on the "passing" side of the cut-point. Such a strategy might be appropriate for an admissions decision wherein there are more students applying than

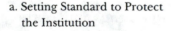
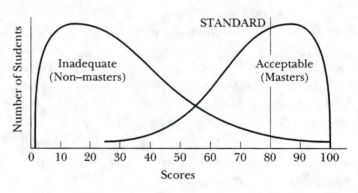

a. Setting Standard to Protect the Institution

b. Setting Standard to Protect the Students

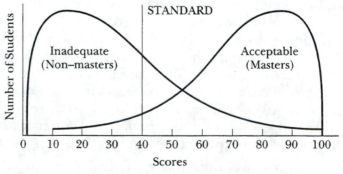

Figure 8.4: Cut-points for Contrasting-groups Method

positions to be had. In that case, a very conservative stance on admissions decisions might make sense because those responsible want as few unqualified students as possible to be mistakenly accepted even if that means that some qualified students will be rejected.

If, on the other hand, the purpose in making the decision warrants protecting the students against mistakes, the cut-point in Figure 8.4b might make more sense. Such a cut-point would protect the students against what Popham (1981, p. 389) calls *false negatives*, or decisions that erroneously put students on the "failing" side of the cut-point. This strategy might be appropriate in an end-of-course achievement decision wherein students who fail must repeat the course (an eventuality that the faculty finds less than pleasing). In that case, the teachers might decide to take a very liberal stance on the pass/fail decisions because they want as few students as possible to be mistakenly failed, even if that means that some very weak students will be passed.

In short, teachers may find themselves protecting the interests of the students or protecting the interests of the institution (and teachers). The way they decide to go will depend on the type of decision being made, its gravity, and the views of those teachers and administrators who are involved in the decision.

Despite the fact that standards setting is political in nature and difficult, teachers are often faced with setting cut-points and making decisions about students' lives. One thing seems clear from all this discussion. In language program decision-making processes, systematic and open standards setting is preferable to no standards because no standards probably means that the decisions are being made unsystematically, covertly, and perhaps, unfairly.

SUMMARY

In this chapter, I defined test validity as the degree to which a test measures what it claims, validity or purports, to measure. Three validity strategies were discussed: content and construct validity (applicable to NRTs and CRTs), as well as criterion-related validity (applicable only to NRTs). I explained content validity as a means for exploring the degree to which a test is a representative sample of the content that it was intended to measure. I described construct validity mostly in terms of the differential-groups studies and intervention studies strategies which are studies set up to investigate the degree to which a test is measuring the psychological construct for which it was designed. I discussed criterion-related validity in terms of setting up an experiment also, but in this case, one group of students simply takes two tests: The test that is being validated and another criterion measure which is already a well-established measure of the construct involved. The result is a validity coefficient that can be squared and then interpreted as the percent of overlapping variance between the new test and another well-respected test of the same construct. The two variations of this criterion-related type of validity are called concurrent validity, when both measures are administered at about the same time, and predictive validity, when the two sets of scores are collected at different times and the purpose of the test is to predict some future behavior or ability.

The last topic that I covered in this chapter was standards setting. I briefly mentioned the state mastery method, which I argued was largely inappropriate for language program decision making. Then I described the continuum methods in more detail including both test-centered and student-centered methods. The most notable of the test-centered methods were the Nedelsky, Anghoff, Ebel, and Jaeger methods, which were discussed in terms of the steps involved in actually doing them as well as in terms of their relative pros and cons. I also covered two student-centered methods known as the borderline-group method and the contrasting-groups method. I ended the chapter with discussion of the relationships between standards setting, test consistency, and test validity, as well as a brief discussion of the political nature of decisions cut-point decisions.

TERMS AND SYMBOLS

coefficient of determination (r_{xy}^2)

concurrent validity

construct validity

content validity

correlation coefficient

criterion measure

criterion-related validity

cut-point

decision validity

differential-groups studies

false negatives

false positives

intervention studies

predictive validity

psychological construct

social consequences

source

standards

standards setting

test validity

validity coefficient (r_{xy})

value implications

REVIEW QUESTIONS

1. What is validity?

2. What are the three basic types of validity?

3. Which type of validity is most typically based on expert opinion?

4. Which type of validity is an experimental demonstration of the existence of an underlying psychological construct?

5. Which type of validity is based on the correlation of the scores on a new test with scores on a previously well-established test of the same construct?

6. What types of validity are appropriate for NRTs, and which for CRTs?

7. In what ways are language programs dependent on good tests?

8. Why are restrictions of range and skewing problems that you should watch out for in performing any correlational analysis?

9. Why are state mastery methods of standards setting generally inappropriate for language programs?

10. How are test consistency (reliability or dependability) and validity related to standards setting?

APPLICATION EXERCISES

A. Table 8.6 is taken from the validity section of *TOEFL Test and Score Manual* (Educational Testing Service 1992, p. 34). This validity section marshals arguments for the validity of the TOEFL from a variety of Educational Testing Service sources and other secondary sources. Much more information is provided in that publication than what is given in Table 8.6, so you should not draw any conclusions about the validity of TOEFL without first obtaining and examining the latest version of the entire publication. Nevertheless, for the sake of practicing what you have learned in this chapter, these tables will suffice.

Table 8.6 displays the degree of relationship between total TOEFL scores and university ratings. At four universities, "the students were ranked in four, five, or six categories based on their proficiency in English as determined by university tests or other judgments of their ability to pursue regular academic courses" (Educational Testing Service 1992, p. 34)

Table 8.6: Correlations of Total TOEFL Scores with Teacher Ratings*

University	Number of Students	Correlations with Teacher Ratings
A	215	.78
B	91	.87
C	45	.76
D	279	.79

*Cited in Educational Testing Service 1992; from American Language Institute 1966.

A1. What type of validity argument does this set of correlations represent? Content? Construct? Criterion-related?

A2. Is this approach concurrent or predictive?

A3. a. What does this information imply about TOEFL's validity?   b. What is the percent of overlapping variance (coefficient of determination) between the total TOEFL scores and the ratings provided by the universities?   c. Is this argument convincing to you?

A4. Are you satisfied with the number of subjects used in the study? Typically, TOEFL is administered to hundreds of thousands of students per year.

B. Table 8.7 summarizes information that was actually presented in prose form in Educational Testing Service 1992.

Table 8.7: Summary of a Variety of Studies Reporting Correlations between TOEFL Total Scores and Various University-Level ESL Placement Procedures

Study	Institution (*N*)	Criterion Measure	Correlation
Maxwell (1965)	University of California at Berkeley (*N* = 238)	English Proficiency Test	.87
Upshur (1966)	San Francisco State (*N* = 50) Indiana University (*N* = 38) Park College (*N* = 12)	Michigan Test of English Language Proficiency	.89
ALI (1966)	Georgetown University (*N* = 104)	American Language Institute Test	.79

B1. What type of validity argument does this set of correlations represent? Content? Construct? Criterion-related?

B2. Is this approach concurrent or predictive?

B3. a. What does this information imply about TOEFL's validity?   b. What is the percent of overlapping variance between the total TOEFL scores and the various sets of university test scores?   c. Do you find this argument convincing?

B4. Are you satisfied with the number of subjects used in these studies? Why, or why not?

C. Table 8.8 is also cited in Educational Testing Service (1992, p. 35) and is taken from Angelis, Swinton, and Cowell (1979). The table presents a comparison of the performances of an experimental group of international students and a group of native speakers. The international students took both the TOEFL and the Graduate Record Examination (GRE) Verbal subtest, while the native speakers took only the GRE.

C1. What type of standardized scores are probably being reported for the GRE results (see Chapter 5)?

C2. a. How do these results support the proposition that the GRE Verbal subtest measures English language ability?   b. What kind of validity argument would this support? Content? Construct? Criterion-related?

Table 8.8: GRE Verbal Score Comparisons*

	Mean	S	Reliability	SEM
TOEFL	523	69	.95	15
(Non-natives) (N = 186)	274	67	.78	30
Native Speakers (N = 1495)	514	128	.94	32

*Cited in Educational Testing Service 1992; adapted from Angelis, Swinton, & Cowell 1979.

C3. Would the GRE Verbal subtest be valid for testing the verbal ability of foreign students who want to pursue graduate studies? Why, or why not?

C4. Why might the standard deviation and reliability on the GRE be lower for foreign students than for native speakers?

C5. Are you satisfied with the number of subjects used in this study? Why, or why not?

D. D1. How would you design an argument for the content validity of the TOEFL?

D2. Do you believe the TOEFL is a valid test of overall English language proficiency?

E. Decide on a standards setting method that you would like to use for a particular type of test in a real or fictitious language program. Write a list of the steps you would have to take in getting the appropriate people to cooperate and provide the decisions/information necessary to actually set the standard. List steps all the way through the standards setting process, including the actual decision making.

CHAPTER 9

TESTING AND CURRICULUM

Many of the articles in the field of language testing, indeed some of the chapters in this book, have treated tests as though they are somehow isolated entities floating free of any language teaching reality. In most of this book, however, I have tried to stress the importance of looking at tests within the context of real, living language programs. For this reason, I paid a good deal of attention to the differences and similarities between NRTs and CRTs, and I always discussed these two categories of tests in terms of adopting, developing, and adapting sound language tests for making decisions in real language programs. In addition, I explained strategies for developing and improving real test items and for describing and interpreting actual test results. Finally, I explored the issues related to correlation with particular emphasis on how correlation relates to the study of the reliability and validity of actual tests. Clearly, the point of view that I take in this book is that tests can and should be integral parts of the larger curriculum in a language program. Although tests may be isolated for purposes of study, they should never be treated as though they are somehow divorced from the language teaching and learning processes that are going on in the same context. In this final chapter, I address the issue of where tests fit into language programs and discuss the place of testing in curriculum planning and implementation.

THE PLACE OF TESTS IN CURRICULUM PLANNING

Curriculum planning, or development, is viewed here as a series of activities that provide a support framework that helps teachers to design effective activities and learning situations to promote language learning. The model shown in Figure 9.1 (from Brown 1989b) describes six broad types of activities that are often identified in the curriculum design literature with promoting good teaching and learning: needs analysis, goals and objectives setting, testing (both NRT and CRT), materials development, teaching, and program evaluation. The model is a simplified, yet complete, version of the widely accepted *systems approach* used in educational technology and curriculum design circles. Dick and Carey (1985) discuss the systems approach to curriculum in terms of what a system is (p. 2):

> A system is technically a set of interrelated parts, all of which are working together toward a defined goal. The parts of the system depend on each other for input and output, and the entire system uses feedback to determine if its desired goal has been reached. If it has not, then the system is modified until it does reach the goal.

A curriculum that has interrelated parts working toward a clearly defined goal with input and output as well as feedback is a system. A quick glance at the curriculum development process described in Figure 9.1 reveals that it is a systems approach with all the characteristics described in the above quotation.

Teachers can use the model shown in Figure 9.1 as both a set of stages for developing and implementing a course or program and a set of components that they can monitor for the improvement and maintenance of an already existing course or program. Either way, using this model helps teachers to focus on and encourage a continuing process of curriculum development and maintenance.

In discussing this model and the associated curriculum activities, I use examples drawn from recent curriculum development efforts in the English Language Institute at the University of Hawaii at Manoa. To show where and how testing fits into all this, I first give a brief explanation of each of the individual components of the model, followed by a more general discussion of the importance of testing to all the other curriculum elements. Because of the scope and topic of this book, only the central issues involved in each curriculum component are discussed here. The focus is on what makes each component a crucial element in the development and maintenance of a sound language curriculum and how testing relates to it. (For more extensive discussion of the elements of this model, see Brown 1989b, Brown & Pennington 1991, or Brown 1995).

Needs Analysis

In language teaching, needs analysis is often seen as the identification and selection of the language forms that the target students are likely to require in actually using a particular language. Most often, the focus is on the learners and what they need to learn, and these needs are usually expressed in linguistic terms. Such a focus seems reasonable because learners are the primary "clients" in a language program, and the curriculum should be designed to serve the clients' needs.

Two dangers may arise, however, in taking this narrow view that learners' needs only include their linguistic requirements. One danger results from the fact that teachers, administrators, employers, institutions, societies, and even nations have needs that may influence the delivery of language teaching and the effectiveness of language learning that follows. Thus, learners are not the only people with needs who are involved in a language program. Perhaps the solution to this dilemma is for needs analysts to view the learner as the focus of any needs analysis while simultaneously gathering information from as many sources as possible so

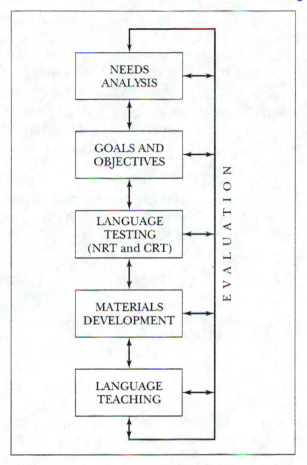

Figure 9.1: Systematic Design of Language Curriculum (adapted from Brown 1989b)

that they remember to include the needs of all program participants (especially the teachers and administrators).

A second danger arises from the fact that a needs analysis usually focuses solely on the linguistic factors involved. Students are people and therefore have needs and concerns that are not solely linguistic. Since such nonlinguistic factors as fatigue, stress, motivation, learning styles, and other psychological and affective factors may be directly related to language learning, information must also be gathered about the students as people in any needs analysis. The solution to this problem may be found in making the linguistic forms the focus of the needs analysis, but gathering information from as many sources as possible on the students' other needs (including physical, personal, familial, professional, cultural, societal, and so forth).

To avoid the dangers just described, ***needs analysis*** is defined rather broadly here (after Brown 1995) as "the systematic collection and analysis of all relevant information that is necessary to satisfy the language learning needs of the students within the context of the particular institution(s)."

Various forms of needs analysis were conducted at UHM as the basis for curriculum development in each of the skill areas. Examples of these needs analyses can be found in Kimzin and Proctor (1986) for the Academic Listening Skills; Asahina and Okuda (1987), Weaver, Pickett, Kiu, and Cook (1987), and Brown, Chaudron, and Pennington (1988) for Foreign Teaching Assistant Speaking Skills; Loschky, Stanley, Cunha, and Singh (1987), and Asahina, Bergman, Conklin, Guth, and Lockhart (1988) for Academic Reading; and Power 1986 for Academic Writing.

Goals and Objectives

If the purpose of doing a needs analysis is to satisfy the language learning needs of the students, one outcome of analyzing those needs might be the specification of formal ***program goals***. Such goals are general statements of what must be accomplished in order to satisfy the students' needs. For example, the students in the ELI at UHM are taking ESL courses for the purpose of improving their ability to study in English at university level. For these students, one appropriate goal might be to enable them to satisfy their potential need to write term papers. Writing such papers is one thing the students need to be able to do with the language while in the university—one thing that can be expressed as a program goal.

Objectives, on the other hand, are statements of the exact content, knowledge, or skills that students must learn in order to achieve a given goal. For instance, taking the goal mentioned in the previous paragraph— being able to write a term paper—the teachers might realize that students first need to develop important library skills. One such skill might be the ability to find a book in the library. To do this, the student needs several subskills: knowing the English alphabet, pinpointing a particular book in the catalog, locating the call number for that book, and finding the book by locating its call number in the stacks, to name just a few. These subskills might be included in the objectives for a lower-level reading or writing course.

Thus, objectives are derived from considering how to best achieve the program goals. Recall that the goals were in turn derived from perceptions of what the students needed to learn. But this process works in two directions. The specification of objectives can help to clarify the program goals and objectives, and the newly clarified goals and objectives can in turn modify the view of what students need to learn. This bidirectional relationship is shown in Figure 9.1 by the arrows that interconnect all elements of the model in both directions.

Language Testing

According to Mager (1975, p. 2), the next logical step in curriculum development is the drafting of tests based on a program's objectives. However, as I have shown throughout this book, putting tests in place is not simple. The goals, objectives, and administrative necessities of a program may require extensive test development. This may in turn necessitate adopting, developing, or adapting tests for a wide variety of decisions including the proficiency, placement, diagnostic, and achievement decisions—all of which are discussed in some detail in Chapters 1 and 2. The strategy explained in the next main section ("The Place of Tests in Curriculum Implementation") offers one set of examples of how such divergent types of testing and decision making can be implemented, at least in a very supportive academic setting.

The supportive environment in which tests have been developed at UHM has been crucial because such implementation involves considerable work and often requires a certain amount of funding as well. However, the investment of resources, time, talent, and energy in developing a sound testing program at UHM has proven worthwhile because the resulting tests are serving all of our decision-making needs as well as our long-range needs to evaluate and fine-tune the entire curriculum on a continual basis. The dividends have been particularly large in terms of what has been learned about our original needs analyses, and the goals and objectives that resulted. Our testing program has taught us about our student's needs and our course objectives, as those two curriculum elements relate to the actual performances of students, and helped us to minimize waste in the crucial, and often expensive, materials development and teaching stages that follow.

Many teachers have asked me (rather suspiciously) why testing comes before materials development and teaching in my model. Aside from the fact that Mager (1975, p. 2) suggests that testing be developed before materials, experience has convinced me that it is much more efficient to develop at least tentative tests of the objectives before plunging ahead with materials development. The tests can then help teachers to investigate the degree to which the objectives are appropriate for the students in question *before* investing the time and energy needed to adopt, develop, or adapt the materials needed to teach those objectives. While NRT proficiency and placement test results may be useful for determining approximately the level for the materials and teaching, only CRTs can directly measure students' abilities with regard to the course objectives. With CRT results in hand, teachers can then determine the degree to which the objectives are appropriate for the particular students involved in the particular course of study.

At UHM for example, we developed a CRT to analyze the tentative objectives of our lower-level reading course (ELI 72 in Figure 9.2, p. 282). We knew from our proficiency results that the students would all be somewhere between 500 and 600 in TOEFL score terms. We also knew from our placement results that these ELI 72 level students would mostly be in the bottom half of that 500–600 TOEFL score range. We had used this information, along with our assessment of the students' needs in academic English and with intuition derived from experience to develop a set of tentative objectives for the course. Fortunately, we then chose to develop a CRT to test those objectives. We first administered this CRT as a diagnostic test early in the Spring semester of 1987. To our great chagrin, over 90% of the students had nearly perfect scores on most of the objectives. In other words, they apparently did not need to learn the objectives that we had outlined as the basis of our curriculum for the course—that is, they did not need to learn what we intended to teach them.

This revelation had a dramatic effect on us as curriculum designers. At first, we felt that we had created a total disaster, but a little reflection made us realize that we had actually been very lucky. The disaster would have been far worse if we had discovered this mismatch between the objectives and the students' abilities *after* having also developed elaborate sets of materials and teaching strategies. Of course, the situation would be even worse if we had never developed CRTs and hence had never discovered the mismatch at all.

In short, we found that developing CRTs to diagnose the students' weaknesses and strengths also afforded us the opportunity to analyze the appropriateness of our course objectives for their abilities. Unfortunately, our perceptions of their needs were pitched far too low. I suppose that few of the students would have complained about a curriculum that was too easy because in the short run they would prefer the easy materials and exercises and the relatively high grades that they would get with little or no effort. The teachers might not have noticed anything out of the ordinary either. In fact, the teachers might be ecstatic that they were "teaching so well" that the students were doing superbly on all the exercises and tests. The only potential problem here is that the students might not be learning anything—at least nothing that was new or challenging to them. We did not want this situation to continue.

As a result of what we learned on the diagnostic CRT, we kept many of our skills-based objectives but raised considerably the difficulty level of material to which the students would be expected to apply those skills. Instead of requiring the students to be able to handle reading materials that averaged about 8th- to 10th-grade readability on the Fry readability scale (Fry 1976), we found and adapted texts that averaged about 13th- to 15th-grade level—that is, university-level readings. Based on later test results, this turned out to be a sound strategy for moving our expectations and the curriculum up to the level of the students. However, we would never have known to do this if we had not first analyzed the appropriateness of the objectives by using a diagnostic CRT.

You may, of course, choose to develop your tests after you put energy into materials development, but at the very least, it would be prudent to use some pilot tests related to the objectives and materials. The point is that needs, objectives, tests, materials, teaching, and program evaluation are so tightly connected in a good curriculum that they all should be developed in the same instant. Since this is obviously not possible, teachers and administrators will have to allocate carefully any curriculum resources that they can muster and decide which areas of focus deserve and require those resources. In our priorities at UHM, testing came before materials development and teaching (even though they are obviously going on all the time) in terms of the support that the program gives to individual teachers.

As explained elsewhere in this book, the process of developing and refining tests is by no means mystical, nor is it particularly easy. However, at UHM, testing has become a crucial element in the curriculum because we feel that it is helping in an unprecedented manner to unify the curriculum and give it a sense of cohesion and purpose. Tests have also been useful for shaping the students' expectations as well as those of the teachers. Students naturally seem to study and practice the types of language and language skills encountered in the content of the tests that they take along the way. In short, tests are viewed as a critical element in the curriculum at UHM and may prove equally useful in other language programs.

Materials Development

Once tentative needs analyses, objectives, and tests have been put into place, materials can be developed in a rational manner to fit the specific needs and abilities of the participants in the program. With appropriate testing information in hand, adopting, developing, or adapting materials become relatively easy because the course is fairly clearly defined. Indeed, the very decisions about whether to adopt, develop, or adapt materials become much easier. For instance, teachers can easily assess existing materials and decide whether these materials could be adopted to fill the needs of the students, or whether they will have to be adapted to meet the students' needs and program goals. Teachers could also estimate whether adaptation would be a minor undertaking or a major project. Even if there are no suitable materials available and teachers must develop them, having clear-cut objectives and tests will aid considerably in the planning, organization, and creation of materials.

The purpose in this section is not to prescribe any particular type of syllabus or materials for any program but rather to argue that materials should be based on the needs analysis, objectives, and test results of the specific curriculum in question. Such decisions must be left to the teachers and administrators who are on site and know the situation best. Among those professionals, however, a strategy should be worked out wherein students' needs, objectives, tests, teaching, and program evaluation are all related to each other and to the materials. In such a strategy, materials will be affected by what is learned from each of the other components of a program and will in turn have an effect on the other components. The main point is that materials should be put into place rationally (whether adopted, developed, or adapted) on the basis of the best available information and planning rather than on the sporadic, random basis that I have seen in so many language programs (and some published materials).

Language Teaching

Contrary to what many teachers may think, the type of curriculum development described here can allow teachers more freedom than usual in the classroom to teach in the ways that they judge to be correct. In such a curriculum, both the teachers and students are aware of the objectives for each course and are aware that these objectives will be tested at the end of the course. This structure is not meant to threaten the teacher but rather to provide support. Instead of having to do a personal needs analysis and course objectives for every class, the teacher can be provided with at least a tentative framework of core objectives upon which to base the teaching. In order for such a curriculum to work, the teachers must have a stake in it—a large stake. In other words, the teachers must be involved in the process of curriculum development, feedback, and revision, and they must be consulted often along the way.

There is strength to be found in numbers, so curriculum planners will find it useful to involve teachers, administrators, and students in defining the needs within a particular program and establishing the course objectives and tests. Such cooperation works at UHM. However, all too often in some language programs, all these curriculum development activities fall solely on the teachers' shoulders. Teachers are typically required to determine what the students need to learn, define the course goals and objectives, select or develop course tests and materials, and do the teaching. At UHM, all these tasks except the teaching are done in groups. The primary reason for this is that most teachers are in no position to do all such tasks well, sometimes because they lack the expertise but more often because they lack the time to do an adequate job. In fact, it is absurd to expect teachers to do all these curricular activities well. They were hired to teach. Needs, objectives, tests, and materials development should be group efforts, drawing on the collective expertise, time, talent, and energy, to do a more effective job of curriculum development than any one teacher could hope to do. This kind of cooperation and support can help teachers to not only do a superior job at the teaching that they were hired to do but also to share ideas with other teachers and develop new teaching skills.

Program Evaluation

Often the terms *testing* and *evaluation* are linked to each other and sometimes are even used interchangeably. In this book, I systematically use them to mean two different things. Evaluation may involve some testing as one source of information, but evaluation is not limited in any way to testing. Information from a wide variety of other sources may prove useful. Certainly test scores are one possible source, but interviews, classroom observations, diaries, notes from meetings, institutional records, and many other sources of information may also prove useful in an evaluation (see Brown 1989b or 1995 for a list of such information sources). *Evaluation* is defined here as the systematic collection and analysis of all relevant information necessary to promote the improvement of the curriculum and analyze its effectiveness within the context of the particular institution(s). This definition is purposely very similar to the one provided above for needs analysis because I view the evaluation process as a sort of ongoing needs analysis.

However, because evaluation takes place after all the other elements of the curriculum have at least been tentatively put into place, evaluation should be based on considerably more and better information than any needs analysis. A needs analysis is usually conducted at the beginning of a curriculum development project and is focused on the linguistic needs of the participants. In the needs analysis phase, information is gathered using interviews, questionnaires, linguistic analyses, guesswork, and a good deal of professional judgment. In contrast, evaluation strategies can be broader, using all available information to analyze the effectiveness of the program. Thus, evaluation can use all the information gathered in (a) doing the initial needs analysis, (b) developing, listing, and refining objectives, (c) writing, piloting, and revising tests, (d) adopting, developing, or adapting materials, and (e) putting all the above in place through teaching. The evaluation process can use the information gained from each curriculum element to modify and improve each of the other elements. This interaction between evaluation and all the other components explains why the arrows in Figure 9.1 connect all the curriculum elements to evaluation in two directions.

In short, evaluation allows a language program to profit from ongoing information gathering, analysis, and synthesis, for purposes of improving each component of a curriculum based on information about all the other components separately and collectively. This ongoing process is what makes the systems approach to curriculum development so potentially powerful and effective. Curriculum that is viewed as a "product" is inflexible once it is "finished." Curriculum that is viewed as a "process" can change and adapt to new conditions, whether they be new types of students, changes in language theory, or new political exigencies within the institution. This process is known as the "systems approach" to curriculum design. As shown in Figure 9.1, tests clearly have an important role in such a systematic curriculum.

THE PLACE OF TESTS IN CURRICULUM IMPLEMENTATION

Curriculum implementation involves actually putting in place the elements developed in the curriculum planning and making them work and fit together within the existing program in a way that will help administrators, teachers, and students. I cover implementation as a separate topic because putting the curriculum into action involves a whole set of new issues. Because of the topic of this book and its length, the focus is on those issues related to the role of *tests* in curriculum implementation. Once again, examples are drawn from the ELI at the University of Hawaii at Manoa to illustrate one way that tests can fit into a program. The discussion includes a brief description of the program as well as information about the various types of tests that have been adopted, developed, or adapted at UHM. The central thesis is that it is important to get all the tests to fit together into a decision-making matrix. Of course, NRTs and CRTs are mentioned along the way, but the focus in this section is on how the various types of tests all feed information into the program—information that not only has positive affects on the students' lives but also influences all the elements of the curriculum itself.

To help with testing, curriculum developers may want to hire an outside consultant or provide special release time or training for program personnel to learn about language testing. In either case, the rewards for the program should be commensurate with the investment because of the important position that testing holds in the curriculum development process.

The ELI as a Language Program

In order to use examples from the testing program at UHM, it is necessary to describe the program itself briefly. After all, tests do not exist in a vacuum but rather are used for decision-making purposes within a specific program.

Briefly then, all ELI courses follow the University of Hawaii's regular schedule for length of term and class hours required. All courses receive three units of credit and meet either 3 days per week for 50 minutes, or twice a week for 75 minutes. The Fall and Spring semesters are each 15 weeks in duration with an extra week for final examinations. Two 6-week Summer Sessions are offered each year, during which most ELI courses meet daily, Monday through Friday, for approximately 2 hours per class. Every effort is made to hold the maximum class size to 20 students. The courses in the ELI are as follows:

ELI 70   Listening Comprehension I

ELI 80   Listening Comprehension II

ELI 72   Reading for Foreign Students

ELI 82   Advanced Reading for Foreign Students

ELI 71   Fundamentals of Writing for Foreign Students

ELI 73   Writing for Foreign Students

ELI 81   Speaking for Foreign Teaching Assistants

ELI 83   Writing for Foreign Graduate Students

ESL 100 Expository Writing: A Guided Approach

I now discuss the four steps that we use in our decision making from a chronological perspective with a particular emphasis on how each step affects the students at UHM. The four steps are as follows:

1. Initial screening procedures

2. Placement procedures

3. Second-week diagnostic procedures

4. Achievement procedures

To accomplish these steps, a number of different tests are used: the ELI Placement Test (ELIPT), the *Test of English as a Foreign Language* (TOEFL), and the CRTs developed for diagnosis and achievement testing in the individual courses (for a full report and description of these CRTs, see Brown 1993). The emphasis is on organization and implementation of the tests within the program as well as on the actual decisions being made with the results. I hope that the strategies which we find so useful can be generalized and adapted to various kinds of second and foreign language programs. Procedures similar to these should help teachers to integrate their testing procedures into one cogent testing program and help to integrate the testing program into the overall curriculum.

Initial Screening and Proficiency Procedures

Each year about 600 new foreign students are admitted to UHM for undergraduate (41%) or graduate (59%) programs. As would be expected from our geographical location, roughly 82% of these students come from Asia, with the four largest contingents coming from Hong Kong, the People's Republic of China, Taiwan, and Japan. Before being admitted, students must be screened by the Office of Admissions and Records. The students' previous academic records, letters of recommendation, and TOEFL scores are all reviewed, and only those students with good academic records and total TOEFL scores of 500 or higher are admitted. Applicants exempt from the TOEFL examination and ELI training are those who:

1. speak English as a native language,

2. hold a bachelor's or a graduate degree from an accredited university in the United States, Canada (except Quebec), Britain, Australia, or New Zealand,

3. have SAT verbal scores of 500 or better, and

4. have completed all their education (K–12 or more) in countries listed in category 2.

This information, including each student's three TOEFL subtest scores and total score, is then sent to the ELI. If students' scores on the TOEFL are above 600, the students are notified that they are exempt from any ELI requirement. Those students who have scored between 500 and 599 on the TOEFL are notified that they must take the ELI Placement Test (ELIPT) when they get to UHM. Clearly, the initial screening procedures are designed to narrow the range of English proficiencies with which the ELI must ultimately deal. Note, however, that even after these broad screening decisions have been made, any student may request an interview with the Director, or Assistant Director, at any time to appeal our decisions. This allows us some flexibility and an initial opportunity to spot students who actually do not need ELI training and should therefore be exempt from the ELIPT. Students who fall into this category are typically those who meet at least one of the following criteria:

1. They received an Associate of Arts or Sciences degree from an American community college with a GPA of 3.0 or higher.

2. They attended school in the United States, Canada (except Quebec), Britain, Australia, or New Zealand for a minimum of 5 years.

3. They attended English medium schools in any Commonwealth country for a minimum of 10 years.

Falling into any one of these categories does not mean that the student is automatically exempted but rather that the student is given an opportunity to present a case for exemption in an interview with the Director or Assistant Director. When we have any doubt, however, we insist that the student take the ELIPT. Thus, some students may have to take a test that is not necessary, but few students who really need ELI training will be missed.

In the end, most students who scored between 500 and 599 on TOEFL are required to take the ELIPT because we want more information on their language abilities in the three main academic skill areas with which our courses deal. (Note that testing for the fourth skill, speaking, is conducted outside of the main placement system because only a relatively small group of graduate students is effected.) We are also interested in getting information that is a bit more recent than their TOEFL scores and more directly related to the teaching and learning that go on in the ELI.

Many teachers may find themselves in a position in which they need *proficiency procedures* to determine how much of a given language their students have learned during their lives. At first, they will only be concerned with knowing about the students' proficiency in general terms without reference to any particular program. This is likely to be the case when students are brand new to a language program and the teachers want to get a general notion of how much of the language they know, as in the admissions decisions at UHM. To do this, teachers will probably need tests that are general in nature, such as the TOEFL in the ELI example. These same teachers may also want to establish guidelines for which types of students are automatically exempt from training, for which students need to take the placement test, and for which students deserve an interview or further information gathering (because they fall into the gray area where a decision may not be clear-cut).

At the same time that they are using such initial screening measures, teachers may be able to get a tentative estimate of the general level of language proficiency among their students. For those familiar with the TOEFL, the TOEFL bracketing on the left side of Figure 9.2 gives a general idea of the overall ability parameters involved in the ELI course structure. Such information may aid in determining entrance standards (or exit) for a

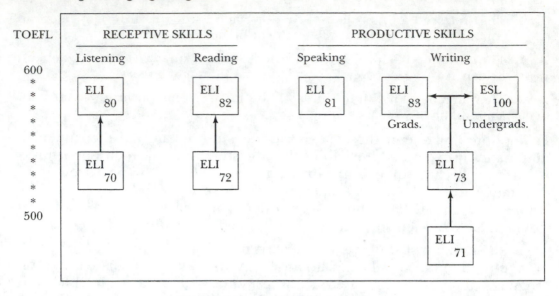

Figure 9.2: ELI Course Structure

curriculum, in adjusting the level of goals and objectives to the true abilities of the students, or in making comparisons across programs. As a result, initial screening procedures are often based on proficiency tests that are general in nature but nonetheless important and globally related to curriculum structure.

Placement Procedures

The duties of the Director of the English Language Institute (ELI) include placing the students into levels of study that are as homogeneous as possible in order to facilitate the overall teaching and learning of ESL. To that end, the ELI has quite naturally developed its own *placement procedures*. These procedures are not based entirely on the placement test results as is the case in some language programs. In addition to the test scores, we use the information gained from the initial screening, as well as the second-week diagnostic and achievement procedures (discussed later in the chapter). Using all this information helps to ensure that we are being maximally fair to the students and that they are working at the level which will most benefit the students, teachers, and administrators alike.

The present English Language Institute Placement Test (ELIPT) is a 3-hour test battery made up of six subtests: the Academic Listening Test, Dictation, Reading Comprehension Test, Cloze, Academic Writing Test, and Writing Sample. Placement into the academic listening skills courses is based primarily on the Academic Listening Test and Dictation, while placement into the reading courses is based on the Reading Comprehension Test and Cloze, and placement into the writing courses is based on the Academic Writing Test (multiple-choice proofreading) and Writing Sample (composition task). We have systematically designed our tests so that two subtest scores can be used for each of the three skill areas: one is discrete-point in nature, and the other is integrative (see Chapter 2 for more on discrete-point and integrative tests). We feel that having these two types of subtests for each skill area provides us with two different views of the students' abilities in each skill.

However, relying solely on these test scores to place students would be very irresponsible. We ensure a more human touch in a face-to-face interview with a member of the ELI faculty. The interviewers have all the information that they may need (including the student's records, TOEFL scores, and ELIPT test scores) when they conduct the interview. The interviewers are told to base their placement decisions for each skill area on the two subtest scores while taking into consideration other information in the student's records and any information gained by talking to the student. If the faculty member is unsure of the appropriate level for a student, or if the student contests the placement decisions, the ELI Director, or Assistant Director, takes over and makes any necessary decisions. The students then register for the appropriate courses, and the semester begins.

The interview procedure allows us to place students more accurately than any test score alone because the placement is based on many sources of information considered together. Indeed, the ELIPT subtest scores (both integrative and discrete-point for each skill) are considered. But more importantly, other factors are taken into account, such as the length of time that the students have studied English, the amount of time since the students studied it, the amount of time in the United States, their TOEFL subtest scores, their spoken language during the interview, their academic records, and any other information available at the time. All these details help us to place students in a way that respects them as human beings who are important to us.

Sooner or later, most teachers will find themselves having to make placement decisions. In most language programs, students are grouped according to ability levels. Such grouping is desirable so that teachers can focus in each class on the problems and learning points appropriate for students at a particular level. As discussed in Chapter 1, placement tests can help teachers to make such decisions. Such tests are typically norm-referenced and therefore fairly general in purpose, but, unlike proficiency tests, placement tests should be designed (through careful item writing, item analysis, and revision—see Chapter 2) to fit the abilities and levels of the students in the particular program. The purpose of such tests is to show

how much ability, knowledge, or skill the students have. The resulting scores are then used to place students into levels of study, or at times to exempt them entirely.

To do this, teachers need tests that are general in nature but designed specifically for the types and levels of their students as well as for the goals of their program. Teachers may also need to establish guidelines for using as many types of test information as possible along with other types of data. In addition, they might want to conduct placement interviews wherein all available information is marshalled for making the placement decisions. They might also consider further testing or information gathering for those students who fall close to their cut-points—say, plus or minus one SEM of any division point between levels (see Chapter 7).

The ELI students are placed in each skill, as shown in Figure 9.2, on the basis of a complete set of placement procedures. Remember that two placement subtest scores are available for each skill along with considerable additional information. The placement decisions are made on the basis of all this information, and the students have recourse to a second interview with the Director or Assistant Director if they want. We feel that our placement decisions are as fair as possible because they are based on a relatively large and varied collection of information sources, and there is a line of appeal that students can follow if they feel that they have been treated unfairly. However, the process of determining whether or not a student has been placed in the proper level does not stop here. The process continues as long as the students are associated with the ELI.

Second-Week Diagnostic Procedures

During the second week of instruction, ELI teachers are required to give a diagnostic test of the skill that they are teaching and to keep a close watch on their students to see if any have been misplaced. When a student is identified who appears to be in the wrong level, the teacher consults with the ELI Director and, if necessary, an interview with the student is arranged. In most cases, a student who is found to be misplaced is encouraged to change registration for the course at the appropriate level of ESL study.

The tests that are used in the second week of classes are provided by the ELI. One teacher is given 10 hours per week release time (and the title "Lead Teacher") for the sole purpose of developing and improving these tests. This teacher works with other lead teachers (one for each skill area) and the various groupings of teachers within the skill areas to create CRTs for each course. The lead teacher does not actually write the tests. Rather, the lead teacher's responsibility is to coordinate groups of teachers who actually do the item writing and test production. Then the lead teacher takes care of duplicating the tests, helping the teachers to administer them, scoring the tests, reporting the results to the teachers, analyzing the pretest and posttest results (for CRT statistics), revising the tests (again, in consultation with the teachers), and starting the whole process over again the next semester.

So far, CRTs in two forms (A and B) have been produced for each of the nine courses (see Brown 1993 for a description of these CRTs at an earlier stage of development). These CRTs are designed to measure the specific objectives of each course. Hence, they can be administered at the beginning of the courses as diagnostic tests and at the end as achievement tests. The tests are administered in a *counterbalanced design* such that half of the students take Form A at the beginning of the course while the other half take Form B. At the end of the course, all students take the opposite form. This counterbalancing is done so that students do not see exactly the same test twice.

Many teachers may find themselves using such *diagnostic procedures* for purposes of checking if their placement decisions were correct, but also for purposes of identifying and diagnosing strengths and weaknesses that students may have with relation to the course objectives and the material to be covered in the course. These procedures may be based extensively on test results, but other factors should probably also come into play. The teachers' observations of the students' classroom performances and attitudes may be one source of information; an interview with the Director may be another. The point is that procedures should be put in place to help students and their teachers to focus their efforts where they will be most effective.

These diagnostic procedures are clearly related to achievement procedures. After all, diagnosis and achievement decisions can be based on two administrations of the same test (preferably in two counterbalanced forms, as described above). However, while diagnostic decisions are usually designed to help identify students' strengths and weaknesses at the beginning or during instruction, achievement procedures are typically focused on the degree to which each student has accomplished the course objectives at the end of instruction. In other words, diagnostic procedures are usually made along the way as the students are learning the language, while achievement procedures come into play at the end of the course.

Achievement Procedures

In the ELI, the CRT posttests are administered as part of the *achievement procedures*. The CRT achievement tests are administered during the students' regularly scheduled final examination periods, which are 2 hours long. Since the CRTs are designed to last no more than 50 minutes, the

English Language Institute   Moore Hall, Room 570

ELI STUDENT PERFORMANCE REPORT

Student's Name _____

           (Family name)   (Other names)

ELI ____ Section ____ ☐ Fall ☐ Spring ☐ SSI ☐ SSII   19 __

☐ Undergraduate   ☐ Graduate   ☐ Unclassified   ☐ EWC Grantee

Academic Dept. _____ Academic Advisor _____

(DO NOT WRITE BELOW THIS LINE!!!)

1. Hours Absent (circle)   0   1   2   3   4   5   [ ] More than 5

2. Class Participation   Very Little   1   2   3   4   5   6   7   Very Much

3. Class Motivation   Very Poor   1   2   3   4   5   6   7   Excellent

4. Overall Improvement   Very Little   1   2   3   4   5   6   7   Very Much
     in this Skill Area

5. Mastery of Course   50% or 60% 65% 70% 75% 80% 85% 90% 95% 100%
     Objectives (approx.)   lower

6. Recommended Action for Next Semester

☐ EXEMPT in this skill area   ☐ ENROLL in _____

7. Course Grade – ELI Courses   Course Grade – ESL Courses
                                 (A B C D F or I) = _____

☐ No credit   ☐ Credit   ☐ Incomplete

8. Remarks

(Rev. JDB 11/89)   _____
                                                 ELI Instructor

Figure 9.3: ELI Student Performance Report

remaining hour and 10 minutes can be utilized by the teacher to administer a personal final examination if desired. In terms of grading, the results of these achievement tests must be counted as at least 10% of the students' grades so that the tests will be taken seriously. The students are, of course, told all this at the beginning of the course. Since until recently our criterion-referenced tests were more or less experimental, we were very careful about treating them as *minimal competency tests* on which students must achieve a certain minimum score in order to pass the course. However, now that the tests are more fully developed, standards are being established for what it means to succeed in our courses (see "Standards Setting" in Chapter 8).

Again, the administration and scoring of these tests is coordinated by the lead teacher in charge of testing. In addition to the tests, our achievement procedures include the requirement that each teacher fill out an evaluation report form (see Figure 9.3) for each student. Since most of our courses are taken on a credit/no credit basis, these evaluation reports serve much the same function as grades in that they are a statement of the students' overall achievement in the course. Unlike grades, these reports are fairly detailed and give a prose description of each student's performance. In addition, the teachers must state specifically what level of ELI course the students should take in the next semester. In some cases, the teacher may suggest that a student skip a level or be exempt from any further study in that skill area. In such a case, the teacher petitions the ELI Director and, if the petition is approved, the teacher advises the student on which course to take.

One copy of the student performance report is kept on file in the ELI, and another is sent to the student's academic department so that the student's academic advisor is apprised of the student's progress and remaining ELI requirements. In this way, students who no longer fit in the particular course level to which we initially assigned them can be identified and adjustments in their placement can be made—even after they have studied for a full semester or more.

Most teachers will probably agree that they would like to foster achievement, particularly in the form of language learning, in their course or program. In order to find out if their efforts have been successful and to help them maximize the possibilities for student learning, achievement procedures like our tests and performance reports may prove useful. Remember that the tests used to monitor such achievement should be developed to measure the very specific objectives of a given course or program and that they must be flexible in the sense that they can be made to change readily in response to what is learned from them in terms of the tests themselves or other curriculum elements. In other words, carefully designed achievement procedures are most useful to a language program when they are flexible and responsive for affecting curriculum changes and continually analyzing those changes with reference to the program realities.

Testing as an Integrated System

At UHM, we believe that the vast majority of the students who are served by the initial screening, proficiency, placement, second-week diagnostic, and achievement procedures are correctly classified and placed and are systematically learning a substantial amount within our program (see Figure 9.4). We feel confident that most of our students are being helped with their language learning needs. Nonetheless, decisions are made by human beings. Since humans are known to make mistakes, and since incorrect decisions can cost the students dearly in the form of extra tuition or unnecessary time spent studying ESL, we must continue to base our decisions on the best and most varied information available and continue to maintain avenues for double-checking those decisions and for appeal on the part of the students.

Testing, though an essential component of any sound language curriculum, is only *part* of the curriculum. Likewise, test results should form part of the basis for any decision, but only part. Other sources of information may prove equally important. For instance, teachers might want to consider admissions scores, letters of recommendation, interviews, student evaluation reports, transcripts of academic work at other institutions, teacher judgments, or any other available sources. However, all sources of information will be most useful if they are systematically sorted and integrated into a regular systematic testing program like the initial screening, proficiency, placement, second-week diagnostic, and achievement procedures recently established for decision making in the University of Hawaii ELI.

Multiple opportunities exist for cross-verifying and changing decisions, and these opportunities should be provided at various points of time within the curriculum process. Above all else, no decision should be made on the basis of a single piece of information. Even a tried-and-true test that has proven reliable and valid can generate some error variation. A second, different, source of information minimizes the chances that such error will influence the reliability of the related decisions.

Certainly, all the decision-making procedures described here will take a great deal of effort on the part of the administrators and teachers, but the benefits gained from effective and humane decision-making procedures accrue to all participants in a program—students, teachers, and administrators.

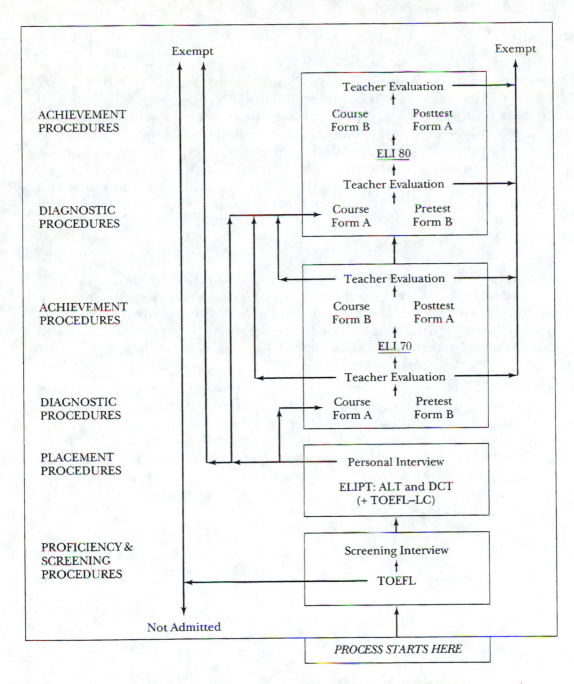

Figure 9.4: ELI Decision–Making Processes for the Listening Skill Area

SUMMARY

I began this chapter by describing a systems approach to curriculum development and implementation. The systems approach involves six different categories of curriculum activities: needs analysis, goals and objectives, testing (NRT and CRT), materials development, teaching, and the never-ending process of evaluation and curriculum improvement. The purpose of the systems framework for curriculum development activities is to help the teachers do the teaching job for which they were hired by drawing on the collective strength of the entire program. Thus, the teaching and curriculum development activities are viewed as independent but closely related. I also argued that all the curriculum components are interrelated in that information about any one component may influence all other components.

I also provided examples of how testing can fit into a curriculum as well as how tests can be an important part of an overall decision-making program. Based on examples from the ELI at UHM, I described procedures more or less in chronological order in terms of when they affect the students: initial screening, proficiency, placement, second-week diagnostic, and achievement procedures.

All in all, this chapter drew on many of the issues covered throughout the book and also summed up the importance of testing and its place within any sound language curriculum. I hope that this chapter has provided an adequate explanation of how tests can fit into a language program because a central theme throughout this book has been that language tests should never be divorced from the central job of fostering language teaching and language learning.

TERMS

achievement procedures

counterbalanced design

curriculum implementation

curriculum planning

diagnostic procedures

evaluation

minimal competency tests

needs analysis

objectives

placement procedures

proficiency procedures

program goals

systems approach

testing (as a curriculum element)

REVIEW QUESTIONS

1. What is the purpose of a needs analysis? Why would needs analysis activities logically end in the formulation of at least some tentative statements of goals and objectives?

2. How do goals differ from objectives as they are defined here? Why might it be necessary to allow a wide variety of different types of objectives—from some that are very specific to others that are more general?

3. Why are tests shown in the middle of the model in Figure 9.1? In other words, why might test development, especially diagnostic tests, best be done directly after formulating the curriculum objectives but before materials development and teaching?

4. Would you adopt, develop, or adapt materials for your curriculum, or would some combination of the three work better? What are some of the advantages of working with a group of teachers on materials development rather than working alone? Some disadvantages?

5. Consider a language teaching situation in which curriculum activities like those described in this chapter are implemented so that all elements are developed cooperatively by all the teachers. Would this help you to do your job as a teacher? What dangers or other potential political problems do you think should be avoided in such a situation?

6. What is the difference between *testing* and *evaluation* as the terms are used in this chapter? How are needs analysis and program evaluation similar and different?

7. What is the purpose in the ELI at UHM of each of the following types of information-gathering procedures:

   a. initial screening and proficiency procedures

   b. placement procedures

   c. first-week diagnostic procedures

   d. achievement procedures

8. What types of information, other than test scores, would be useful in your program for each of the four sets of decision-making procedures listed in question 7?

9. What differences and similarities in test content, format, and logistics would be necessary for tests designed to make the following types of decisions?

   a. initial screening and proficiency

   b. placement

   c. first-week diagnostic

   d. achievement

10. Can you list the main topics covered in this book? Do you see why each topic is important and how they fit together? Why not write the author and let him know what you think? (JD Brown, Dept. of ESL, UHM, 1890 East-West Road, Honolulu, Hawaii 96822)

APPLICATION EXERCISES

A1. Write a list of all the different things that you do in your teaching. Take some time. You will be surprised at how many different things you really do. Now separate the items on your list into those activities that are essentially related to teaching and those that are basically curriculum responsibilities. Which curriculum activities are most closely related to the needs analysis, goals and objectives, testing, materials development, teaching, and program evaluation categories described in this chapter?

A2. Can you now augment the list of activities that you perform in each of these categories? How many of the curriculum responsibilities have been delegated to you? How much release time, or secretarial help, have you been given to perform all these curriculum development functions? Did you have any idea how many different activities would be involved in your job before you started working?

B1. Think about your language program (or one that you know about) from a curriculum standpoint. List the ways in which the program addresses needs analysis, setting goals and objectives, testing, materials development, teaching, and program evaluation.

B2. Are the teachers helped by the administration with these activities, or are they solely responsible for teaching *and* for curriculum development? How could these curriculum processes be improved to help you better do the teaching job for which you were hired?

C. What are the equivalents in your program (or one that you know about) for each of the following information-gathering procedures:

1. initial screening and proficiency procedures
2. placement procedures
3. first-week diagnostic procedures
4. achievement procedures

If any of these four sets of procedures does not exist in your program, should it be instituted? Why, or why not?

ANSWER KEY FOR APPLICATION EXERCISES

CHAPTER 1

Application Exercises for Chapter 1 are too specific to your situation for an Answer Key to be provided. (Please compare your answers to material presented in the chapter.)

CHAPTER 2

Application Exercises for Chapter 2 are too specific to your situation for an Answer Key to be provided. (Please compare your answers to material presented in the chapter.)

CHAPTER 3

A. All the answers that you need are in the accompanying table.

Application Answers for Item Statistics (from Table 3.11 Data)

Statistic	1	2	3	4	5	6	7	8	9	10	11	12	13	14	15	16	17	18	19	20	21	22	23	24	25	26	27	28	29	30
IF	.57	.77	.20	.87	.80	.83	.80	.87	.90	.93	.67	.23	.47	.23	.73	.13	.43	.07	.93	.93	.90	.13	.83	.30	.20	.70	.70	.73	.07	.37
ID	.20	.40	.50	.40	.50	.20	.60	.40	.30	.10	.60	.30	.40	.40	.30	.40	.50	.20	.20	.20	.30	.30	.20	.60	.40	.60	.60	.10	.10	.50

B. You should probably begin by noticing that the item numbers are in the first column and that there is some kind of grouping going on as indicated by the High and Low labels in the second column. Next, you will want to look for the item facility values, which are listed in the third column under Difficulty. The output then gives the number of students (not the percents as in the chapter example) in the High and Low groups who chose each of the four options, a.–d. Based on my knowledge of the test and of the numbers of students tested, I can tell you that there was no option e. and that the High and Low groups are not the upper and lower thirds but rather the upper half and lower half. Finally, you probably looked for the item discrimination index and ended up guessing that it was in the last column labeled Correlation. This last column presents the point-biserial correlation coefficient (this statistic is explained much more fully in Chapter 6). As I mentioned in the chapter, the point-biserial correlation coefficient functions much the same as the item discrimination index.

My top five choices for items to keep are Items 7, 9, 10, 12, and 13. They are generally the best discriminators, and all but one fall within the range of .30 to .70 in item facility. Item 12 is outside that range, but it is such a good discriminator that I decided to keep it as a counterweight to Item 10, which is fairly difficult. In the process of choosing these five items, I also considered Item 6 but was disturbed by the fact that it was so easy and the fact that almost as many people in the Low group answered correctly as in the High group.

In terms of distractor efficiency, I would like to have a look at distractor *a.* of Item 9, *c.* of Item 12, and *a.* of Item 13 to see if I could make them a bit more attractive to those students who do not know the answer. Notice also that Item 5 may be an item that has two possible answers or at least one distractor that is very close to correct. Because so many students, especially High students, were attracted to distractor *c.*, I would want to have a careful look at the item before using it again for anything.

C. In the case of the items in Table 3.9, the easiest approach to choosing fifteen out of the twenty items solely on the basis of the difference index would be to eliminate the worst five items. The lowest DIs are clearly items 45, 46, 52, 56, and 58. The remaining items would therefore be the ones that I would select under these conditions. The highest of the rejected items, at .082, is considerably lower than the lowest of the remaining selected items, at .131, so this serves as a logical breaking point for making this kind of selection.

However, you must also think about what the DIs in the selected items mean in terms of percentage of gain among your students. In this case, you must decide whether you are willing to accept items that show as little as a 13.1% gain in the number of students answering the item correctly. Perhaps items that are as low as 13% should be revised to fit the course objectives better, or perhaps the particular objectives involved should be taught better or practiced more thoroughly. Nevertheless, before making any selections on real items, you would want to insist on examining the items themselves so that format and content analyses could be brought into the selection process along with the DIs shown in Table 3.9.

D. The *B*-indexes for the item data given in Table 3.13 are shown in the accompanying table. The interpretation of these items is comparable to that described in the text for the items in Table 3.10. This is because the results in Tables 3.10 and 3.13 are very similar in the sense that those items which performed very poorly in Table 3.10 (items 2, 3 & 4) also did so in Table 3.13—despite the fact that a different cut-point was used. However, actual choices from among the remaining "good" items might differ somewhat depending on which set of results was used, on the number of items that were ultimately needed, and on the purpose and quality of the items being analyzed.

Application Answers for *B*-indexes (from Table 3.13 Data)

					Item Number							
Student ID	1	2	3	4	5	6	7	8	9	10	Total	Percent
IF$_{pas}$	0.82	0.18	0.53	1.00	0.82	0.88	0.88	0.82	0.76	0.94	7.65	76% Mean$_{pass}$
IF$_{fail}$	0.00	1.00	0.67	1.00	0.33	0.33	0.33	0.00	0.00	0.00	3.67	37% Mean$_{fail}$
B-index	0.82	−0.82	−0.14	0.00	0.49	0.55	0.55	0.82	0.76	0.94	3.98	40% Pass–Fail

CHAPTER 4

A. A1. a. A cloze test is a test developed by deleting words in a text and replacing them with blanks. The student is then required to fill in the blanks. The one indicated in Table 4.9 was scored such that any answer that was acceptable to native speakers of English for a given blank was counted correct. b. 3. c. *The Test of English as a Foreign Language* (see Educational Testing Service 1994).

A2. a. 51.3. b. 100. c. 16.01. d. 107.

A3. a. Probably because each student's Total CESL was an average of the three subtest scores. b. The TOEFL score is a standardized score (see next chapter) that theoretically has no upper limit. But for all practical purposes, 700 is in reality about (or circa "ca.") as high as they go. (The actual top possible score at the moment is 677.)

A4. a. Cloze. b. Total TOEFL. c. 50.

A5. a. Total TOEFL. b. Most probably, some of the students had not taken TOEFL, either because they were not university-bound or because SIU does not require TOEFL scores from foreign students. In other cases, students' scores may not have been reported to SIU or may not have arrived yet, even though the students had taken the test.

A6. a. Total TOEFL, but this is a standardized score (see next chapter) so it may turn out that CESL Structure had the widest dispersion in terms of raw scores (the actual number of items answered correctly by each student).   b. Total TOEFL has the highest standard deviation.

A7. a. It would always be nice to also have the low–high scores and the range plus a graph of each set of scores. However, this is not always feasible, and what Hinofotis does present in this table is adequate to visualize how the students performed on each of the subtests. It most certainly is adequate for the study in which it was found, the focus of which was something quite different.

B. B1.

Test A:

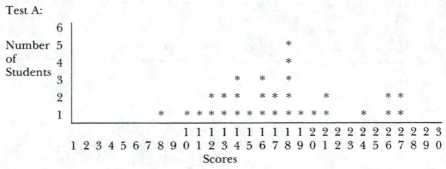

Test B:

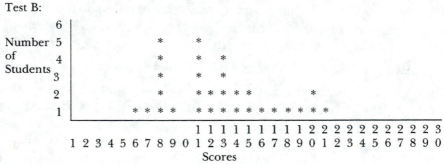

Test C:

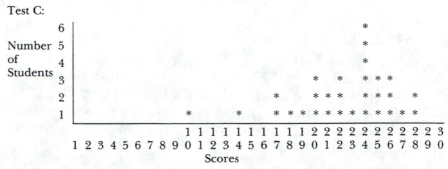

Test D:

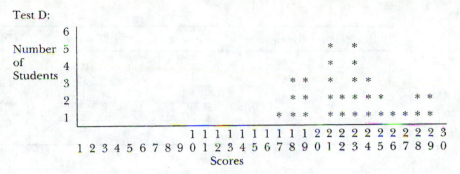

B2.
Sri Lankan High-School Cloze Test Results

Statistic	Test A	Test B	Test C	Test D
N	30	30	30	30
k	30	30	30	30
Mean	17.30	12.73	22.20	22.70
Mode	18	8, 11	24	21, 23
Median	17.00	12.50	23.50	23.20
Midpoint	17.50	13.50	19.00	23.00
S	4.97	4.10	4.05	3.35
Variance	24.68	16.80	16.43	11.21
Low–High	8–27	6–21	10–28	17–29
Range	20	16	19	13

CHAPTER 5

A. A1. About the 16th percentile because a student at 85 would be −1 standard deviations below the mean.

A2. Between 81% and 82% (34.13 + 34.13 + 13.59 = 81.85).

A3. About 5 standard deviations (177 − 100 = 77; 77 ÷ 15 = 5.13 ≈ 5). No, this score would not necessarily mean that Iliana is intelligent. You have no idea what type of measure is involved so you simply cannot draw any conclusions except that, whatever the scale, Iliana is unusually high on it.

A4. $z = 5.13 ≈ 5$; $T = 101.3 ≈ 100$; CEEB = 1013 ≈ 1000.

B.

Student	Raw score	z score	T score	CEEB score
A	64	+2	70	700
B	50	0	50	500
C	43	−1	40	400
D	39.5	−1.5	35	350
etc.				

C. C1. a. z scores = Test C

b. T scores = Test B

c. CEEB scores = Test A

C2. a. the largest standard deviation = Test A

b. the lowest mean = Test C

c. the largest number of items = Test A

d. a negatively skewed distribution = Test B

C3. In Test C:

a. a raw score of 11 equals a z score of 0.

b. a raw score of 7 equals a T score of 40.

c. a raw score of 19 equals a CEEB score of 700.

D.

Raw Scores and Standardized Scores

Students	Score	z	T	CEEB
Robert	77	2.00	70.0	700
Millie	75	1.50	65.0	650
Dean	72	.75	57.5	575
Shenan	72	.75	57.5	575
Cuny	70	.25	52.5	525
Bill	70	.25	52.5	525
Corky	69	.00	50.0	500
Randy	69	.00	50.0	500
Monique	69	.00	50.0	500
Wendy	69	.00	50.0	500
Henk	68	− .25	47.5	475
Elisabeth	68	− .25	47.5	475
Jeanne	67	− .50	45.0	450
Iliana	64	−1.25	37.5	375
Archie	64	−1.25	37.5	375
Lindsey	61	−2.00	30.0	300

E. You are entirely on your own for this one.

CHAPTER 6

A. You will find all the information that you need to check your calculations in the accompanying table. You may have noticed that these calculations are suspiciously similar to those shown in Table 6.2. You are right. Test Z here is exactly the same as Test Y in Table 6.2 except that each score is ten points lower. This also results in a mean that is ten points lower. Notice, however, that this makes no difference in the resulting correlation coefficient. As long as the scores are in the same order and the distances between them remain constant, the correlation will remain the same.

Application Answer for Pearson r (from Table 6.12 Data)

Column 1 Name	2 3 4 $Z - \bar{Z} = (Z-\bar{Z})$	5 6 7 $Y - \bar{Y} = (Y-\bar{Y})$	8 $(Z-\bar{Z})(Y-\bar{Y})$
Robert	87 − 56.94 = 30.06	77 − 69.00 = 8.00	240.48
Millie	75 − 56.94 = 18.06	75 − 69.00 = 6.00	108.36
Iliana	72 − 56.94 = 15.06	64 − 69.00 = −5.00	−75.30
Dean	61 − 56.94 = 4.06	72 − 69.00 = 3.00	12.18
Cuny	60 − 56.94 = 3.06	70 − 69.00 = 1.00	3.06
Bill	60 − 56.94 = 3.06	70 − 69.00 = 1.00	3.06
Corky	59 − 56.94 = 2.06	69 − 69.00 = 0.00	0.00
Randy	58 − 56.94 = 1.06	69 − 69.00 = 0.00	0.00
Monique	57 − 56.94 = 0.06	69 − 69.00 = 0.00	0.00
Wendy	57 − 56.94 = 0.06	69 − 69.00 = 0.00	0.00
Henk	57 − 56.94 = 0.06	68 − 69.00 = −1.00	−0.06
Shenan	56 − 56.94 = −0.94	72 − 69.00 = 3.00	−2.82
Jeanne	52 − 56.94 = −4.94	67 − 69.00 = −2.00	9.88
Elisabeth	49 − 56.94 = −7.94	68 − 69.00 = −1.00	7.94
Archie	30 − 56.94 = −26.94	64 − 69.00 = −5.00	134.70
Lindsey	21 − 56.94 = −35.94	61 − 69.00 = −8.00	287.52
N	16	16	$\Sigma(Z-\bar{Z})(Y-\bar{Y}) = 729.00$
Mean	56.94	69.00	
S	15.01	3.87	
Range	67	17	

$$r_{xy} = \frac{\Sigma(Z-\bar{Z})(Y-\bar{Y})}{NS_y S_z}$$

$$= \frac{729.00}{16(15.01)(3.87)}$$

$$= \frac{729.00}{929.42} = .7843601$$

$$\approx .78$$

B. You will find the calculations for the Spearman ρ in the accompanying table. Notice that the result of .68 is considerably lower than the Pearson r of .78 calculated for the original interval scale raw data, which were converted into these ranks. It will often be true that ρ will be lower than r in this manner.

Application Answer for Spearman *rho* (from Table 6.12 Data)

Students	Test Z Scores	Test Y Scores	Test Z Ranks	Test Y Ranks	D	D²
Robert	87	77	1.0	1.0	0.0	0.00
Millie	75	75	2.0	2.0	0.0	0.00
Iliana	72	64	3.0	14.5	−11.5	132.25
Dean	61	72	4.0	3.5	0.5	0.25
Cuny	60	70	5.5	5.5	0.0	0.00
Bill	60	70	5.5	5.5	0.0	0.00
Corky	59	69	7.0	8.5	−1.5	2.25
Randy	58	69	8.0	8.5	−0.5	0.25
Monique	57	69	10.0	8.5	1.5	2.25
Wendy	57	69	10.0	8.5	1.5	2.25
Henk	57	68	10.0	11.5	−1.5	2.25
Shenan	56	72	12.0	3.5	8.5	72.25
Jeanne	52	67	13.0	13.0	0.0	0.00
Elisabeth	49	68	14.0	11.5	2.5	6.25
Archie	30	64	15.0	14.5	0.5	0.25
Lindsey	21	61	16.0	16.0	0.0	0.00

$$\Sigma D^2 = 220.50$$

$$\rho = 1 - \frac{6 \times \Sigma D^2}{N(N^2 - 1)} = 1 - \frac{6 \times 220.5}{16(256 - 1)} = 1 - \frac{1323}{4080}$$

$$= 1 - .32 = .68$$

C. The answers that you should have obtained are the following:

Item 1

$$r_{pbi} = 1 - \frac{\overline{X}_p - \overline{X}_q}{S_t} \sqrt{pq} = \frac{80 - 60}{10} \sqrt{.5 \times .5} = \frac{20}{10} \sqrt{.25}$$

$$= 2 \times .5 = .100$$

You should have calculated the mean of the total scores for those students who answered Item 1 correctly ($\overline{X}_p$ of those coded as 1) and gotten $(90 + 80 + 70) \div 3 = 80$. Doing the same for those students who answered incorrectly ($\overline{X}_q$ of those coded as 0), the result should have been $(65 + 60 + 55) \div 3 = 60$. In addition, the standard deviation given below Table 6.13 is 10, and the proportion of students in the p group is .50, so the proportion in the q group is also .50. Substituting all these values into the formula for Item 1 and solving it as shown, you should have obtained a correlation of 1.00. The same processes should also have been used in solving Items 2–4.

Item 2

$$r_{pbi} = \frac{\overline{X}_p - \overline{X}_q}{S_t} \sqrt{pq} = \frac{60 - 80}{10} \sqrt{.5 \times .5} = \frac{-20}{10} \sqrt{.25}$$

$$= -2 \times .5 = -1.00$$

Item 3

$$r_{pbi} = \frac{\overline{X}_p - \overline{X}_q}{S_t} \sqrt{pq} = \frac{70 - 0}{10} \sqrt{1.0 \times 0} = \frac{70}{10} \sqrt{.00}$$

$$= 7 \times 0 = .00$$

Item 4

$$r_{pbi} = \frac{\overline{X}_p - \overline{X}_q}{S_t} \sqrt{pq} = \frac{0 - 70}{10} \sqrt{0 \times 1.00} = \frac{-70}{10} \sqrt{0}$$

$$= -7 \times 0 = .00$$

CHAPTER 7

A. A1.

$$\alpha = 2(1 - \frac{S_{odd}^2 - S_{even}^2}{S_t^2}) = 2(1 - \frac{2.11^2 + 2.39^2}{4.18^2})$$

$$= 2(1 - \frac{4.4521 + 5.7121}{17.4724}) = 2(1 - \frac{10.1642}{17.4724})$$

$$= 2(1 - .5817289) = 2(.4182711) = .8365422$$

$$\approx .84$$

A2.

$$K - R21 = \frac{k}{k-1} (1 - \frac{\overline{X}(k - \overline{X})}{kS^2}) = \frac{20}{19} (1 - \frac{10.5(20 - 10.5)}{20 \times 4.18^2})$$

$$= 1.0526(1 - \frac{99.75}{349.448}) = 1.0526(1 - .2855) = 1.0526 \times .7145$$

$$= .7521 \approx .75$$

A3.

$$K - R20 = \frac{k}{k-1} \left(1 - \frac{\Sigma\ IV}{S_t^2}\right) = \frac{20}{19} \left(1 - \frac{3.50}{4.18^2}\right) = 1.0526\left(1 - \frac{3.50}{17.4724}\right)$$

$$= 1.0526(1 - .2003) = 1.0526 \times .7997 = .8418 \approx .84$$

A4. Split-half correlation $\qquad r = .7208$
Full-test reliability
(Adjusted by Spearman-Brown) =

$$r_{xx'} = \frac{2 \times r}{1 + r} = \frac{2 \times .7208}{1 + .7208} = \frac{1.4416}{1.7208} = .8377 \approx .84$$

B. These estimates indicate that the test is about 84% consistent and about 16% inconsistent when interpreted as an NRT. Put another way, about 84% of the variation in scores is meaningful variance, and about 16% is measurement error.

C.

$$SEM = S\sqrt{1 - r_{xx'}} = 4.18\sqrt{1 - .84} = 4.18\sqrt{.16}$$

$$= 4.18 \times .40 = 1.672$$

D. The best strategy would be to calculate the correlation coefficient between the two sets of scores. This procedure is called *interrater reliability*. Unless you are only interested in the reliability of single ratings, the results of the interrater correlations should be adjusted using the Spearman-Brown Prophecy formula to reflect the actual number of ratings used for each student's work.

E. E1.

$$\text{agreement coefficient} = p_o = \frac{A + D}{N} = \frac{51 + 24}{100} = \frac{75}{100}$$

$$= .75$$

E. E2.

$$p_{chance} = [(A+B)(A+C)+(C+D)(B+D)]/N^2$$
$$= [(61)(66)+(39)(34)]/10000$$
$$= [4026+1326]/10000 = 5352/10000 = .5352$$
$$\approx .54$$

$$\kappa = \frac{(p_o - p_{chance})}{(1 - p_{chance})}$$

$$= \frac{.75 - .54}{1 - .54} = \frac{.21}{.46} = .4565 \approx .46$$

F. F1. agreement coefficient (using Table 7.9) =

$$z = \frac{(c - .5 - \overline{X})}{S}$$

$$= \frac{(24 - .5 - 22.70)}{3.3481} = \frac{.8}{3.3481} = .2389 \approx .2$$

$$\text{K-R20} = \frac{k}{k-1}\left(1 - \frac{\Sigma IV}{S_i^2}\right) = \frac{30}{29}\left(1 - \frac{4.1767}{3.34^2}\right) = 1.0345\left(1 - \frac{4.1767}{11.1556}\right)$$

$$= 1.0345(1 - .3744) = 1.0345 \times .6256 = .6471832 \approx .65$$

Based on z of .20 (remember that it is used without regard to the sign) and K-R20 of .65, Table 7.9 shows a value somewhere between .71 and .75. Let's call it .73.

F2. Following the same steps as for exercise F1 (but using Table 7.10) yields a kappa coefficient somewhere between .41 and .49, or approximately .45.

F3. phi (lambda) dependability index =

$$\Phi(\lambda) = \Phi(.80) = 1 - \frac{1}{k-1}\left[\frac{\overline{X}_p(1-\overline{X}_p) - S_p^{\,2}}{(\overline{X}_p - \lambda)^2 + S_p^{\,2}}\right]$$

$$= 1 - \frac{1}{30-1}\left[\frac{.7566667(1-.7566667) - .1116033^2}{(.7566667 - .80)^2 + .1116033^2}\right]$$

$$= 1 - \frac{1}{29}\left[\frac{.1841222 - .0124552}{.0018777 + .0124552}\right]$$

$$= 1 - .0344828\left[\frac{.1716670}{.0143329}\right]$$

$$= 1 - (.0344828 \times 11.977129)$$

$$= 1 - .4130049 = .5869951 \approx .59$$

F4. Based on statistics in Table 7.10 and the information given in the question, phi dependability index =

$$\Phi = \frac{\dfrac{nS_p^{\,2}}{n-1}[K - R20]}{\dfrac{nS_p^{\,2}}{n-1}[K - R20] + \dfrac{\overline{X}_p(1-\overline{X}_p) - S_p^{\,2}}{k-1}}$$

$$= \frac{\dfrac{30 \times (.1116033)^2}{30-1}[.6471832]}{\dfrac{30 \times (.1116033)^2}{30-1}[.6471832] + \dfrac{.7566667(1-.7566667) - .1116033^2}{30-1}}$$

$$= \frac{\dfrac{.3736560}{29}[.6471832]}{\dfrac{.3736560}{29}[.6471832] + \dfrac{.1716670}{29}}$$

$$= \frac{.0083386}{.0083386 + .0059195} = \frac{.0083386}{.0142581} = .5848324 \approx .58$$

CHAPTER 8

A. A1. Criterion-related validity—because the argument is based on the degree of correlation between the scores on the test and a criterion measure (university ratings).

A2. Predictive—because the correlations show the degree of relationship between the scores and future predicted performance as judged at various universities.

A3. a. It could be inferred that this information is valid for predicting overall performance in university academic English as judged by various universities. Of course, such results are open to a variety of interpretations.   b. The coefficients of determination range from a low of .5776 (for $r = .76^2$) to a high of .7569 (for $r = .87^2$).   c. As part of the overall pattern of validity evidence, these coefficients seem to me to form a fairly convincing argument—though I must wonder what direct bearing a 1966 study has on a 1987 test. Has the population of students changed at all? Has the test changed substantially?

A4. You must decide for yourself the answers to these questions and the implications of those answers.

B. B1. Criterion-related—because the argument is based on the degree of correlation between the scores on the test and a criterion measure (university placement procedures).

B2. Probably concurrent—though it is hard to know from this table alone whether the two sets of tests were administered at about the same time. In well-designed studies, they would be administered at roughly the same time, so let's give them the benefit of the doubt.

B3. a. It could be inferred that this information indicates that TOEFL is valid for making placement decisions in ESL programs. However, ETS makes it very clear elsewhere in the publication that such is not the case and that TOEFL scores should not be used as the sole basis for placement. It would be safer to look at these correlations as indicating that TOEFL scores are fairly highly correlated with other large-scale NRTs at various universities and are therefore related to overall ESL proficiency to a reasonably high degree.   b. The coefficients of determination range from a low of .6241 (for $r^2 = .79^2$) to a high of .7921 (for $r^2 = .89^2$).   c. Again, as part of the overall pattern of validity evidence, this seems to me to be a fairly convincing argument—though once again I must wonder what direct bearing studies from 1965 and 1966 have on a 1987 test. Has the population of students changed at all? Has the test changed substantially?

B4. You must again decide for yourself the answers to these questions and the implications of those answers.

C. C1. CEEB

C2. a. Students who are strong in the construct of concern (English language ability, i.e., native speakers) score much higher than students who are not so strong (i.e., non-natives). b. Construct validity—because this is a differential-groups type of study.

C3. You must once again decide for yourself the answers to these questions and the implications of those answers.

C4. The standard deviation and reliability are probably lower for the non-natives than for the natives because the GRE was designed for natives, which means that the scores for the non-natives are uniformly low and fairly homogeneous (i.e., they do not vary as much as the scores for the natives).

C5. You must once again decide for yourself the answers to these questions and the implications of those answers.

D. D1. Personally, I would set up the test items for review by a panel of experts with some sort of rating scale for each question so that the judges can decide the degree to which each item is measuring overall ESL proficiency (like that shown in Table 8.1).

D2. One last time, this is the type of question that you should answer for yourself based on the evidence presented. I could tell you what I believe, but it is more important for you to decide for yourself what you think. It would also be wise to form no opinion at all until you have reviewed all the latest available information on the validity of the TOEFL. Remember that the information presented here is only part of a larger pattern of information that ETS marshalled in 1992 to defend the validity of the test.

E. The answer to this standards setting exercise will depend on the method that you have chosen and the nature of the language program and decision that you have in mind. However, the steps listed should include at least those given in the body of the chapter for the method that you have chosen, plus some application of the SEM or CI discussed later in the chapter, and recognition of the political nature of standards setting and related decisions.

CHAPTER 9

Application Exercises for Chapter 9 are too specific to your situation for an answer key to be provided. (Please compare your answers to material presented in the chapter.)

REFERENCES

Alderson, J. C., K. J. Krahnke, & C. W. Stansfield (1987). *Reviews of English Language Proficiency Tests.* Washington, D.C.: TESOL.

American Council on the Teaching of Foreign Languages. (1986). *ACTFL proficiency guidelines.* Hastings-on-Hudson, NY: American Council on the Teaching of Foreign Languages.

American Language Institute. (1966). *A report on the results of English testing during the 1966 pre-university workshop at the American Language Institute.* Unpublished ms. Washington, D.C.: American Language Institute, Georgetown University.

American Psychological Association. (1994). *Publication manual of the American Psychological Association* (4th ed.). Washington, D.C.: American Psychological Association.

American Psychological Association. (1985). *Standards for educational and psychological testing.* Washington, D.C.: American Psychological Association.

Angelis, P. J., S. S. Swinton, & W. R. Cowell. (1979). *The perfomance of non-native speakers of English on TOEFL and verbal aptitude tests* (TOEFL Research Report 3). Princeton, NJ: Educational Testing Service.

Anghoff, W. H. (1971). Scales, norms, and equivalent scores. In R.L. Thorndike (Ed.), *Educational measurement* (2nd ed.). Washington, D.C.: American Council on Education.

Asahina, R., & J. M. Okuda. (1987). Lecture skills for foreign teaching assistants: goals, microskills and objectives. Honolulu, HI: ELI Documents, Department of ESL, University of Hawaii at Manoa.

Asahina, R., M. Bergman, G. Conklin, J. Guth, & C. Lockhart. (1988). ELI 82 curriculum development project. Honolulu, HI: ELI Documents, Department of ESL, University of Hawaii at Manoa.

Bachman, L. F. (1987). The development and use of criterion-referenced tests of language proficiency in language program evaluation. In A. Wangsotorn, K. Prapphal, A. Maurice, & B. Kenny (Eds.), *Trends in language programme evaluation.* Bangkok: Chulalongkorn University.

Bachman, L. F. (1990). *Fundamental considerations in language testing.* Oxford: Oxford University Press.

Bachman, L. F., & A. S. Palmer. (1981). A multitrait–multimethod investigation into the construct validity of six tests of speaking and reading. In A. S. Palmer, P. J. M. Groot, & G. A. Trosper (Eds.), *The construct validation of tests of communicative competence.* Washington, D.C. : TESOL.

Bachman, L. F., & A. S. Palmer. (1982). The construct validation of some components of communicative proficiency. *TESOL Quarterly, 16,* 449–465.

Bachman, L. F., & A. S. Palmer. (1983). The construct validity of the FSI oral interview. In J. W. Oller, Jr. (Ed.), *Issues in language testing.* Cambridge, MA: Newbury House.

Bachman, L., & S. Savignon. (1986). The evaluation of communicative language proficiency: A critique of the ACTFL oral interview. *Modern Language Journal, 70,* 380–397.

Belanoff, P., & M. Dickson (Eds.). (1991) *Portfolio grading: Process and product.* Portsmouth, NH: Boynton/Cook.

Berk, R. A. (Ed.). (1980). *Criterion-referenced measurement: The state of the art.* Baltimore: Johns Hopkins University Press.

Berk, R. A. (Ed.). (1984a). *A guide to criterion-referenced test construction.* Baltimore: Johns Hopkins University Press.

Berk, R. A. (1984b). Selecting the index of reliability. In R.A. Berk (Ed.), *A guide to criterion-referenced test construction.* Baltimore: Johns Hopkins University Press.

Berk, R. A. (1986). A consumer's guide to setting performance standards on criterion-referenced tests. *Review of Educational Research, 56,* 137–172.

Bolus, R. E., F. B. Hinofotis, & K. M. Bailey. (1982). An introduction to generalizability theory in second language research. *Language Learning, 32,* 245–258.

Brennan, R. L. (1980). Applications of generalizability theory. In R.A. Berk (Ed.), *Criterion-referenced measurement: The state of the art.* Baltimore: Johns Hopkins University Press.

Brennan, R. L. (1984). Estimating the dependability of the scores. In R. A. Berk (Ed.), *A guide to criterion-referenced test construction.* Baltimore: Johns Hopkins University Press.

Brière, E. J. (1979). Testing communicative language proficiency. In R. Silverstein (Ed.), *Proceedings of the third international conference on frontiers in language proficiency and dominance testing.* Occasional papers on linguistics, No. 6. Carbondale, IL: Southern Illinois University.

Brown, J. D. (1981). Newly placed versus continuing students: Comparing proficiency. In J. C. Fisher, M. A. Clarke, & J. Schachter (Eds.), *On TESOL '80 building bridges: Research and practice in teaching English as a second language.* Washington, D.C.: TESOL.

Brown, J. D. (1983a). A closer look at cloze: Validity and Reliability. In J. W. Oller, Jr. (Ed.), *Issues in language testing.* Cambridge, MA: Newbury House.

Brown, J. D. (1983b). An exploration of morpheme-group interactions. In K. M. Bailey, M. H. Long, & S. Peck (Eds.), *Second language acquisition studies.* Cambridge, MA: Newbury House.

Brown, J. D. (1984a). Criterion-referenced language tests: What, how and why? *Gulf Area TESOL Bi-annual, 1,* 32–34.

Brown, J. D. (1984b). A cloze is a cloze is a cloze? In J. Handscombe, R. A. Orem, & B. P. Taylor (Eds.), *On TESOL '83: The question of control.* Washington, D.C.: TESOL.

Brown, J. D. (1984c). A norm-referenced engineering reading test. In A. K. Pugh & J. M. Ulijn (Eds.), *Reading for professional purposes: Studies and practices in native and foreign languages.* London: Heinemann Educational Books.

Brown, J. D. (1988a). *Understanding research in second language learning: A teacher's guide to statistics and research design.* London: Cambridge University.

Brown, J. D. (1988b). Components of engineering–English reading ability. *System, 16,* 193–200.

Brown, J. D. (1988c). Tailored cloze: Improved with classical item analysis techniques. *Language Testing, 5,* 19–31.

Brown, J. D. (1989a). Improving ESL placement tests using two perspectives. *TESOL Quarterly, 23,* 65–83.

Brown, J. D. (1989b). Language program evaluation: A synthesis of existing possibilities. In K. Johnson (Ed.), *Program design and evaluation in language teaching.* London: Cambridge University.

Brown, J. D. (1990). Short-cut estimates of criterion-referenced test consistency. *Language Testing, 7*, 77–97.

Brown, J. D. (1993). A comprehensive criterion-referenced language testing project. In D. Douglas, & C. Chapelle (Eds.), *A new decade of language testing research* (pp. 163–184). Washington, D.C.: TESOL.

Brown, J. D. (1995). *The elements of language curriculum: A systematic approach to program development.* New York: Heinle & Heinle Publishers.

Brown, J. D. (forthcoming a). *Sony communicative ability language examination* (SCALE–Written Test, Forms I–IV). Tokyo: Sony Enterprises.

Brown, J. D. (forthcoming b). Differential subtest performance and test-taker characteristics. Unpublished ms. University of Hawaii at Manoa, Honolulu, HI.

Brown, J. D., & K. M. Bailey. (1984). A categorical instrument for scoring second language writing skills. *Language Learning, 34*, 21–42.

Brown, J. D., C. Chaudron, & M. Pennington. (1988). Foreign teaching assistant training and orientation pilot project. *report on the educational improvement fund 1987/1988.* Honolulu, HI: Office of Faculty Development and Academic Support, University of Hawaii at Manoa.

Brown, J. D., H. G. Cook, C. Lockhart, & T. Ramos. (1991). Southeast Asian Languages Proficiency Examinations. In S. Anivan (Ed.), *Current developments in language testing* (pp. 210–226). Singapore: SEAMEO Regional Language Centre.

Brown, J. D., & M. C. Pennington. (1991). Unifying curriculum processes and curriculum outcomes: The key to excellence in language education. In M. C. Pennington (Ed.), *Building better English language programs: Perspectives on evaluation in ESL.* Washington, D.C.: NAFSA.

Brown, J. D., T. Ramos, H. G. Cook, & C. Lockhart. (1990). *SEASSI placement examinations* (including Listening, Cloze, Dictation, and Interview tests in Indonesian, Khmer, Tagalog, Thai, and Vietnamese with user's manual, test booklets, answer sheets, answer keys, and tapes). Honolulu, HI: Department of Indo-Pacific Languages, University of Hawaii at Manoa.

Brown, J. D., & J. A. Ross. (forthcoming). Decision dependability of subtests, tests and the overall TOEFL test battery. In the *Proceedings of the 1993 language testing research colloquium.*

Burton, N. W. (1978). Societal standards. *Journal of Educational Measurement, 15*, 263–271.

Busch, J. C., & R. M. Jaeger. (1990). Influence of type of judge, normative information, and discussion on standards recommended for the national teacher examinations. *Journal of Educational Measurement, 27*, 145–163.

Butler, C. (1985). *Statistics in linguistics.* Oxford: Blackwell.

Canale, M. (1983). On some dimensions of language proficiency. In J. W. Oller, Jr. (Ed.), *Issues in language testing.* Cambridge, MA: Newbury House.

Canale, M., & M. Swain. (1980). Theoretical bases of communicative approaches to second language teaching and testing. *Applied Linguistics, 1*, 1–47.

Canale, M., & M. Swain. (1981). A theoretical framework for communicative competence. In A. Palmer, P. J. M. Groot, & G. A. Trosper (Eds.), *The construct validation of tests of communicative competence.* Washington, D.C.: TESOL.

Carroll, J. B. (1972). Fundamental considerations in testing for English language proficiency of foreign students. In H. B. Allen, & R. N. Campbell (Eds.), *Teaching English as a second language: A book of readings* (2nd ed.). New York: McGraw-Hill.

Carroll, J. B., & S. M. Sapon. (1958). *Modern language aptitude test.* New York: The Psychological Corporation.

Cartier, F. (1968). Criterion-referenced testing of language skills. *TESOL Quarterly, 2,* 27–32.

Chaudron, C., G. Crookes, & M. H. Long. (1988). *Reliability and validity in second language classroom research* (Technical Report #8). Social Science Research Institute, University of Hawaii at Manoa.

Chomsky, N. (1965). *Aspects of the theory of syntax.* Cambridge, MA: M.I.T Press.

Cohen, J. (1960). A coefficient of agreement for nominal scales. *Educational and Psychological Measurement, 20,* 37–46.

Cowan, J. R. (1974). Lexical and syntactic research for the design of EFL materials. *TESOL Quarterly, 8,* 389–399.

Cronbach, L. J. (1970). *Essentials of psychological testing* (3rd ed.). New York: Harper & Row.

Cronbach, L. J., G. C. Gleser, H. Nanda, & N. Rajaratnam. (1970). *The dependability of behavioral measurements.* New York: Wiley.

Cziko, G. A. (1983). Psychometric and edumetric approaches to language testing. In J. W. Oller, Jr. (Ed.), *Issues in language testing research.* Cambridge, MA: Newbury House.

Dick, W., & L. Carey. (1985). *The systematic design of instruction* (2nd ed.). Glenview, IL: Scott Foresman.

Dixon, W. J., & F. J. Massey, Jr. (1951). *Introduction to statistical analysis.* New York: McGraw-Hill.

Ebel, R. L. (1979). *Essentials of educational measurement* (3rd ed.). Englewood Cliffs, NJ: Prentice-Hall.

Educational Testing Service. (1968). *Modern Language Association foreign language proficiency tests for teachers and advanced students.* Princeton, NJ: Educational Testing Service.

Educational Testing Service. (1992). *TOEFL test and score manual: 1992–1993 edition.* Princeton, NJ: Educational Testing Service.

Educational Testing Service. (1994). *Test of English as a foreign language.* Princeton, NJ: Educational Testing Service.

Emrick, J. A. (1971). An evaluation model for mastery testing. *Journal of Educational Measurement, 8,* 321–326.

Erickson, M., & J. Molloy. (1983). ESP test development project for engineering students. In J. W. Oller, Jr. (Ed.), *Issues in language testing research.* Cambridge, MA: Newbury House.

Farhady, H. (1979). The disjunctive fallacy between discrete-point and integrative tests. *TESOL Quarterly, 13,* 347–357.

Farhady, H. (1982). Measures of language proficiency from the learner's perspective. *TESOL Quarterly, 16,* 43–59.

Feldt, L. S., & R. L. Brennan. (1989). Reliability. In R. L. Linn (Ed.), *Educational measurement* (3rd ed.). New York: ACE/Macmillan.

Fisher, R. A, & F. Yates. (1963). *Statistical tables for biological, agricultural and medical research.* London: Longman.

Fry, E. B. (1976). *Fry readability scale (extended).* Providence, RI: Jamestown Publishers.

Fusco, E., M. C. Quinn, M. Hauck. (1993). *The portfolio assessment handbook.* Roslyn, NY: Berrent.

Glaser, R. (1963). Instructional technology and the measurement of learning outcomes: Some questions. *American Psychologist, 18,* 519–521.

Glass, E. V. (1978). Standards and criteria. *Journal of Educational Measurement, 15,* 237–261.

Guilford, J. P. (1954). *Psychometric methods.* New York: McGraw-Hill.

Guilford, J. P., & B. Fruchter (1973). *Fundamental statistics in psychology and education* (5th ed.). New York: McGraw-Hill.

Halliday, M. A. K., & R. Hasan. (1976). *Cohesion in English.* London: Longman.

Hambleton, R. K. (1978). On the use of cut off scores with criterion-referenced tests in instructional settings. *Journal of Educational Measurement, 15,* 277–290.

Harris D. P., & L. A. Palmer. (1970). *Comprehensive English language test for speakers of English as a second language.* New York: McGraw-Hill.

Hatch, E., & H. Farhady. (1982). *Research design and statistics for applied linguistics.* Cambridge, MA: Newbury House.

Hatch, E., & A. Lazaraton. (1990). *The research manual: Design and statistics for applied linguistics.* Cambridge, MA: Newbury House.

Hewitt, G. (1995). *A portfolio primer: Teaching, collecting, and assessing student writing.* Portsmouth, NH: Heinemann.

Hinofotis, F. B. (1980). Cloze as an alternative method of ESL placement and proficiency testing. In J. W. Oller, Jr., & K. Perkins (Eds.) *Research in language testing.* Cambridge, MA: Newbury House.

Hinofotis, F. B. (1981). Perspectives on language testing: Past, present and future. *Nagoya Gakuin Daigaku Gaikokugo Kyoiku Kiyo, 4,* 51–59.

Hinofotis, F. B. (1983). The structure of oral communication in an eduational environment: A comparison of factor-analytic rotational procedures. In J. W. Oller, Jr. (Ed.), *Issues in language testing.* Cambridge, MA: Newbury House.

Hudson, T., & B. Lynch (1984). A criterion-referenced approach to ESL achievement testing. *Language Testing, 1,* 171–201.

Huff, D., & I. Geis (1954). *How to lie with statistics.* New York: W. W. Norton.

Huynh, H. (1976). On the reliability of decisions in domain referenced testing. *Journal of Educational Measurement, 13,* 253–264.

Hymes, D. H. (1967). Models of interaction of language and social setting. *Journal of Social Issues, 33,* 8–28.

ILR (1982). Interagency Language Roundtable Language Skill Level Descriptions: Speaking. Appendix B in Liskin-Gasparro (1982).

Inman, M. (1978). Lexical analysis of scientific and technical prose. In M. Todd-Trimble, L. Trimble, & K. Drobnic (Eds.), *English for specific purposes sciences and technology.* Oregon: Oregon State University.

Jacobs, H. L., S. A. Zinkgraf, D. R. Wormuth, V. F. Hartfiel, & J. B. Hughey. (1981). *Testing ESL composition: A practical approach.* Rowley, MA: Newbury House.

Jaeger, R. M. (1982) An iterative structured judgment process for establishing standards on competency tests: Theory and application. *Educational Evaluation and Policy Analysis, 4,* 461–476.

Jaeger, R. M. (1989a). An iterative structured judgment process for establishing standards on competency tests: Theory and application. *Educational Evaluation and Policy Analysis, 4,* 461–476.

Jaeger, R. M. (1989b). Certification of student competence. In R. L. Linn (Ed.), *Educational measurement* (3rd ed.). London: Collier Macmillan.

Kimzin, G., & S. Proctor. (1986). An ELI academic listening comprehension needs assessment: Establishing goals, objectives and microskills. Honolulu, HI: ELI Documents, Department of ESL, University of Hawaii at Manoa.

Koffler, S. L. (1980). A comparison of approaches for setting proficiency standards. *Journal of Educational Measurement, 17,* 167–178.

Kuder, G. F., & M. W. Richardson. (1937). The theory of estimation of test reliability. *Psychometrika, 2,* 151–160.

Lackstrom, J. E., L. Selinker, & L. Trimble. (1973). Technical rhetorical principles and grammatical choice. *TESOL Quarterly, 7,* 127–136.

Lado, R. (1961). *Language testing: The construction and use of foreign language tests.* London: Longman.

Linn, R. L. (1978). Demands, cautions, and suggestions for setting standards. *Journal of Educational Measurement, 15,* 301–308.

Liskin-Gasparro. (1982). *Testing & teaching for oral proficiency.* Boston: Heinle & Heinle.

Livingston, S. A., & M. J. Zieky (1982). *Passing scores: A manual for setting standards of performance on educational and occupational tests.* Princeton, NJ: Educational Testing Service.

Lord, F. M., & M. Novick. (1968). *Statistical theories of mental test scores.* Reading, MA: Addison-Wesley.

Loschky, L. J. Stanley, C. Cunha, & S. Singh. (1987). Evaluation of the University of Hawaii English Language Institute Reading Program. Honolulu, HI: ELI Documents, Department of ESL, University of Hawaii at Manoa.

Macready, G. B., & C. M. Dayton. (1977). The use of probabilistic models in the assessment of mastery. *Journal of Educational Measurement, 14,* 99–120.

Mager, R. F. (1975). *Preparing instructional objectives* (2nd ed.). Belmont, CA: Fearon-Pitman.

Marshall, J. L. (1976). *The mean split-half coefficient of agreement and its relation to other test indices* (Technical Report #350). Madison, WI: Wisconsin Research and Development Center for Cognitive Learning.

Maxwell, A. (1965). A comparison of two English as a foreign language tests. Unpublished ms. Davis, CA: University of California (Davis).

Meskauskas, J. A. (1976). Evaluation models for criterion-referenced testing: Views regarding mastery and standard-setting. *Review of Educational Research, 45,* 133–158.

Messick, S. (1988). The once and future issues of validity: Assessing the meaning of consequences of measurement. In H. Wainer, & H. I Braun (Eds.), *Test validity.* Hillsdale, NJ: Lawrence Erlbaum.

Moy, R. H. (Unpublished ms.) Proficiency standards and cut-scores for language proficiency tests. Los Angeles: University of California.

Mullen, K. A. (1980). Rater reliability and oral proficiency evaluations. In J. W. Oller, Jr. and K. Perkins (Eds.), *Research in language testing.* Cambridge, MA: Newbury House, 91–115.

Nedelsky, L. (1954). Absolute grading standards for objective tests. *Educational and Psychological Measurement, 14,* 3–19.

Oller, J. W., Jr. (1979). *Language tests at school: A pragmatic approach.* London: Longman.

Popham, W. J. (1978). *Criterion-referenced measurement.* Englewood Cliffs, NJ: Prentice-Hall.

Popham, W. J. (1981). *Modern educational measurement.* Englewood Cliffs, NJ: Prentice-Hall.

Popham, W. J., & T. R. Husek. (1969). Implications of criterion-referenced measurement. *Journal of Educational Measurement, 6,* 1–9.

Power, K. M. (1986). Needs analysis for ESL 100. Honolulu, HI: ELI Documents, Department of ESL, University of Hawaii at Manoa.

Powers, D. E., & C. S. Stansfield. (1982). *Towards standards of proficiency on the Test of Spoken English* (TOEFL Final Report). Princeton, NJ: Educational Testing Service.

Premaratne, G. K. (1987). A close study of the cloze procedure: A comparison of three cloze types used in ESL testing. Unpublished MA thesis, University of Hawaii at Manoa.

Richards, J. C., J. Platt, & H. Weber. (1985). *Longman dictionary of applied linguistics.* London: Longman.

Rowley, G. L. (1982). Historical antecedents of the standard-setting debate: An inside acount of the minimal-beardedness controversy. *Journal of Educational Measurement, 19,* 87–95.

Savignon, S. J. (1972). *Communicative competence: An experiment in foreign-language teaching.* Philadelphia: Center for Curriculum Development.

Savignon, S. J. (1985). Evaluation of communicative competence: The ACTFL provisional proficiency guidelines. *Modern Language Journal, 69,* 129–142.

Scriven, M. (1978). How to anchor standards. *Journal of Educational Measurement, 15,* 273–275.

Selinker, L., R. M. Todd-Trimble, & L. Trimble. (1976). Presuppositional rhetorical information in EST discourse. *TESOL Quarterly, 10,* 281–290.

Selinker, L., R. M. Todd-Trimble, & L. Trimble. (1978). Rhetorical function shifts in EST discourse. *TESOL Quarterly, 12,* 311–320.

Shannon, G. A., & B. A. Cliver. (1987). An application of item response theory in the comparison of four conventional item discrimination indices for criterion–referenced tests. *Journal of Educational Measurement, 24,* 347–356.

Shepard, L. (1980). Standard setting issues and methods. *Applied Psychological Measurement, 4,* 447–467.

Shepard, L. A. (1984). Setting performance standards. In R. A. Berk (Ed.) *A guide to criterion-referenced test construction.* Baltimore: Johns Hopkins University Press.

Skakun, E. N., & S. Kling. (1980). Comparability of methods for setting standards. *Journal of Educational Measurement, 17,* 229–235.

Spolsky, B. (1978). Introduction: Linguists and language testers. In B. Spolsky (Ed.), *Advances in language testing series: 2.* Arlington, VA: Center for Applied Linguistics.

Stanley, J. C. (1971). Reliability. In R. L. Thorndike (Ed.), *Educational measurement* (2nd ed.). Washington, D.C.: American Council on Education.

Subkoviak, M. J. (1980). Decision-consistency approaches. In R. A. Berk (Ed.), *Criterion-referenced measurement: The state of the art.* Baltimore: Johns Hopkins University Press, 129–185.

Subkoviak, M. J. (1988). A practitioner's guide to computation and interpretation of reliability indices for mastery tests. *Journal of Educational Measurement, 25,* 47–55.

Thorndike, R. L. (1951). Reliability. In E. F. Lindquist (Ed.), *Educational measurement* (2nd ed.). Washington, D.C.: American Council on Education.

University of Michigan. (1961). *Michigan test of English language proficiency: Form A.* Ann Arbor, MI: University of Michigan Press.

Upshur, J. A. (1966). Comparison of performance on "Test of English as a Foreign Language" and "Michigan Test of English Language Proficiency." Unpublished ms. Ann Arbor, MI: University of Michigan.

Weaver, J., A. Pickett, L. Kiu, & J. Cook. (1987). Foreign TA training project needs analysis. Honolulu, HI: ELI Documents, Department of ESL, University of Hawaii at Manoa.

Widdowson, H. G. (1978). *Teaching language as communication.* Oxford: Oxford University Press.

Woods, A., P. Fletcher, & A. Hughes. (1986). *Statistics in language studies.* Cambridge: Cambridge University Press.

Zieky, M. J., & S. A. Livingston. (1977). *Manual for setting standards on the basic skills assessment tests.* Princeton, NJ: Educational Testing Service.

INDEX